Smyslov's Best Games of Chess

My Rise to the World Championship

V. V. Smyslov

Translated and edited by
P. H. Clarke

HARDINGE SIMPOLE PUBLISHING

Hardinge Simpole Publishing,
Aylesbeare Common Business Park,
Exmouth Road,
Aylesbeare,
Devon,
EX5 2DG,
England

For a complete list of titles, visit
http://www.hardingesimpole.co.uk

e-mail: admin@hardingesimpole.co.uk

This edition, with new material and Tournament Tables, transferred to
Digital Printing in 2003

First published in 1952 in Russian as Izbrannie Partii
First published in English in 1958 as My Best Games of Chess 1935-1957
by Routledge and Kegan Paul.

ISBN 1 84382 115 X

Cover design by Robert Parsons, 1987, 2001 © Hardinge Simpole
Limited

Hardinge Simpole Chess Classics

It is often said that chess has the most extensive literature of any game, sport or pastime. This may well be true, but the literature of chess, while vast, is also by its very nature ephemeral. Each week new treatises on the openings pour out of databases, like an unstemmable flood from the hand of some demented sorcerer's apprentice. Beneath this deluge, works of lasting value have all too frequently been submerged.

It is our intention to fulfill a twofold mandate. The first is to rescue from oblivion any worthwhile publication by the pen of an acknowledged master of chess writing - in particular, books on World Chess Championships by such eminent authors as Harry Golombek, perhaps the greatest stylist ever to write a chess book, have been unjustly consigned to history. Hardinge Simpole Publishing is resurrecting them. Similarly games anthologies selected and annotated by connoisseurs such as Larry Evans and Peter Clarke are being revived. Books like this will be published as Hardinge Simpole Chess Classics.

Our second task has been to give an opportunity to talented writers who would otherwise have found it difficult to get into print. Hardinge Simpole Publishing has commercial aims, in common with all publishers. But we do not rely on the mass market for all our books. We are fully prepared to commit to what may be caviar to the general, so long as the product is indeed genuine.

With our blend of the classic and the experimental Hardinge Simpole publishing strives at all times to offer quality. We hope that you the readers will endorse our choice.

Descriptive Notation

For decades there were two primary modes of chess notation – algebraic and descriptive. Algebraic was popular on the European continent, while descriptive prevailed in the English speaking world. With the advent of computers, however, descriptive notation gradually died out.

Nevertheless, many of the classics *which we are reviving in this series* are published in the descriptive form, so we have thought it prudent to explain it briefly here for those who may have forgotten it or indeed never before come into contact with it.

To convert all moves and commentaries from the classics produced by Hardinge Simpole publishing into algebraic notation would not only alter the flavour of the text but add many pounds to the price of each book.

What follows, therefore, is a description of the conventions of descriptive notation which assumes knowledge of the algebraic system only.

First here is an empty chess board with algebraic co-ordinates - this should be quite familiar to you:

(see following diagram)

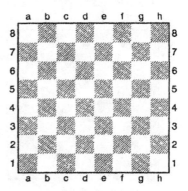

It is common in algebraic notation to show the pieces as figurines but in descriptive notation the pieces are almost always denoted by their initial letters:

K = king
Q = queen
B = bishop
N or Kt = knight
R = rook
P = pawn

Castling king side is sometimes written out in full or rendered 0-0. Castling queen side can be written as 0-0-0. Check (+) is standardly rendered ch. In descriptive notation the files take their names from the pieces which start on them – thus the a-file becomes the QR file – the b-file the QN file etc. Ranks retain numbers from 1-8 but we number them from Black's or White's side depending on whose move it is – thus the square c3 in algebraic notation becomes QB3 for White but QB6 for Black.

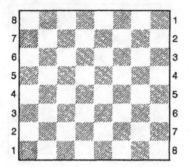

QR QN QB Q K KB KN KR

To specify a move completely we just state which piece or pawn makes the move and the square to which it is moved. Captures are denoted by an x. If there is a possibility of an ambiguous move extra specification is brought into play – see the following example:

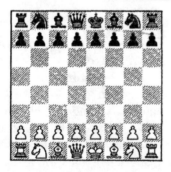

Now just play through these moves on your chess board:

1 P-K4 P-K4

2 P-Q4 PxP
3 QxP N-QB3

3 ... N-B3 would not be precise since the Black KN can also go to its B3 square.

4 Q-K3 B-N5ch
5 P-B3 B-R4

Note that P-B3 adequately describes White's move since P-KB3 fails to stop the check.

6 N-QR3

We need to say N-QR3 since N-KR3 is also possible.

6 ... B-N3
7 Q-B3 N-B3
8 B-KN5 0-0

If the position you have now reached on your chess board duplicates that in the following diagram then you can be confident that you have mastered descriptive notation and will be able to follow the games in this book with no difficulties! **Use the diagrams in the main body of this book as sign posts to help you with the notation if you are unsure about anything!**

Comments and Corrections, 2003

(1) Smyslov - Botvinnik, 1943, *page 19*

In the note to 30 P-Q R 4 add the variation:
After 30...P-Q Kt 5 White wins with 31 P x P P x P;
32 R-K 1

(2) Smyslov - Euwe, 1948, *page 76*

Subsequent analysis has revealed - in the note to
14...Kt-K 2 - VARIATION 3:
after the correct 14..Kt-Kt5!; 15 B-Kt 5 P-Q B 3; 16
R-Q 8+ Q x R; 17 B x Q R x B
that Black could still have had counterplay.

(3) Petrosian - Smyslov, 1949, *page 85*

Note to White's 43rd, not 42nd as printed, move
K-B 1

This deserves a? A considerably more stubborn
resistance follows:
After 43 R-Q 3! R-K 4+; 44 K-B 2 R-K 8; 45 B-B 3 K-
B 3; 46 B-K 2 P-Kt 3; 47 P x P P x P; 48 B-B 3 P-Kt 4;
49 B-K 2 R-KR 8; 50 B-B 1 B-Kt 6+; 51 K-Kt 2 R-R 7+;
52 K-Kt 1 R-B 7; 53 R-Q 5 R-B 6; 54 R x P R x Kt P
Though black still has real chances to win.

(4) Smyslov - Letelier, 1950, *page 95*

As an addendum to the note to 27...Kt x Kt:
After 27 ...Kt-K 2 it was also possible to continue
with
28 R-K 5! R x R; 29 P x R Kt-B 3; 30 Kt x Kt P x Kt;
31 R-K 1! R-Kt 3; 32 R-Q Kt 1 with advantage to
White,
for example: 32...B-B 1; 33 R-Kt 8 R-Kt 1; 34 R-R
8 P-R 3; 35 R-R 7+ K-Kt 3; 36 R-Q B 7 winning a
pawn.

(5) Smyslov - Taimanov, 1951, *page 105*

The black pawn on the d4 square in diagram 125
should be white.

(6) Smyslov - Botvinnik, 1955, *page 134*

In the note to 25...Q x P it should be mentioned
that 25...P-R 3 loses to 26 R(1)-K B 6 R-Kt 2; 27 Kt-
B 7!

(7) Smyslov - Bisguier, 1955, *page 135*

See the note to 19...Kt-Q 2. This move in
retrospect does not deserve a "?".Even the
apparently stronger defence 19...P-Kt 5; 20 Kt-K
2 Kt-K 5; 21 B x Kt P x B; 22 Kt-Q 4 Q-Kt 3 gives
White a very strong attack with 23 B-K 1!

V. V. Smyslov, 2003

World Championship 1948

		1	2	3	4	5	
1	Botvinnik,Mikhail	* * * * *	½ ½ 1 ½ ½	1 ½ 0 1 1	1 1 1 1 0	1 ½ 1 ½ ½	14.0 / 20
2	Smyslov,Vassily	½ ½ 0 ½ ½	* * * * *	½ ½ 1 ½ ½	0 0 ½ 1 ½	1 1 0 1 1	11.0 / 20
3	Reshevsky,Samuel Herman	0 ½ 1 0 0	½ ½ 0 ½ ½	* * * * *	1 ½ 0 1 ½	1 ½ ½ 1 1	10.5 / 20
4	Keres,Paul	0 0 0 0 1	1 1 ½ 0 ½	0 ½ 1 0 ½	* * * * *	1 ½ 1 1 1	10.5 / 20
5	Euwe,Max	0 ½ 0 ½ ½	0 0 1 0 0	0 ½ ½ 0 0	0 ½ 0 0 0	* * * * *	4.0 / 20

World Championship 1954

		1	2	3	4	5	6	7	8	9	0	1	2	3	4	5	6	7	8	9	0	1	2	3	4	
1	Botvinnik,Mikhail	1	1	½	1	½	½	0	½	0	0	0	1	1	0	1	1	½	½	½	0	½	½	0	½	12.0 / 24
2	Smyslov,Vassily	0	0	½	0	½	½	1	½	1	1	1	0	0	1	0	0	½	½	½	1	½	½	1	½	12.0 / 24

World Championship 1957

		1	2	3	4	5	6	7	8	9	0	1	2	3	4	5	6	7	8	9	0	1	2	
1	Smyslov,Vassily	1	½	½	0	0	1	½	1	½	½	½	1	0	½	½	½	1	½	½	1	½	½	12.5 / 22
2	Botvinnik,Mikhail	0	½	½	1	1	0	½	0	½	½	½	0	1	½	½	½	0	½	½	0	½	½	9.5 / 22

Candidates Tournament 1953

		1	2	3	4	5	6	7	8	9	0	1	2	3	4	5	
1	**Smyslov,Vassily**	* *	½ ½	½ 1	1 1	½ ½	½ ½	1 1	½ 0	½ ½	½ ½	½ ½	½ ½	1 ½	1 1	1 ½	18.0 / 28
2	**Bronstein,David I**	½ ½	* *	1 1	1 ½	½ ½	½ ½	½ 0	½ ½	1 ½	½ ½	½ ½	0 1	1 ½	½ ½	½ ½	16.0 / 28
3	**Reshevsky,Samuel Herman**	½ 0	0 0	* *	½ ½	½ ½	½ ½	½ ½	1 0	½ ½	½ 1	½ 1	1 ½	½ 1	1 1	1 ½	16.0 / 28
4	**Keres,Paul**	0 0	0 ½	½ ½	* *	½ 1	½ ½	½ 1	½ ½	½ ½	0 ½	1 1	1 ½	½ 1	½ ½	1 1	16.0 / 28
5	**Petrosian,Tigran V**	½ ½	½ ½	½ ½	½ 0	* *	0 ½	½ ½	½ ½	0 0	½ ½	½ ½	1 1	½ 1	1 ½	1 1	15.0 / 28
6	**Najdorf,Miguel**	½ ½	½ ½	½ ½	½ ½	1 ½	* *	0 0	1 ½	1 ½	½ 0	½ ½	½ ½	½ ½	0 ½	1 1	14.5 / 28
7	**Geller,Efim P**	0 0	½ 1	½ ½	½ 0	½ ½	1 1	* *	½ 0	0 1	½ ½	0 1	1 ½	½ 1	0 1	½ ½	14.5 / 28
8	**Kotov,Alexander**	½ 1	½ ½	0 1	½ ½	½ ½	0 ½	½ 1	* *	1 0	1 ½	0 0	1 0	1 ½	0 ½	0 1	14.0 / 28
9	**Taimanov,Mark E**	½ ½	0 ½	½ ½	½ ½	1 1	0 ½	1 0	0 1	* *	1 0	½ ½	½ ½	½ 0	0 ½	1 1	14.0 / 28
10	**Averbakh,Yuri L**	½ ½	½ ½	½ 0	1 ½	½ ½	½ 1	½ ½	0 ½	0 1	* *	½ ½	½ ½	0 ½	1 1	0 0	13.5 / 28
11	**Boleslavsky,Isaak**	½ ½	½ ½	½ 0	0 0	½ ½	½ ½	1 0	1 1	½ ½	½ ½	* *	½ 0	½ ½	½ 1	½ ½	13.5 / 28
12	**Szabo,Laszlo**	½ ½	1 0	0 ½	0 ½	0 0	½ ½	0 ½	0 1	½ ½	½ ½	½ 1	* *	1 ½	½ ½	1 ½	13.0 / 28
13	**Gligoric,Svetozar**	0 ½	0 ½	½ 0	½ 0	½ 0	½ ½	½ 0	0 ½	½ 1	1 ½	½ ½	0 ½	* *	½ 1	1 1	12.5 / 28
14	**Euwe,Max**	0 0	½ ½	0 0	½ ½	0 ½	1 ½	1 0	1 ½	1 ½	0 0	½ 0	½ ½	½ 0	* *	1 ½	11.5 / 28
15	**Stahlberg,Gideon**	0 ½	½ ½	0 ½	0 0	0 0	0 0	½ ½	1 0	0 0	1 1	½ ½	0 ½	0 0	0 ½	* *	8.0 / 28

URS-ch22 Moscow 1955

		1	2	3	4	5	6	7	8	9	0	1	2	3	4	5	6	7	8	9	0	
1	Smyslov,Vassily	*	1	0	½	½	1	½	1	1	½	½	½	1	½	½	0	1	½	½	1	12.0 / 19
2	Geller,Efim P	0	*	½	0	½	1	0	½	1	1	0	1	0	1	½	1	1	1	1	1	12.0 / 19
3	Ilivitzki,Georgi A	1	½	*	½	½	½	0	1	½	1	½	½	½	½	½	½	½	1	½	1	11.5 / 19
4	Spassky,Boris V	½	1	½	*	½	½	1	½	½	0	1	0	0	½	1	½	½	1	1	1	11.5 / 19
5	Petrosian,Tigran V	½	½	½	½	*	½	1	½	½	½	½	½	½	½	½	½	1	1	½	1	11.5 / 19
6	Botvinnik,Mikhail	0	0	½	½	½	*	½	0	½	1	1	1	½	½	1	½	1	½	1	1	11.5 / 19
7	Taimanov,Mark E	½	1	1	0	0	½	*	0	1	½	1	1	½	½	½	1	0	1	½	½	11.0 / 19
8	Keres,Paul	0	½	0	½	½	1	1	*	0	0	½	½	1	½	½	1	1	1	½	1	11.0 / 19
9	Mikenas,Vladas	0	0	½	½	½	½	0	1	*	½	½	1	0	½	½	1	1	1	½	1	10.5 / 19
10	Furman,Semen Abramovich	½	0	0	1	½	0	½	1	½	*	0	1	½	1	½	½	0	1	½	1	10.0 / 19
11	Antoshin,Vladimir S	½	1	½	0	½	0	0	½	½	1	*	0	1	½	½	0	1	1	½	1	10.0 / 19
12	Kotov,Alexander	½	0	½	1	½	0	0	½	0	0	1	*	1	½	0	1	1	½	1	½	9.5 / 19
13	Borisenko,Georgy K	0	1	½	1	½	½	½	0	1	½	0	0	*	½	½	½	½	0	½	1	9.0 / 19
14	Flohr,Salo	½	0	½	½	½	½	½	½	½	0	½	½	½	*	1	½	0	½	1	½	9.0 / 19
15	Averbakh,Yuri L	½	½	½	0	½	0	½	½	½	½	½	1	½	0	*	½	½	½	½	½	8.5 / 19
16	Lisitsin,Georgy	1	0	½	½	½	½	0	0	0	½	1	0	½	½	½	*	½	0	1	1	8.5 / 19
17	Kan,Ilia Abramovich	0	0	½	½	0	0	1	0	0	1	0	0	½	1	½	½	*	0	1	½	7.0 / 19
18	Simagin,Vladimir	½	0	0	0	0	½	0	0	0	0	0	½	1	½	½	1	1	*	1	0	6.5 / 19
19	Kortschnoj,Viktor	½	0	½	0	½	0	½	½	½	½	½	0	½	0	½	0	0	0	*	1	6.0 / 19
20	Sherbakov,Vitaly S	0	0	0	0	0	0	½	0	0	0	0	½	0	½	½	0	½	1	0	*	3.5 / 19

Zagreb 1955

		1	2	3	4	5	6	7	8	9	0	1	2	3	4	5	6	7	8	9	0	
1	Smyslov,Vassily	*	½	½	½	½	½	1	½	½	½	1	1	1	1	1	½	1	1	1	1	14.5 / 19
2	Matanovic,Aleksandar	½	*	½	0	1	½	½	½	½	½	1	1	1	1	1	0	1	1	½	½	12.5 / 19
3	Ivkov,Borislav	½	½	*	0	1	1	½	½	½	½	½	½	1	½	1	½	1	1	1	½	12.5 / 19
4	Gligoric,Svetozar	½	1	1	*	0	1	½	0	½	0	0	1	1	½	1	½	1	½	1	1	12.0 / 19
5	Geller,Efim P	½	0	0	1	*	½	1	½	½	½	1	½	½	½	½	1	½	1	1	1	12.0 / 19
6	O'Kelly de Galway,Alberic	½	½	0	0	½	*	½	1	½	1	½	½	½	1	½	1	½	0	1	1	11.0 / 19
7	Trifunovic,Petar	0	½	½	½	0	½	*	½	½	½	½	½	1	1	½	½	1	1	½	1	11.0 / 19
8	Bisguier,Arthur Bernard	½	½	½	1	½	0	½	*	½	½	½	1	1	½	½	1	0	1	0	½	10.5 / 19
9	Filip,Miroslav	½	½	½	½	½	½	½	½	*	1	0	½	½	½	1	0	1	½	½	½	10.0 / 19
10	Rabar,Braslav	½	½	½	1	½	0	½	½	0	*	1	½	0	½	½	½	½	½	1	½	9.5 / 19
11	Milic,Borislav	0	0	½	1	0	½	½	½	1	0	*	½	1	0	0	½	½	1	½	½	8.5 / 19
12	Dueckstein,Andreas	0	0	½	0	½	½	½	0	½	½	½	*	0	1	1	½	0	1	½	1	8.5 / 19
13	Barcza,Gedeon	0	0	0	0	½	½	0	0	½	1	0	1	*	0	½	1	1	1	1	½	8.5 / 19
14	Minev,Nikolay N	0	0	½	½	½	0	0	½	½	½	1	0	1	*	0	½	½	½	½	1	8.0 / 19
15	Fuderer,Andrija	0	0	0	0	½	½	½	½	0	½	1	0	½	1	*	1	½	½	½	½	8.0 / 19
16	Porreca,Giorgio	½	1	½	½	0	0	½	0	1	½	½	½	0	½	0	*	0	0	0	1	7.0 / 19
17	Karaklajic,Nikola	0	0	0	0	½	½	0	1	0	½	½	1	0	½	½	1	*	0	½	½	7.0 / 19
18	Udovcic,Mijo	0	0	0	½	0	1	0	0	½	½	0	0	0	½	½	1	1	*	½	1	7.0 / 19
19	Pirc,Vasja	0	½	0	0	0	0	½	1	½	0	½	½	0	½	½	1	½	½	*	0	6.5 / 19
20	Bertok,Mario	0	½	½	0	0	0	0	½	½	½	½	0	½	0	½	0	½	0	1	*	5.5 / 19

Candidates Tournament 1956

		1	2	3	4	5	6	7	8	9	0	
1	Smyslov,Vassily	**	½ ½	½ ½	0 ½	½ ½	½ 1	1 1	½ 1	1 ½	½ 1	11.5 / 18
2	Keres,Paul	½ ½	**	½ ½	½ ½	½ ½	½ 1	½ ½	½ 0	1 ½	1 ½	10.0 / 18
3	Szabo,Laszlo	½ ½	½ ½	**	1 ½	½ ½	½ ½	½ 1	0 ½	½ ½	0 1	9.5 / 18
4	Spassky,Boris V	1 ½	½ ½	0 ½	**	½ ½	½ 1	0 ½	½ ½	½ ½	½ 1	9.5 / 18
5	Petrosian,Tigran V	½ ½	½ ½	½ ½	½ ½	**	0 ½	0 1	1 ½	½ ½	1 ½	9.5 / 18
6	Bronstein,David I	½ 0	½ 0	½ ½	½ 0	1 ½	**	½ 1	1 ½	½ ½	½ 1	9.5 / 18
7	Geller,Efim P	0 0	½ ½	½ 0	1 ½	1 0	½ 0	**	1 1	½ 1	1 ½	9.5 / 18
8	Filip,Miroslav	½ 0	½ 1	1 ½	½ ½	0 ½	0 ½	0 0	**	1 0	½ 1	8.0 / 18
9	Panno,Oscar	0 ½	0 ½	½ ½	½ ½	½ ½	½ ½	½ 0	0 1	**	1 ½	8.0 / 18
10	Pilnik,Herman	½ 0	0 ½	1 0	½ 0	0 ½	½ 0	0 ½	½ 0	0 ½	**	5.0 / 18

Alekhine mem 1956

		1	2	3	4	5	6	7	8	9	0	1	2	3	4	5	6	
1	Botvinnik,Mikhail	*	½	½	½	½	1	0	½	½	1	1	1	1	1	1	1	11.0 / 15
2	Smyslov,Vassily	½	*	½	½	½	½	½	½	½	1	1	1	1	1	1	1	11.0 / 15
3	Taimanov,Mark E	½	½	*	½	1	1	½	½	½	½	½	1	½	1	1	1	10.5 / 15
4	Gligoric,Svetozar	½	½	½	*	0	½	½	½	1	½	½	1	1	1	1	1	10.0 / 15
5	Bronstein,David I	½	½	0	1	*	½	½	½	½	½	1	½	1	½	1	1	9.5 / 15
6	Najdorf,Miguel	0	½	0	½	½	*	½	½	1	½	½	½	1	1	1	1	9.0 / 15
7	Keres,Paul	1	½	½	½	½	½	*	1	0	½	0	½	½	½	1	1	8.5 / 15
8	Pachman,Ludek	½	½	½	½	½	½	0	*	½	½	½	½	½	1	1	1	8.5 / 15
9	Unzicker,Wolfgang	½	½	½	0	½	0	1	½	*	1	½	½	½	1	0	1	8.0 / 15
10	Stahlberg,Gideon	0	0	½	½	½	½	½	½	0	*	½	½	1	1	1	1	8.0 / 15
11	Szabo,Laszlo	0	0	½	½	0	½	1	½	½	½	*	½	½	½	0	½	6.0 / 15
12	Padevsky,Nikola	0	0	0	0	½	½	½	½	½	½	½	*	0	½	1	½	5.5 / 15
13	Uhlmann,Wolfgang	0	0	½	0	0	0	½	½	½	0	½	1	*	1	½	½	5.5 / 15
14	Ciocaltea,Victor	0	0	0	0	½	0	½	0	0	0	½	½	0	*	1	½	3.5 / 15
15	Sliwa,Bogdan	0	0	0	0	0	0	0	0	1	0	1	0	½	0	*	½	3.0 / 15
16	Golombek,Harry	0	0	0	0	0	0	0	0	0	0	½	½	½	½	½	*	2.5 / 15

CONTENTS

                                       Page

Translator's Note   ix

Vassily Vassilievitch Smyslov, by P. A. Romanovsky   xi

V. V. Smyslov—1952-1957, by the Translator   xxix

Preface   xxxiii

1   Gerasimov – Smyslov — Championship of the Moscow House of Pioneers, Moscow, 1935   1

2   Smyslov–Lilienthal—Moscow Championship, 1938   2

3   Belavenetz – Smyslov — Training Tournament, Moscow–Leningrad, 1939   5

4   Kotov–Smyslov—Twelfth Soviet Championship, Moscow, 1940   8

5   Smyslov–Rabinovitch—Telephone Match, Moscow–Leningrad, 1941   11

6   Smyslov–Boleslavsky—Tournament for the Absolute Championship of the U.S.S.R., Moscow–Leningrad, 1941   13

7   Smyslov–Lilienthal—Moscow Championship, 1942   15

8   Smyslov–Botvinnik—Moscow Championship, 1943   18

9   Smyslov–Kotov—Moscow Championship, 1943   20

10   Ravinsky–Smyslov—Thirteenth Soviet Championship, Moscow, 1944   23

11   Smyslov–Makogonov—Thirteenth Soviet Championship, Moscow, 1944   26

12   Smyslov–Konstantinopolsky—Moscow Championship, 1944   29

13   Smyslov–Rudakovsky—Fourteenth Soviet Championship, Moscow, 1945   31

14   Smyslov–Reshevsky—Radio Match, U.S.S.R.–U.S.A., 1945   32

15   Reshevsky–Smyslov—Radio Match, U.S.S.R.–U.S.A., 1945   35

16   Smyslov–Kotov—Moscow Championship, 1946   39

17   Bondarevsky–Smyslov—Moscow   Championship,
     1946   41
18   Sajtar–Smyslov—Match-Tournament,   Moscow–
     Prague, 1946   43
19   Smyslov–Konig—Radio Match, U.S.S.R.–Great
     Britain, 1946   45
20   Smyslov–Steiner—Groningen, 1946   47
21   Smyslov–Euwe—Groningen, 1946   49
22   Boleslavsky–Smyslov—Groningen, 1946   52
23   Smyslov–Kottnauer—Groningen, 1946   54
24   Smyslov – Denker — Match, U.S.S.R. – U.S.A.,
     Moscow, 1946   56
25   Tolush–Smyslov—Fifteenth Soviet Championship,
     Leningrad, 1947   59
26   Smyslov–Ragosin—Fifteenth Soviet Championship,
     Leningrad, 1947   60
27   Smyslov – Golombek   (Ending) — Match,   Great
     Britain–U.S.S.R., London, 1947   62
28   Smyslov–Sokolsky—Tchigorin Memorial Tourna-
     ment, Moscow, 1947   64
29   Tsvetkov–Smyslov (Ending)—Tchigorin Memorial
     Tournament, Moscow, 1947   66
30   Smyslov–Euwe (Ending)—World Championship
     Tournament, 1948   67
31   Smyslov–Reshevsky—World Championship Tour-
     nament, 1948   69
32   Smyslov–Keres—World   Championship Tourna-
     ment, 1948   72
33   Smyslov–Euwe—World   Championship Tourna-
     ment, 1948   75
34   Euwe–Smyslov—World   Championship Tourna-
     ment, 1948   77
35   Boleslavsky–Smyslov—Soviet Team Championship,
     Leningrad, 1948   81
36   Petrosian–Smyslov—Seventeenth Soviet Champion-
     ship, Moscow, 1949   83
37   Smyslov–Lublinsky—Seventeenth Soviet Champion-
     ship, Moscow, 1949   85
38   Smyslov–Florian—Match-Tournament, Moscow–
     Budapest, 1949   87

39   Gereben–Smyslov—Match-Tournament, Moscow–
Budapest, 1949   89

40   Smyslov – Bronstein — Candidates' Tournament,
Budapest, 1950   91

41   Smyslov–Letelier—Venice, 1950   94

42   Bondarevsky–Smyslov—Eighteenth Soviet Championship, Moscow, 1950   96

43   Aronin–Smyslov—Eighteenth Soviet Championship, Moscow, 1950   99

44   Smyslov–Tolush—Tchigorin Memorial Tournament,
Leningrad, 1951   101

45   Smyslov–Taimanov—Tchigorin Memorial Tournament, Leningrad, 1951   104

46   Smyslov–Botvinnik—Nineteenth Soviet Championship, Moscow, 1951   107

47   Lipnitsky–Smyslov—Nineteenth Soviet Championship, Moscow, 1951   109

48   Smyslov–Bronstein—Nineteenth Soviet Championship, Moscow, 1951   111

49   Smyslov–Simagin—Nineteenth Soviet Championship, Moscow, 1951   113

50   Smyslov–Barcza—International Team Tournament,
Helsinki, 1952   117

51   Smyslov–Stahlberg—Candidates' Tournament,
Zurich, 1953   119

52   Keres–Smyslov—Candidates' Tournament, Zurich,
1953   121

53   Smyslov–Botvinnik, World Championship Match,
Moscow, 1954   124

54   Botvinnik–Smyslov, World Championship Match,
Moscow, 1954   125

55   Smyslov–Fuderer—Hastings, 1954-55   128

56   Smyslov–Scherbakov—Twenty-second Soviet Championship, Moscow, 1955   131

57   Smyslov–Botvinnik—Twenty-second Soviet Championship, Moscow, 1955   133

58   Smyslov – Bisguier—Match, U.S.S.R. – U.S.A.,
Moscow, 1955   135

59   Smyslov–Trifunovic—Zagreb, 1955   137

60   Smyslov–Duckstein—Zagreb, 1955   138

61   Geller–Smyslov—Candidates' Tournament, Amsterdam, 1956   140
62   Smyslov–Panno—Candidates' Tournament, Amsterdam, 1956   143
63   Smyslov–Filip—Candidates' Tournament, Amsterdam, 1956   145
64   Ivkov – Smyslov — Match, Yugoslavia – U.S.S.R., Belgrade, 1956   147
65   Uhlman–Smyslov—Alekhine Memorial Tournament, Moscow, 1956   149
66   Smyslov–Botvinnik—World Championship Match, Moscow, 1957   150
67   Smyslov–Botvinnik—World Championship Match, Moscow, 1957   152

TRANSLATOR'S NOTE

THE Russian text of *Izbrannie Partii* published in 1952 contained 60 of grandmaster Smyslov's best games up to 1951. To produce an English edition of this work it was felt desirable to round it off by adding a selection of his games from the period 1952–1957 and at the same time to omit a few of the original games for the sake of balance. In fact I have left out 11 games and added a further 18 to bring the total to 67 in all. Wherever possible, though not in every case, I have made grateful use of Smyslov's own notes to these additional games taken from various numbers of the magazine *Chess in the U.S.S.R.* ('Shakhmaty v. S.S.S.R.'). As in the original there is a description and appreciation of Smyslov's chess career by the Soviet master P. A. Romanovsky and a short article by the author illustrating his attitude towards chess. To complete the picture I have written an account of his career from 1952 onwards to the gaining finally of the World Championship.

I wish to record my humble thanks to the World Champion for so kindly permitting me to undertake this task. Indeed I regard it as a great honour to be associated with his work and I only hope that what little I have added will not prove too unworthy. The World Champion can be sure that his games will be avidly studied and appreciated by all English-speaking chessplayers.

P. H. CLARKE.

VASSILY VASSILIEVITCH SMYSLOV

by P. A. ROMANOVSKY

I

V. V. SMYSLOV was born in Moscow on March 24th, 1921, the son of an engineering technologist, V. O. Smyslov. From his father, who was an experienced chessplayer, Vassily Vassilievitch inherited a love for chess, and by the time he was six and a half years old he had already learnt the rules of the game and how to handle the pieces intelligently.

At fourteen the young Smyslov began to take part in classification tournaments and successfully mastered the first difficult steps along the path of official tournament play. As a result of a successful appearance in 1935 in one of the summer classification tournaments in the Central Park of Culture and Rest Smyslov became a third category player. Successes encouraged the young player, and thereafter he quickly climbed the tournament ladder. In 1936 he entered the second category, and in the autumn of the same year the first category. His development took place in the congenial atmosphere of the Moscow House of Pioneers, where the young man's gifts attracted the attention of both his youthful comrades and his instructors.

In 1938, the year in which he finished school, Smyslov gained first place in the All-Union Schoolboys' Championship and that same summer competed in the All-Union tournament in Gorky for players of the first category. At that time his play already displayed the assurance of maturity. He confidently took the lead in his group, showing, alongside his ability to attack, great skill in the defence of difficult positions; he shared first and second places in this tournament with Anatole Ufimtsev.

Successes following one after the other earned for the talented young man the title of candidate master. Only a few months later, in the autumn, we find him making great new advances: then seventeen years old and a first-year student at the Moscow Institute of Aviation, Vassily Smyslov took part in the tournament for the championship of Moscow. The entry was very strong, including not only grandmaster Lilienthal and such experienced masters as Panov, Yudovitch, Zubarev and Belavenetz but also a number of candidate masters, the leading representatives of the chess-playing youth of the capital. Smyslov was the youngest competitor in the championship.

A fierce struggle developed for first place, and Smyslov was involved in it. As the decisive stage of the tournament drew nearer the more dangerous he became to his rivals. One by one the masters Zubarev, Panov and Yudovitch were overtaken and even grandmaster Lilienthal had to admit defeat in a heated encounter. But still in front was Belavenetz who had drawn with Smyslov. Before the last round the scores were: Belavenetz 12, Smyslov and Lilienthal 11½. The deciding games went well for Smyslov: both Belavenetz and Lilienthal drew, while Smyslov, playing energetically with the black pieces, defeated Slonim. So by sharing first and second places in this tournament, the strongest of its kind, Vassily Vassilievitch Smyslov earned the title of Master of Sport of the U.S.S.R.

The magazine, *Chess in the U.S.S.R.*, in its appreciation of the result of the championship described the outstanding success of the talented young player in the following way: "The creative road of Smyslov has only just begun, but already his play gives an impression of great artistic maturity, of accomplished mastery. Scarcely any of the Moscow masters look more deeply into all the nuances of opening strategy than Smyslov does. Moreover it is especially worthy that his opening knowledge is not just the result of the mechanical study of variations recommended by the theorists; for he not only "knows" the openings, but he understands their essentials, and this understanding guarantees him an opening advantage in most of his games. The whole middle-game he plays with great creative drive and disarming accuracy. And he plays the endings equally well. The value of Smyslov's result is very high indeed: it is sufficient to say that from six games against grandmaster and masters he made five points without losing a game. The figure of Smyslov in many ways brings to mind M. M. Botvinnik at the beginning of his distinguished chess career. It stands to reason that there still remains much work for Smyslov to do, but broad avenues have opened before him for his further creative development. The family of Soviet masters has received a valuable addition in the person of Smyslov."

The year 1940 brought new successes to Smyslov. For the first time he was one of the competitors in the Soviet Championship—the twelfth in number. The flower of Soviet chess thought, headed by the Champion of the U.S.S.R. M. Botvinnik, took part in this memorable tournament. Youth was represented by a wide surge of talent: side by side with the well-tried V. Makogonov, P. Keres, V. Mikenas, V. Panov and A. Lilienthal there appeared the names of Stolberg—the youngest player—and the young Smyslov and Boleslavsky. Smyslov began the tournament brilliantly and after fourteen rounds, five rounds before the end, having won five games in succession, he headed the table with 10½ points without the loss of a game. Bondarevsky, playing very well, had 10 points, while Lilienthal and Botvinnik had 9½ each. It seemed that first place and the title of grandmaster was almost assured to Smyslov, however in the fifteenth round he suffered his one and only loss in the tournament at the hands of Makogonov. In the four remaining rounds he conceded three draws, and with 13 points finished behind Bondarevsky and Lilienthal, who each had 13½. Keres, Botvinnik and Boleslavsky were below Smyslov. By this success Smyslov showed himself to be of grandmaster strength.

In 1941 in the hexagonal tournament for the title of Absolute Champion of the U.S.S.R., Smyslov came third behind Botvinnik and Keres; for this he was awarded the highest-ranking title—grandmaster of the U.S.S.R.

Of his achievements since the war his successful encounters with foreign opponents deserve special attention. In the Radio Match, U.S.S.R.–U.S.A., in 1945 he won both his games against the American grandmaster Reshevsky, and in the big international tournament in Groningen he took third place in front of a number of Soviet and foreign grandmasters.

In events in the U.S.S.R. Smyslov had excellent results and three times (in 1942, 1943 and 1944) won the championship of

Moscow, and successfully took part in the Soviet Championships. In the seventeenth in 1949 he shared first and second places with grandmaster Bronstein.

Smyslov gained a notable sporting and creative result in the World Championship Tournament in 1948. He defeated the Dutch grandmaster Euwe 4—1 and the American grandmaster Reshevsky 3–2. In the final result Smyslov scored 11 points from 20 games and took second place behind Botvinnik.

As a result of this new outstanding success numerous judges of Smyslov's talent and ability hailed him as the second-best chessplayer in the world. In 1950 in the Candidates' Tournament in Budapest Smyslov took third place.

Smyslov's last two appearances in the Eighteenth and Nineteenth Soviet Championships were, as always, creatively very valuable, but from the sporting point of view they were beneath his capabilities. In the Nineteenth Championship, which resulted in a victory for grandmaster Keres, Smyslov was fourth; the young masters Geller and Petrosian were in front of him.

For seventeen years the gifted Soviet grandmaster has bestrode the arena of chess mastery. In these years, during which the steady rise of the Soviet School of chess has led to a whole series of victories for its representatives over foreign opponents, victories firmly asserting the supremacy of Soviet chess thought throughout the whole world, the creative ideas of Vassily Vassilievitch Smyslov have finally been moulded.

His *Selected Games*, with his own notes, clearly reveals the picture of the creative path, which Smyslov has chosen for himself in the art of chess.

II

To understand the sources of Smyslov's creative strivings we must once again recall that the first and perhaps the fundamental guiding principles in the development of the young man's chess talent were nurtured by his father, V. O. Smyslov. Vassily Osipovitch Smyslov, the name of a student at the St. Petersburg Technological Institute, we meet in the beginning of this century in Tchigorin's chess classes.

In matches between the St. Petersburg University and the Technological Institute V. O. Smyslov played on one of the top boards for the Institute.

Thus Vassily Vassilievitch's father was a contemporary of Tchigorin and studied in St. Petersburg at the same time that the Tchigorin School was growing and gaining strength. This circumstance, no doubt, played its part in bestowing upon Smyslov's father the clear artistic traditions under the influence of which the talent of the young Smyslov naturally began to grow and develop.

If you also take into consideration that the representatives of the first generation of Soviet masters—F. I. Dus-Khotimirsky, I. L. Rabinovitch, V. I. Nenarokov, N. D. Grigoriev, P. A. Romanovsky and others—were all pupils of the Russian School, which had passed on its legacy and traditions to the rising generation, then it becomes clear that Smyslov's gifts were bound to develop on the basis of the creative traditions of Tchigorin.

In fact, leaving aside for the moment the clearest and most characteristic episodes in Smyslov's creative work, we may see from one of his statements how close to his own both in spirit and actuality were the views, behind which we can clearly perceive the figure of the founder of the Russian School of chess, Michael Ivanovitch Tchigorin.

In the concluding lines of a short essay on Tchigorin, which is to be found in the famous work of N. Grekov, *The Great Russian Chess Master, M. I. Tchigorin,* Smyslov expressed both his own attitude and that of the Soviet chessplayers towards Tchigorin.

"We, the Soviet chessplayers", writes Smyslov, "follow the artistic legacy of Tchigorin and respect the memory of this Russian coryphæus of chess thought."

When considering Smyslov's statements in the commentaries on his games and his decisions in many problem-like positions, it is easy to be convinced that these lines are by no means only a declaration. Smyslov actually does follow the artistic legacy of Tchigorin, and this very circumstance constrains him to refer sceptically to an appraisal of any sort based only on general considerations and to be ironical, for example, about the "advantage" of the two Bishops, which is still sufficient for many chessplayers, among whom there are even some Soviet players. In the light of this, the notes to the game with Euwe (white) from the last round of the World Championship Tournament are interesting.

About 19. ... B × P Smyslov writes: "Euwe hoped with the help of his two Bishops to win back the pawn on Q Kt 3 and obtain the better ending. So great"—exclaims Smyslov—"is the conviction nowadays in the advantage of the two Bishops! Here it is interesting to recall"—he continues—"that M. I. Tchigorin readily carried on the struggle with two Knights and obtained repeated successes. In the art of chess"—states Smyslov in conclusion—"there are no unalterable laws governing the struggle, which are appropriate to every position, otherwise chess would lose its attractiveness and eternal character."

In this statement a sharp protest rings out against the routine, the stereotype, the dogma, against everything which also aroused the indignation of M. I. Tchigorin in his day.

Below in those same notes, Smyslov disputes the analysis on the two Bishops which P. Keres gives in his book on the World Championship; "The white Bishops"—observes Smyslov —"did not show any superiority in the fight against the Knights ... therefore the lengthy discussion by Keres concerning the use of the two Bishops arouses surprise."

Smyslov, let it be understood, has no intention of denying the fact that in some positions the two Bishops can be more active. More than that, it is possible to bring forward not a few examples from Smyslov's own games, where he took brilliant advantage of the activity of the two Bishops. There is another thing that does not please grandmaster Smyslov: he takes great exception to the dogmas about the advantage of the two Bishops, to the idea that their mobility should be deliberately emphasized even where there is only the possibility of obtaining them. Not only Bishops can be active, but Queens, Rooks and Knights as well; it is therefore incorrect to consider only the two Bishops as an advantage. "It is not a matter of two Bishops or two Knights," as Tchigorin once wrote, "but how they are placed and how they co-operate with the other pieces." Smyslov also talks about the same point in the notes mentioned above.

Thus the creative views of Smyslov find their source first of all in the ideas of Tchigorin. Therefore it is not surprising that in his opinion the processes of a game of chess are transformed into a great art, and he, like an artist, invests in this art his innermost thoughts, deep emotion and genuine creative pathos.

III

THE art of chess interests V. Smyslov most of all from the point of view of all the unsolved problems inherent in it. The genius of Smyslov is experimental; he is an innovator, a stranger to the stereotype. Technical solutions and variations found in his play are not ends in themselves but a means of creating, a way of artistically instrumenting his ideas.

One of the most important questions of contemporary chess is the problem of the strong pawn centre and the struggle of the pieces against it. Today a deep and pointed discussion is going on around this question. The dogmatic over-estimation of the significance of pawn configurations, which were tied down to rules by the orthodox disciples and interpreters of the "new" school of Steinitz, provoked a certain belittling of the role of the pieces in a number of positions, and this in its turn led to a notorious narrowing of the range of creative ideas in the art of chess. The gradually increasing influence of Russian chess thought and finally the clear opinions of Alekhine made very important corrections to the barren and narrow positional interpretation of the German and Viennese Schools on the questions of pawn positions. However the question of the strong pawn centre will continue to provoke bitter quarrels as long as there is chess.

An inquisitive seeker of the new, Smyslov has not been able to stand aside from this discussion. More than that, a great part of his creative quests have been directed primarily at the clarification of the "central pawn problem".

This is what he himself says about it in his notes to the move 3. ... P—Q 4 after 1. P—Q 4, Kt—K B 3; 2. P—Q B 4, P—K Kt 3; 3. P—K Kt 3 (see the game Smyslov—Lilienthal, page 15). The advance of the central pawn reflects the influence of the new ideas, characteristic of the modern understanding of the questions of opening strategy. The struggle against the pawn centre by the pieces acting on the centre squares—that is the real problem. . . ."

Perhaps there is not a single Soviet chessplayer, although many have worked on this problem, who has invested in it as many valuable and original ideas as Smyslov, who has bravely applied his findings on this question in the most important competitions.

In addition it is impossible not to emphasize that V. Smyslov appears in this connection as the direct developer of the heritage and ideas of Tchigorin, the expression of which we find, for example, in Tchigorin's own move 2. ... Kt—Q B 3 in the Queen's Gambit (1. P—Q 4, P—Q 4; 2. P—Q B 4).

Not only in the above-mentioned opening but also in many other openings questions concerning the influence of the pieces on the centre and in general the play of the pieces have arrested the serious attention of Smyslov and have served as material for his experimental investigations. Thus, in the Catalan Opening not only the stoic defence of the Q P—the bulwark of the pawn centre—has received his attention, but also the continuation Q P × P with the manœuvre B—Q 2—B 3 to follow. This very manœuvre he used in his game with Sajtar (see page 43) in another opening system, and self-critically called his solution experimental.

With his critical outlook on the routine and stereotype, Smyslov is constantly choosing "unusual" continuations. In the notes to his moves one is continually coming across such a note: "Usual here is. . . ."

However the "unusual" continuations adopted by Smyslov are not at all a yearning for the original, for novelty for novelty's sake, for finesses to attract the attention of the spectator or reader in some way. Indeed, in Smyslov's play there is not even a hint of what might be called an anti-classical approach to the game, an approach in which the classical clarity and depth are substituted for by flowery, unnatural constructions contrary to the classical spirit.

In the course of his daring denial of the routine and commonplace Smyslov does not in the least depart from classical principles and testaments; quite the reverse, he creates a deepening understanding of these principles, widens their effect and opens new avenues for their development.

A specially characteristic feature of Smyslov's style is the breadth of his creative ideas, for he does not let slip even the slightest essential detail of the process of the struggle as it takes place. Thanks to this Smyslov is often confronted with ample scope for choosing among a variety of continuations. This allows him to be swayed not only by a criterion of the strength when choosing this or that move or variation, but among variations of approximately equal worth to dwell on those which seem to him the more interesting artistically and which respond more to his artistic tastes. From this then spring those original decisions in many positions, which unexpectedly unfold before the astonished spectator tactical finesses the existence of which it was difficult even to suspect. Such, for example, are the 18th and 26th moves in the game he won from Reshevsky in the World Championship Tournament (see page 69), or his 12th move in the famous game with Tolush from the Fifteenth Soviet Championship (see page 59), in which Smyslov began to demonstrate the paradoxical character of his decisions almost from the first moves in the opening (7. ... B—K 3).

The sacrifice of the exchange in the opening in the game with Steiner (page 47) and the pawn sacrifice, prepared inconspicuously by the modest move of the Rook, 19. R—Q 2, in the game with Sokolsky appear sudden and at first incomprehensible. In almost every game we come across moves and manœuvres, the point of which is deeply veiled. However when the whole of the further course of events uncovers this point and indeed uncovers it with marked clarity, Smyslov's artistry and depth of thought become apparent to us.

Smyslov's play, especially in attack—once the real object of attack has been created—is exceptionally purposeful. He never lacks singleness of purpose on such occasions, but delivers blows on the uncovered targets energetically, consistently and without loss of time. In Smyslov's games there are many examples of such attacks which completely disorganize the opponent.

Let us at least cite the already-mentioned game with Sokolsky or his victories over Boleslavsky in the sextangular tournament for the Absolute Championship of the U.S.S.R. in 1941. Lastly his 19-move defeat of Kottnauer at Groningen and the 26-move victory over Euwe in the World Championship Tournament (see pages 54 and 75) present examples of the inexorable, searching blows inflicted one after the other on the opponent's weaknesses.

The technical side of Smyslov's play stands at a very high level; nevertheless even here he does not deny himself the pleasure, if only the opportunity offers itself, of embellishing the purely technical design with one or two artistic patterns. As a clear example of such an artistic setting we may take the almost filigree finished ending of his game with Taimanov from the Tchigorin Memorial Tournament, 1951.

If to all that has been said we add that Smyslov is stoical and skilful in defence, while in the counter-attack energetic and swift, then before us in all fullness appears the figure of a great master artist, reflecting in all his works the deep progressiveness and purposeful creative direction of the Soviet School of chess.

IV

THEY quarrel about Smyslov: some consider that his main strength is tactical skill, others say that he is exceptionally tenacious in defence, and still others assert that the strongest aspect of his play is the depth of his strategical ideas.

And there are critics, who suggest that Smyslov has not yet found his true artistic self and that the direction of his ideas in the arena of the chessboard is contrary to the characteristic features of his gifts; in a word, that in the works of Smyslov there exists an estrangement of form from contents.

We believe that such expressions, tending to draw a simplified image of Smyslov the artist, are completely incorrect.

As far as the artistic concepts and views which he has worked out for himself are concerned V. V. Smyslov is an absolutely complete chessplayer. This does not at all mean that he cannot perfect his chess ideas further. On the contrary, the far-reaching views of Smyslov demand of him continual quests; for him the continual striving to enrich the art of chess in the U.S.S.R. with new ideas is characteristic. But, undoubtedly, there is another side: Smyslov has firmly established for himself his chief weapons; they fully satisfy his creative emotions, allow him steadfastly to follow his own tendencies when the play is tense and to mirror his views and moods. In his own foreword to this book Smyslov has defined with sufficient clarity the direction of his genius:

"The play of a master must express the desire to combine a general strategic plan with a skilful use of tactics in the solution of the problem before him. A leaning to one side or another" —writes Smyslov—"an excessive subjectiveness in the appraisal of a position . . . . disturbs the logical development of a game of chess and enters into conflict with the diversity of form of a realistic art, in which living truth is reflected and by which our socialism has been so enriched."

Oneness of form and contents, trueness to his art, logic on the basis of knowledge—these are the principles which serve as the beacons along Smyslov's creative road.

His deep strategy, emphasized not only in the games themselves but also in the notes to them, together with the ingenious and wide use of tactics to solve innumerable problems presents an inner harmony.

V. Smyslov is strikingly realistic in the appraisal of positions, and no sort of "brilliancies" ever lure him from a logical and purposeful playing for the win, if the seed of victory has already been revealed to him and become the object of his thoughts.

His style of play is extremely original. It is most noticeable where the targets for a plan of campaign have not yet appeared, where the struggle takes place in circumstances offering approximately equal chances. In such positions Smyslov strives to increase the tension, to put before his opponent ever more complex problems.

Smyslov's games with Reshevsky from the Radio Match, U.S.S.R. – U.S.A., 1945, with Panov from the Moscow Championship, 1943, and especially with Makogonov from the Thirteenth Soviet Championship, 1944 (see pages 32, 35, and 26) are excellent examples of this strategy.

Also of interest in this respect is the game Aronin–Smyslov from the Eighteenth Soviet Championship, where as early as the opening Smyslov began constantly to increase the tension in the play. His comments on this game are very characteristic. To his 7th move he puts: "A continuation that had not been investigated deeply and that leads to a complicated struggle." The note to 15. . . P—Kt 4 runs: "The unusual pawn structure gives the development of the game a tense character" (it was Smyslov who constructed it). The note to 19. . . Q—B 1 (in reply to 19. Q—Q 6, which offers the exchange of Queens) reads:

"Black declines to exchange Queens, reckoning on . . . catching the enemy Queen in a trap." To 26. ... K—B 2 Smyslov puts an exclamation mark and gives a variation, in which he proves that "26. ... O—O could lead . . . to simplification".

This continual orientation to a "wider field" typifies the breadth of Smyslov's creative opinions.

In his foreword we find even the reason for this breadth. "The chessplayer-artist"—writes Smyslov—"must strive to broaden his outlook in chess. . . . The tendency to try to fill in by individualistic schemes. . . . all the rich expanse of chess ideas lowers the artistic, and consequently the idealist value of a game of chess."

Smyslov's words do not disagree with his deeds; he stands before us not only as a great artist but also as a convinced and resolute teacher of the art of chess.

V

THE games, which have been collected together in this book, give a fairly accurate picture of the style of one of the leading representatives of the Soviet School; they trace its evolution and uncover the creative views and principles, which serve as the fountain and basis of that style. However there are still more games, characteristic of the style of Smyslov, which have not been included in this collection.

In fact the brilliance and originality of Smyslov's attacks, their convincing and long-remembered violence, is rather sparingly reflected here. The attractive patterns of Smyslov's combinational ideas are also a little lost in the deep scientific approach which imbues his strict comments. So the writer of this foreword considers that it would be useful to attract the attention of the reader to this side of the talent of the Soviet grandmaster by illustrating several games not given in this book.

It stands to reason that the examples given below are in no way intended to play the part of a principal addition to the author's material. Our wish is purely to add a little colour and bring closer to the reader the artistic moulds in which the creative ideas of Smyslov are cast.

The position shown in the diagram was reached in the game Alatortsev – Smyslov (Moscow Championship, 1942) after

White's 25th move. The first impression that one gets is that it is rather promising for White, who has an extra and excellently defended passed pawn in the centre. The ensuing denouément is all the more beautiful for its suddenness: 25. ... R × B!!; 26.

V. Smyslov

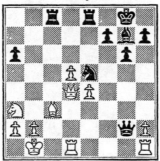

V. Alatortscv

Q × R (if 26. P × R, then 26. ... R—Kt 1 ch; 27. Q—Kt4, Q × K P ch; 28. Kt—B 2, R × Q ch; 29. P × R, Kt—B 5 with a quick finish), Kt—B 5!; 27. Q—Kt 4, P—Q R 4 (the Queen is driven from the square from which it defends Q R 3, Q Kt 2 and, if the Kt moves away, K 4. 27. ... Q × K P ch would have been a mistake on account of 28. Kt—B 2); 28. Q—Kt 3, Kt × Kt ch! (it was much weaker to play for the exchange by 28 ... Kt—Q 7 ch; 29. R × Kt, Q × P ch and 30. ... Q × R); 29. P × Kt (not 29. Q × Kt because of 29. ... R—Kt 1), Q × K P ch; 30. Q—Q 3, R—Kt 1 ch; 31. K—B 1, R—B 1 ch; 32. K—Kt 1, Q—K 4! White resigned.

The following position, Smyslov—Zagoriansky (Moscow Championship, 1944), still bears the mark of the opening. It came about after Black's 12th move in a French Defence.

Play continued: 13. P—B 4! (threatening to advance to B 6), P—B 4; 14. P × P, B × P; 15. P—Q Kt 4!, B—K 2; 16. P—B 5, R—Q B 1; 17. Q R—B 1 (now the Q B P cannot be held back. Bad is 17. ... B—B 3; 18. B × B, R × B; 19. Kt—K 5), K R—Q 1; 18. P—B 6! P × P; 19. Q—R 6, Q—B 5; 20. P—Kt 5!! (White conducts the attack with inexhaustible energy), R—B 2 (if 20. ... Q × B, then 21. P—Kt 6, P × P; 22. Q × P ch, K—R 1; 23. Q—R 5 ch with a quick mate);

E. Zagoriansky

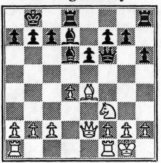

V. Smyslov

21. R—Kt 1, K—R 1; 22. P × P and Black can resign. For violence—a real Smyslov attack!

A sudden calamity struck White in the game Lisitsyn–Smyslov (Thirteenth Soviet Championship, 1944). Black had just played 22. ... Q—R 1, attacking White's Bishop. Blinded by the fact that Black's Bishop was also attacked, Lisitsyn presumed that after he had retreated his Bishop Black would automatically have to move his from K B 5. But the transfer

V. Smyslov

G. Lisitsyn

of the black Queen to R 1 had a hidden combinational idea. Suspecting nothing, White played 23. B—B 4 (23. B—B 1 was necessary), and in reply there came an original and elegant combination, immediately deciding the outcome of the struggle: 23. ... R × B!; 24. Q × R, Kt—K 6! (threatening both the King and the Queen. Obviously 25. P × Kt is followed by 25. ... B × P ch; 26. K—B 1, Q—B 6 ch and mate next move. White must suffer loss of material); 25. Q—K B 1, Kt × Q; 26. P × B, Q × P; 27. K × Kt, Q—Q 4; 28. B—R 3, R—Kt 1; 29. B—B 5, P—Q Kt 4; 30. R (Q 1)—B 1, P—R 4; 31. K—Kt 1, P—R 5; 32. R—B 3, Q—K 5; 33. R—R 1, P—Kt 5; 34. R—Q Kt 3, P—R 6; 35. R × R P, P—Kt 6 and White has to give up his Bishop. Black carried out the attack with great force.

Let us look at the finish of a comparatively recently played Smyslov game. In a tense and protracted encounter, Smyslov-Flohr (Seventeenth Soviet Championship, 1949), the following sharp position was reached.

S. Flohr

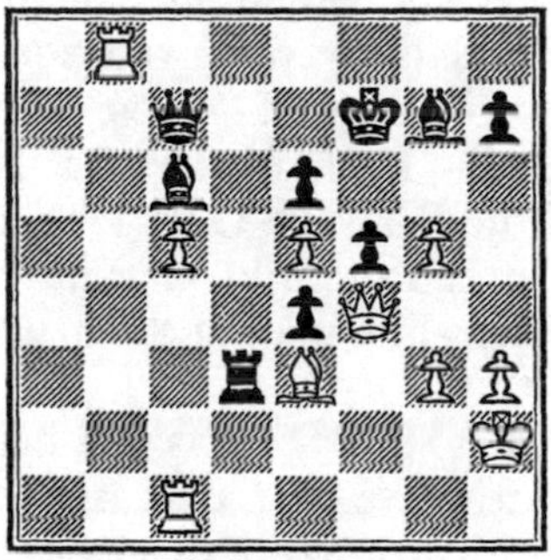

V. Smyslov

White is the exchange and a pawn ahead, but Black wins the K P by force, after which the way is open for a direct attack on the white King.

The impression is such that White's chances even seem inferior and that his chief hope must not be in his material superiority so much as in the fact that Black's King also cannot feel secure. The stormy struggle developed as follows: 44. R (B 1)—Q Kt 1, B × P; 45. Q—R 4! (a deep calculation: if 45. ... R × B, then 46. Q—R 5 ch, K—Kt 2; 47. Q—R 6 ch, K—B 2; 48. P—Kt 6 ch! P × P; 49. Q—B 8 mate), B × P ch! (obviously, this is the best chance!); 46. Q × B, Q × Q ch; 47. K × Q, R × B ch; 48. K—B 4!, R × P; 49. R—B 8, B—Q 4; 50. P—B 6 (now mate in three is threatened by 51. R—Kt 7 ch etc.), R—B 6 ch; 51. K—K 5, R—B 6 (Black reckons to put up

S. Flohr

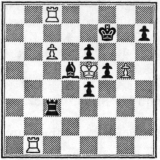

V. Smyslov

further resistance after 52. P—B 7 by 52. ... K—Kt 2 or K—K 2, though even that would not save him. Smyslov, however finds a quicker and more artistic solution).

52. P—Kt 6 ch!!, P × P (or 52. ... K × P; 53. R—Kt 8 ch!, K—B 2; 54. R (Kt 1)—Kt 1, R × P; 55. R—Kt 7 mate. The dynamic quality of the Rook on Q Kt 1, effecting a mate in two directions, is an extraordinarily elegant part of the whole economic and problem-like mating construction); 53. R—Kt 7 mate.

We suggest that these illustrations will help the reader in his study of this collection to get a clearer picture, amidst the complicated labyrinths of strategic ideas, of the attractive sharpness and tactical skill behind Smyslov's thoughts.

VI

THE genius of Smyslov, as we have already noted, is largely experimental. And, naturally, since all experiments cannot be scientifically sound, individual failures are not to be avoided. In chess these failures are almost all responsible for a lowering of the actual sporting results, and these are sometimes most important. But this does not stop Smyslov in his quests.

As Tchigorin before him, Smyslov has no special love for draws nor does he own to playing "by rule of thumb". It is through this that he has won for himself the great affection of our chessplayers, who value in a game of chess daring, courage, risks and a wealth of fantasy.

The publishing of Smyslov's games makes a valuable contribution to the chess literature of the U.S.S.R. The content of games and the detailed commentaries to them by the author represent an interesting account of seventeen years of creative activity in chess. The main theme of this book is the author's tracing of those creative searches which have brought him to his high and respected position as one of the world's leading chess players.

His first literary work must undoubtedly serve to bring his great genius nearer to thousands of chess lovers and further strengthen the ties between the great mass of Soviet players and the leading players of their country.

P. A. ROMANOVSKY,
*Honoured Master of Sport
of the U.S.S.R.*

V. V. SMYSLOV, 1952-57

by THE TRANSLATOR

As master Romanovsky explained, although grandmaster Smyslov achieved good results in the years immediately after the World Championship Tournament of 1948, he did not quite live up to the high reputation he had earnt for himself. Indeed, at that time he was outshone by the genius of Bronstein and Keres, and he even had difficulty in keeping up with the rising Soviet stars, Geller, Petrosian and Taimanov.

In the spring of 1952 a powerful Soviet contingent, headed by the World Champion, took part in the Maroczy Memorial Tournament in Budapest. Smyslov started very badly with 2 points from his first six games, but he then began to play so well that in the end he shared 3rd-5th places with Botvinnik and Stahlberg, behind Keres and Geller. This was perhaps the beginning of Smyslov's second surge forward. In the International Team Tournament at Helsinki Smyslov played with remarkable power and sureness; it was not without reason that grandmaster Bernstein was heard to remark on seeing Smyslov one day, "There goes the best player in the tournament." And then in the Twentieth Soviet Championship there came an astonishing reversal when Smyslov could only take a very moderate place below a number of lesser masters. But this was to be his last set-back.

1953 saw Smyslov greater than ever: in the mighty Candidates' Tournament, in which every leading master except Botvinnik was playing, Smyslov played with a certainty reminiscent of Capablanca at his best. He took first place by two clear points, suffering only one defeat in twenty-eight games. This was a great triumph, and one which confirmed him as the most worthy challenger for the World Championship.

So the following year sees Smyslov fighting Botvinnik for the Championship. Most experts favoured the Challenger's chances, but in the first six games he suffered three defeats, and the match looked already lost. However, Smyslov recovered, even took the lead, and finally shared the honours of a drawn match with the World Champion. Grandmaster Vassily Smyslov had proved himself the equal of any player in the world both from the point of view of bare results and also on the artistic side. But the final honour, the World Championship, was still not his. Was it too much to expect of him to win the right to challenge a second time?

In the following year Smyslov maintained his high level of play, winning a strong international tournament at Zagreb comfortably, successfully representing the Soviet Union abroad in many matches and finally tying for the Soviet Championship with Geller ahead of Botvinnik. Their individual game resulted in a severe defeat for the World Champion. Unexpectedly Geller defeated Smyslov 4–3 in the play-off for the title.

The three-year-cycle of the World Championship came round to the Candidates' Tournament again in the spring of 1956, this time in Amsterdam. The favourite was Smyslov, but it was asking a great deal of him to win again. And so it seemed, for first Geller and then Keres was in front. But Smyslov was always close behind, and at the critical stage he calmly took his opportunity and went on to finish an easy victor. A significant feature of Smyslov's success in recent years has been this wonderful ability of his to remain calm and unruffled and seemingly above the strain of the conflict while others tire and falter. Thus Smyslov earned the right to challenge Botvinnik a second time.

In his last tournament before the match, the Alekhine Memorial Tournament, Smyslov shared first and second places with the World Champion, a result which lends added interest to their coming encounter.

So the World Championship Match has ended in a great victory for Smyslov by 12½–9½. The chess world salutes its new Champion, grandmaster Vassily Vassilievitch Smyslov. At last after many years of constant endeavour he has reached his goal, and most worthy he is of this final honour.

In the event he has proved himself Botvinnik's better, though the ex-World Champion has a chance to reverse this in a revenge match next year. Few can expect him to do so, for time is not on his side and even this year it was evident that he was not at his best. A sad but inevitable fact it is that World Champions present and future never meet at their peak. If they did, there could be no victories. Who could defeat Capablanca of 1921, Alekhine of 1927, Botvinnik of 1948 or Smyslov of 1957? There is no answer.

To complete the story told by Smyslov's games I have chosen two from the match. In the first Smyslov inflicts a drastic defeat upon the World Champion to draw level at 3–3; in the second, the twentieth match game, we see the mature style of Smyslov at its best; here he is supremely confident, punishing the slightest error with unrelenting accuracy, just as Capablanca did at the height of his powers. In the face of such play Botvinnik could do little but acknowledge defeat, a defeat which meant in fact the loss of the Championship. There only remained two token draws to seal the struggle. The road now lies open to Smyslov to prove himself a great World Champion, to uphold the traditions of his predecessors and to create a new page in the history of chess.

P. H. CLARKE.

PREFACE

I FIRST became interested in chess as early as 1927 when still a child. My father, Vassily Osipovitch Smyslov, was my first teacher. I still have A. A. Alekhine's book *My Best Games*, which my father gave to me in 1928 and which became my constant reference.

My love for the literature of the game began as soon as I had learnt how to play. I was later to read everything that my father had in his library: Dufresne's handbook, separate numbers of the Soviet magazines *Chess* and *Chess Sheet*, the text-books of Lasker and Capablanca, and the collections of games of Soviet and international tournaments. The games of the great Russian chess master M. I. Tchigorin made an indelible impression on me; it was with interest that I read the various declarations on questions of strategy by A. I. Nimzovitch; I studied attentively the genius of prominent Soviet masters.

During my years as a student my enthusiasm for chess began to take on a serious and systematic character. The conditions created in our country for the training and development of a man's talent in the field of culture chosen by him were favourable for me to mature in.

In chess I saw an interesting sphere of creative ideas built up on the opposing thoughts of two chessplayers, who in the process of a tense struggle are striving to create an artistic composition. I always considered the only fruitful approach to chess, as one of the manifestations of the exalted culture of the people, the creative one.

If W. Steinitz and his disciples introduced to chess ideas which limited the fantasy of the chessplayer by their severe laws based on strictly logical thinking, then M. I. Tchigorin, as an artist, saw chess from another point of view—as an original art, impossible to encompass and express by any mathematical formula.

It seems to me that nowadays the chessplayer-artist must strive to broaden his outlook in chess, to seek continually for such means as will lead chess forward and to free himself from the elements of dogmatism alien to the Soviet School of chess. The tendency to try to fill in by individualistic schemes not only in the opening but also in the middle-game all the rich expanse of chess ideas lowers the artistic, and consequently the idealist value of a game of chess. Of course, I in no way wish to lessen the significance of scientific methods of preparation and technique in chess, without which the object of a game of chess may not, strictly speaking, be achieved. That is another matter.

Millions of adherents to chess in the Soviet Union love chess because they find in it, apart from the possibility for sporting competition, the elements of original artistic creation. Therefore technical questions, even when a virtuoso is involved, cannot play a sufficient role in themselves, but must only be a subordinate factor.

I give now a few examples of the deep creative approach to chess of the most prominent representatives of our school.

In the many outstanding games of the founder of the Russian School, M. I. Tchigorin, there are certain new ideas showing an understanding much in advance of his time. For example in the famous game against Pilsbury (St. Petersburg, 1895), in which Tchigorin was Black, we see running throughout the whole game an artistic idea distinct for its strategic novelty, which directly opposed the dogmatic and stereotyped thinking of Pilsbury (immediate seizure of the centre).

In his game with A. I. Nimzovitch (San Remo, 1930) A. A. Alekhine, with the white pieces, created a classic example of the blockade of the opponent's position: with every move the number of threats increased and the means of defence lessened. Such a disproportion must lead to a swift finish. In fact Black resigned on the 30th move, as he did not have a single useful move.

In his game with J. R. Capablanca (Amsterdam, 1938) M. M. Botvinnik gave his opponent the opportunity to win a pawn on the wing so as to deflect an enemy Knight from the chief theatre of action. The strategy of the Soviet grandmaster proved not only more far-sighted but also deeper from the creative point of view. At the critical moment two piece sacrifices following one after the other shattered the position of the Black King and quickly forced Capablanca to acknowledge defeat.

In these games the dénouement came about—and this is very important—not as a consequence of a bad mistake, but as the logical result of the development of the initiative and the exhausting of the defensive resources.

It is possible to give tens and hundreds of such examples, illustrating the breadth of the creative thought of the representatives of our School. Of course in the creative style of individual Soviet chessplayers one or other methods of play prevail which reflect the character and mentality of that particular player; however, there is always a common beginning—a purposeful strategic plan which follows from the structure and true reality of the opening.

Here it is convenient to talk further about the role of tactics and combinations in the art of chess. A correctly set out game often creates, as it develops, culminating points, when the problems can only be decided by means of a combination. That is why the play of a master must express the desire to combine a general strategic plan with a skilful use of tactics in the solution of the problem before him.

A leaning to one side or another, an excessive subjectiveness in the appraisal of a position, all this disturbs the logical development of a game of chess and enters into conflict with the diversity of form of a realistic art, in which living truth is reflected and by which our socialism has been so enriched.

In selecting the games the author was ruled by demands for an entirety of strategic ideas and their consistent solution, and also the basic meaning of a game of chess. In addition to this the author wished to reflect in some way the growth of the Soviet chess movement, which in the recent history of its competition with foreign chess thought has shown the superiority of our school.

If this work, which is now offered to the reader, is able to arouse an even greater interest in the art of chess, the author will consider his task for the most part fulfilled.

V. V. SMYSLOV

No. 1.   Queen's Pawn Opening
K. GERASIMOV   V. SMYSLOV
(Championship of the Moscow House of Pioneers, Moscow, 1935)

1. P—Q 4	P—Q 4
2. Kt—K B 3	Kt—K B 3
3. P—K 3	P—K 3
4. B—Q 3	P—B 4
5. P—Q Kt 3	

The development of the Q B on Q Kt 2 in this variation is based on the idea of seizing the square K 5 with a Kt and starting an attack on the K-side. The alternative is to play P—Q B 3 and Q Kt—Q 2 as a preparation for the advance P—K 4 and the consequent opening of the centre.

5. ...	Kt—B 3
6. B—Kt 2	B—Q 3
7. O—O	Q—B 2

The usual move here is 7 ... O—O so that, while continuing to develop, Black may move the Queen on the next move to a square more appropriate to White's reply. If then 8. Q Kt—Q 2, Q—K 2 (threatening P—K 4); 9. Kt—K 5, P × P; 10. P × P, B—R 6 Black has counterplay on the Q-side. Or 8. Kt—K 5, Q—B 2; 9. P—K B 4, P × P; 10. P × P, Kt—Q Kt 5 and White's dangerous B is removed. The text move is designed to prevent White from playing Kt—K 5.

8. P—Q R 3	P—Q Kt 3
9. P—B 4	B—Kt 2
10. Kt—B 3	P—Q R 3
11. R—K 1	

More energetic is 11. Q P × P, Kt P × P; 12. P × P, P × P; 13. R—B 1, starting the fight against his opponent's hanging pawns in the centre.

11. ...	B P × P
12. K P × P	O—O
13. Kt—Q R 4	B—B 5

Necessary to prevent P—B 5. Now 14. P—B 5 is answered by 14. ... P—Q Kt 4; 15. Kt—Kt 6, Q R—Q 1; 16. P—Q Kt 4, Kt—K 5 and if 17. B × Kt, P × B; 18. R × P, then 18. ... Kt—K 2; 19. R—K 1, B × Kt; 20. Q × B, B × P ch; 21. K—R 1, B—B 5 with chances for both sides.

14. Kt—K 5	P × P

Opening the long diagonal for the B. White's reply is forced on account of the threat of P—Q Kt 4.

15. P × P	Kt × Kt
16. P × Kt	Q—B 3

Suddenly the White King is threatened with a mating attack. Now White had to force the transition to an ending by 17. Q—B 3, Q × Q; 18. P × Q, Kt—Q 2; 19. B—K 4, Q R—Kt 1; 20. Q R—Q 1, Kt—B 4; 21. Kt × Kt, P × Kt etc. With the Queens on the board Black's attack quickly becomes irresistible.

17. B—K B 1

Correct, as already stated, was 17. Q—B 3. In the event of 17. P—B 3, Black builds up his attack by 17. ... Kt—Kt 5; 18. B—K 4 (18. P —Kt 3, B—K 6 ch; 19. K—Kt 2, Kt—B 7; 20. Q—K 2, Kt × B), B × P ch; 19. K—R 1, Kt—B 7 ch; 20. K × B, Kt × Q; 21. B × Q, B × B.

17. ...   K R—Q 1
18. Q—Kt 3   Kt—Kt 5
19. P—R 3   *1*

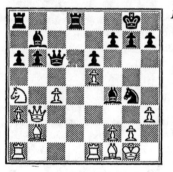

1

19. ...   R—Q 6

The start of an effective combination. Obviously, the R cannot be taken by the B, and if 20. Q × R, then 20. ... B—R 7 ch, 21. K—R 1, Kt × P ch winning the Q.

20. Q × P   R × K R P!

This is the point of Black's combination. Now 21. Q × Q is impossible because of 21. ... B—R 7 ch; 22. K—R 1, Kt × P mate. White tries to stop the mating threats by defending his K B 2, but then his Q is lost by the well-known pendulum manœuvre.

21. B—Q 4   B—R 7 ch
22. K—R 1   B × P ch

White resigned. If 23. K—Kt 1, B—R 7 ch; 24. K—R 1, B—B 2 ch and 25. ... B × Q is decisive.

This was my first tournament game to be published (in the magazine "64").

No. 2. French Defence

V. SMYSLOV A. LILIENTHAL

(*Moscow Championship, 1938*)

1. P—K 4   P—K 3
2. P—Q 4   P—Q 4
3. Kt—Q B 3 Kt—K B 3
4. P—K 5   Kt—Kt 1

In this variation it is usual to retreat the Kt to Q 2. However the text move, which preserves the possibility of playing the Kt to K B 4, is quite playable.

5. Q—Kt 4   P—K R 4
6. Q—B 4   P—Q B 4

The development of the Q B at Q R 3 was in keeping with the spirit of the system chosen by Black. After the exchange of the white-squared B Black could take up play on the white squares on both wings. For example, 6. ... P—Q Kt 3; 7. Kt—B 3, B—R 3; 8. B × B, Kt × B; 9. O—O, Kt—R 3 with Kt—K B 4 to follow.

7. P × P   B × P
8. Kt—B 3   Kt—Q B 3
9. B—Q 3   Kt—Kt 5
10. O—O   Kt × B
11. P × Kt   B—Q 2 *2*

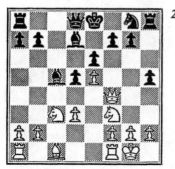

2

12. B—K 3

Before White can organize an attack he must first of all exchange the black-squared Bishops. The text move is the beginning of a manœuvre designed to accomplish this.

12. ...	B—K 2

Clearly bad for Black was 12. ... B × B; 13. P × B and White has strong pressure on the open file.

13. Q—Kt 3	P—K Kt 3
14. B—Kt 5	Kt—R 3
15. B × B	Q × B
16. Q R—B 1	

By exchanging the black-squared Bishops White has obtained a clear positional advantage. The Rook move prevents Black from castling long, which would allow him quite adequate play based on the possibility of a counter-attack on the K-side.

16. ...	Kt—B 4
17. Q—B 4	K—B 1

In this way Black manages an artificial castling, which in this position, however, amounts to a serious loss of time. True, after 17. ... O—O White could prepare a pawn storm by P—K R 3 and P—K Kt 4, so retaining the initiative.

18. Kt—K 2	K—Kt 2
19. R—B 7	K R—Q B 1

Black sacrifices a pawn to create some counterplay. Pure defence by 19. ... Q R—Q Kt 1 is no better because of 20. Q—Kt 5 with great positional advantage to White.

20. R × P	K R—Q Kt 1
21. R × R	R × R
22. P—Q Kt 3	R—Q B 1
23. Q Kt—Q 4	Q—R 6
24. Kt × Kt ch	K P × Kt
25. Q—Kt 5	

White proceeds to take advantage of the weakness of Black's K-side. On 25. ... Q × R P there would follow 26. Q—B 6 ch, K—Kt 1; 27. Kt—Kt 5, R—B 1; 28. P—K 6 with a decisive attack.

25. ...	B—K 3
26. Q—B 6 ch	K—Kt 1
27. Kt—Kt 5	R—K 1 3

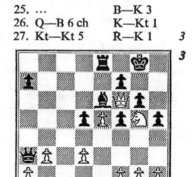

3

28. Kt × B

A simple and entirely correct solution to the problem. White gets nowhere by 28. P—R 4. For example: 28. P—R 4, Q—Kt 7 (preventing R—B 1); 29. R—K 1, Q—B 6; 30. R—K 3, Q—R 8 ch; 31. K—R 2, Q—Q 5 and 32. R—Kt 3 is not possible because of 32. ... Q × P ch; 33. K—Kt 1, R—Q B 1.

28. ...	R × Kt
29. Q—Q 8 ch	K—Kt 2
30. Q × P	Q × R P
31. P—R 3	Q—Kt 7

Best. If 31. ... R—Kt 3, then 32. Q—Q 4, K—Kt 1; 33. R—R1, Q × P; 34. R × P and White's R comes into powerful play.

32. P—Q 4	R—Kt 3
33. Q—Q 7	P—R 4
34. Q—R 7	

A serious oversight allowing Black equal chances. Correct was 34. Q—Q 8 so as to answer 34. ... R × P with 35. Q—B 6 ch, K—Kt 1; 36. P—K 6, and 34. ... Q × Kt P with 35. P—Q 5 followed by P—Q 6 and White wins; lastly, if 34. ... R—K 3, then 35. P—B 4 prepares the advance of the Q P.

After the text move Black cannot, of course, play 34. ... Q × Q P because of 35. P—K 6, but he could play 34. ... R × P!, answering 35. P—K 6 with 35. ... R—Kt 2. However A. Lilienthal failed to take this chance to equalize the game; he lets White's mistake go unpunished.

34. ...	Q × Kt P
35. Q × P	P—B 5

This is the best chance now. Bad is 35. ... R—Kt 4; 36. Q—Q 8, Q—K 3; 37. R—R 1, R—Q 4; 38. Q—Kt 8, R × Q P; 39. R—R 8 with a winning attack. If 39. ... K—R 3, then a possible continuation is 40. P—R 4, R × P; 41. P—Kt 3, R—K 5; 42. P—B 4 and White wins.

36. Q—Q 2	P—B 6
37. P—Q 5	P × P
38. K × P	Q—B 5

39. P—Q6   R—Kt 2

If 39. ... Q—K 5 ch; 40. P—B 3, Q × P; 41. P—Q 7, R—Kt 7; 42. P—Q 8 = Q, White wins.

40. R—Q 1	R—Q 2
41. Q—Q 5	Q—B 5
42. Q—Q 4	Q—Kt 4 ch
43. K—R 2	K—R 2
44. Q—K 4	K—Kt 2
45. R—Q 4	

The simplest plan. The tempting 45. R—K Kt 1 led to unnecessary complications. For example, 45. R—K Kt 1, Q—Q 7; 46. R—Kt 2, R—R 2; 47. P—B 4, Q—Q 8; 48. P—B 5, R—R 8.

45. ...   R—R 2

Passive defence also fails. In that case White could use the following plan: 45. ... K—R 2; 46. Q—B 4, Q—Q 1; 47. P—R 4, K—Kt 2; 48. R—Q 3, K—R 2; 49. Q—B 6, Q—Kt 3; 50. R—Q B 3 followed either by playing the R to the eighth rank or by preparing the advance P—K 6.

46. Q—B 4   Q × Q ch

If 46. ... Q—Q 1, then 47. Q—B 6 ch, and after the exchange of Queens P—Q 7 is decisive.

4

47. R × Q	P—Kt 4		52. P—Q 7	R—R 1
48. R—B 5	K—Kt 3		53. R—Q 6	R—Q 1
49. R—B 6 ch	K—Kt 2		54. P—B 4	K—B 1
50. P—R 4	P × P		55. P—B5	K—K2
51. K—R 3	R—R 5		56. P—B 6 ch	Black
				resigned.

No. 3. Queen's Pawn, King's Indian Defence

S. BELAVENETZ   V. SMYSLOV

(Training Tournament, Moscow–Leningrad, 1939)

1. P—Q 4	Kt—K B 3
2. Kt—K B 3	P—K Kt 3
3. B—B 4	B—Kt 2
4. P—K 3	

White's set-up is directed against the counter-thrust P—K 4. The execution of this break in this variation meets with certain well-known difficulties. However, if Black refrains from a direct attempt to carry out P—K 4 based on the set-up P—Q 3 and Q Kt—Q 2 but instead aims for pressure on the centre with his pieces, then White cannot count on any opening advantage.

4. ...	P—B 4
5. Q Kt—Q 2	O—O
6. P—B 3	P—Kt 3
7. P—K R 3	B—Kt 2
8. B—B 4	

White provokes the advance P—Q 4 in order to seize the square K 5. The loss of time, connected with this plan, allows Black to get a good game without any difficulty. Better was 8. B—Q 3, to which Black could reply 8. ... P—Q 3.

8. ...	P—Q 4
9. B—Q 3	Q Kt—Q 2
10. O—O	5

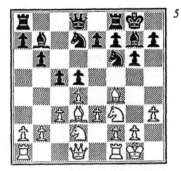

10. ...	Kt—K5

By this move Black prepares the advance P—K 4. Now White could try to win a pawn, but to carry this into effect would expose him to great danger.

Indeed, after 11. B × Kt, P × B; 12. Kt—Kt 5, Kt—B 3; 13. B—K 5, P—K R 3; 14. B × Kt, P × B; 15. K Kt × K P, P—B 4; 16. Kt —K Kt 3, P—K B 5 Black has an active position. Also unsatisfactory for White is 13. Q—B 2 in view of 13. ... P × P; 14. K P × P, Q—Q 4 with the threats P—K R 3 and P—K 6.

11. Q—B 2	Kt × Kt
12. Q × Kt	R—K 1
13. B—Kt 3	P—Q R 3

To prevent B—Kt 5

14. Q R—Q 1	P—K 4
15. P × K P	Kt × P
16. B—K 2	

In this way White threatens to bring pressure to bear on the Q P. Now the correct continuation for Black is 16. ... Q—K 2; 17. Kt × Kt, B × Kt; 18. B × B, Q × B; 19. B—B 3, Q R—Q 1 with complete equality, since 20. P—B 4 is not dangerous because of 20. ... P × P; 21. Q × R, B × B!

16. ...	P—B 3

White takes advantage of this weakening of the King position and the diagonal Q R 2—K Kt 8 by an elegant manœuvre.

17. B × Kt	P × B
18. P—K 4	

After this move Black's position becomes critical.

18. ...	P × P
19. B—B 4 ch	K—B 1
20. Q—K 3!	

Clearly the best continuation. If 20. Kt—Kt 5, Black could continue 20. ... Q × Q; 21. R × Q, B—R 3; 22. R—Q 7, B × Kt; 23. R × B, P—Kt 4; 24. B—Q 5, Q R—Q 1 with equal chances. Now Black is forced to sacrifice the Queen, otherwise Kt—Kt 5 is decisive.   6

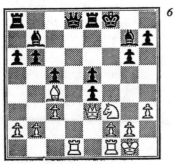

6

20. ...	P × Kt
21. R × Q	Q R × R
22. P × P	R—Q 3

Black has Rook and Bishop and a solid position in exchange for his Queen. In view of the threat of R—K B 3 White transfers his Bishop to K 4 where it will occupy a strong position in the centre of the board.

23. B—Q 3	K R—Q 1
24. B—K 4	B—B 1
25. K—Kt 2	P—Q R 4

The plans of both sides are clear: the only open file—the Q-file—is firmly occupied by the Black Rooks, which can, if need be, break into the seventh rank; Black must aim to block the position on the Q-side so as not to give lines of entry to the White Rook; Black may allow this breakthrough only if all the pawns on the Q-side are exchanged.

26. R—Q Kt 1	B—K 3
27. P—Kt 3	

White is thus able to open lines without the exchange of all the pawns on the Q-side. In the variation 27. P—Kt 4, B P × P; 28. P × P, B × P; 29. R—Q R 1, B—B 2; 30. P × P, P × P; 31. R × P, B—B 3, Black would defend himself more easily. Now the threat is P—Kt 4 after P—R 3.

27. ...	B—B 3
28. P—R 3	

Consistently carrying out his plan. 28. Q—R 6 ch, K—Kt 1 only led to a lessening of the pressure on the Q-side, and 28. P—K B 4 would increase the sphere of activity of the black-squared Bishop after 28. ... P × P; 29. Q × K B P, K—Kt 2.

28. ...   K—Kt 2
29. P—Kt 4   7

29. ...   P—R 3!

The point of the manœuvre
begun by 27. ... B—B 3. Thanks
to the threat of B—Kt 4, the entry
of the Rook to the seventh rank
becomes a serious threat. The
following counterplay is based on
the attack on K B 7.

30. P × B P

The plan of attack started by
this exchange leads to dangerous
complications. 30. P × R P was
better.

After 30. P × R P, B—Kt 4;
31. Q—K 2, R—Q 7; 32. Q—R 6!,
B—K 6; 33. R—K B 1, R—Kt 7;
34. Q—Kt 7 ch, K—B 3; 35. Q—
K R 7 with the threats of Q × P
ch and P—R 6, White had winning chances.

Black would have had to play
35. ... P × P; 36. Q × P ch, K—
K 2; 37. Q—Kt 7 ch, K—Q 3;
38. R—Q 1 ch, R—Q 7 with a
difficult defence in prospect.

30. ...   B—Kt 4
31. Q—K 2

An interesting possibility was
31. Q—K 1, P × P; 32. R—Kt 7
ch, K—B 3; 33. Q—Q Kt 1,
R—Q 7; 34. B × P, B—R 5; 35.
R—B 7 ch (35. R—Kt 6, R × P

ch; 36. K—Kt 1, R × P), B × R;
36. Q—B 5 ch, K—K 2; 37. Q ×
B ch, K—Q 3 and both sides have
chances.

31. ...   R—Q 7
32. Q—Kt 5   B—K 6
33. P × P

White had counted on this
position. He has a strong passed
pawn as well as an attack on the
enemy K P. But he has underestimated his opponent's threats—
Black's   counter-attack   proves
extremely dangerous.

33. ...   R × P ch
34. K—Kt 3

If 34. K—R 1, then 34. ... B—
K B 5; 35. P—Kt 7, R (1)—Q 7;
36. Q—B 5, R—R 7 ch; 37. K—
Kt 1, B—K 6 ch ; 38. Q × B, R
(Q 7)—Kt 7 ch; 39. K—B 1,
B × P and there is no way to
prevent mate; or if 35. B—Q 3,
then 35. ... B × P with a certain
draw by R—R 7 ch and R—Kt 7
ch.

34. ...   K—B 3   8

35. R—K 1

The decisive mistake. Necessary
was 35. P—Kt 7, R (7)—Q 7 (but
not 35. ... R (1)—Q 7 because of
36. Q × P ch); 36. P—Kt 8=Q,
B—B 5 ch; 37. K—R 4, and now

the attempt to win by 37.... P—Kt 4 ch; 38. K—R 5, B—B 2 ch; 39. K × P, P—Kt 5 ch; 40. K—R 7, B—Kt 1 ch; 41. K—R 8, B—B 5 ch? does not work because of 42. Q—K 8! Instead of 41. ... B—B 5 ch Black must play 41.... B —B 2 ch with a draw by perpetual check (pointed out by Yudovitch and Belavenetz).

35. ...   R (1)—Q 7

White had not considered the possibility of this move. The position illustrates beautifully the well-known axiom of the strength of doubled Rooks on the seventh rank.

36. R—K Kt 1

36. R × B is impossible as after 36. ... P—Kt 4 the White King suddenly finds itself in a mating net.

36. ...   P—Kt 4

White exceeded the time limit here. A tense game, if not without mistakes.

No. 4. Queen's Pawn, King's Indian Defence
A. KOTOV   V. SMYSLOV
(*Twelfth Soviet Championship, Moscow, 1940*)

1. P—Q 4	Kt—K B 3
2. P—Q B 4	P—K Kt 3
3. Kt—Q B 3	B—Kt 2
4. P—K 4	O—O
5. K Kt—K 2	P—Q 3
6. P—B 3	

White has built up a strong pawn centre and intends to adopt the well-known Samisch System: B—K 3, Q—Q 2 and O—O—O. This plan of development is one of the best means of combating the King's Indian Defence. Therefore adherents of the King's Indian Defence sometimes play the opening moves in a different order: 1. P—Q 4, Kt—K B 3; 2. P—Q B 4, P—Q 3; 3. Kt—Q B 3, P—K 4, as in this way the Samisch System is excluded.

6. ...   P—K 4
7. B—K 3

7. P—Q 5 is more careful, blocking the centre and at the same time not allowing Black the following counterplay.

7. ...   P × P

The exchange of centre pawns not only frees the diagonal for the black-squared Bishop but also is linked in this instance with the sharp attempt to open up the game by P—B 3 and P—Q 4.

8. Kt × P   P—B 3
9. Q—Q 2   9

9. Kt—B 2 made it more difficult for Black to play P—Q 4.

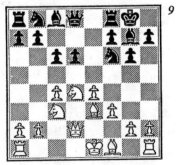

9

9. ...	P—Q 4!
10. B P × P	P × P
11. P—K 5	Kt—K 1
12. P—B 4	P—B 3

Black consistently opens the position, not fearing the continuation 13. P—K 6, Kt—B 3; 14. Kt × Kt, P × Kt; 15. B—B 5, Kt—Q 3; 16. Kt × P, P × Kt; 17. Q × P, as after 17. ... Kt—Kt 2; 18. Q—B 4, R—K 1; 19. P—K 7 ch, K—R1, the White K P is pinned.

13. P × P

After this exchange Black's pieces become very active. 13. O—O—O deserved attention.

13. ...	Kt × P
14. B—K 2	Kt—B 3
15. O—O	R—K 1
16. K—R 1	B—Kt 5

Black has succeeded in obtaining a good development. As a result of the opening complications not a trace of his opponent's pawn centre remains; on the contrary, the position of the White pawn on K B 4 and the congestion of minor pieces on the open K-file forces White to go over to the defence of the weak points in his position.

17. B × B

An unfortunate reply which considerably increases the activity of Black's pieces and which was provoked, evidently, by an underestimation of the tactical peculiarities of the position. He should have continued 17. B—Kt 1, Kt—K 5; 18. Kt × K Kt, B × B; 19. Kt × B, P × Kt; 20. Q R—Q 1, maintaining material equality, although, in my opinion, after 20. ... Q × Q; 21. R × Q, Q R—Q 1; 22. K R—Q 1, R—Q 6!, Black's chances are preferable.

17. ...	Kt × B
18. B—Kt 1	

Another possibility was 18. Kt × Kt, P × Kt; 19. B—Kt 1, but by 19. ... P—Q 5; 20. Kt—R 4, Q—Q 4; 21. K R—K 1, Kt—K 6 Black would have preserved a positional advantage.

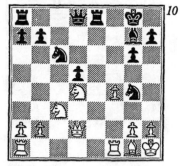

18. ...	Kt × P!

An unexpected combination. It is not possible to play 19. K × Kt on account of 19. ... Q—R 5 mate, and if 19. Kt × Kt, Kt × R; 20. Kt × Q, Kt × Q, Black is left the exchange up. White is therefore forced to resign himself to the loss of a pawn.

19. B × Kt	Kt × Kt
20. Q R—K 1	Q—Q 2
21. Q—Q 3	Q R—Q 1
22. R × R ch	R × R
23. B—Kt 1	Q—B 4!

By transferring his Queen to an active position with a gain of tempo Black maintains his advantage. If 24. Q × Q, Kt × Q, the Q P is invulnerable because of the threat of Kt—Kt 6 ch, and if then 25. R—Q 1, then 25. ... P—Q 5; 26. Kt—Kt 5, P—Q R 3! and again the pawn cannot be taken because of the reply 27. ... R—Q 1. White's difficulties have arisen not only from the loss of a pawn but also from the open position of his King.

24. Q—Q 1   *11*

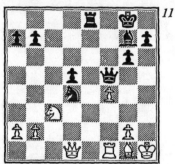

11

24. ...   Kt—K 7!
25. Kt × Kt   Q—R 4 ch

This is the point of Black's simplifying combination, which is intended to repel the enemy's attack on the Q P. Now Black regains his piece and settles down to the prosaic task of realizing his material advantage.

26. B—R 2   R × Kt
27. R—K 1   R—K 5
28. Q—B 1   R × R ch
29. Q × R   P—K R 3
30. Q—Q 2   Q—B 4
31. B—Kt 1   Q—R 4 ch
32. B—R 2   K—R 2

Preventing the threat of 33. P—K Kt 4, Q × P; 34. Q × P ch with Q × P and the liquidation of the pawns to follow.

33. P—Q Kt 3   P—Q 5
34. Q—Q 3   Q—K B 4
35. Q—Q 2

The exchange of Queens is unsatisfactory because of the variation: 35. Q × Q, P × Q; 36. K—Kt 1, P—Q 6; 37. K—B 2, B—Q 5 ch; 38. K—B 3, K—Kt 3; 39 B—Kt 3, P—Q 7; 40. K—K 2, B—K 6 and White is helpless against the advance of the Black King to K Kt 5.

35. ...   Q—K 5

The Queen has taken up an active position in the centre of the board.

36. B—Kt 1   P—Q Kt 4

Intending, after 37, continuing ... P—Q 6; 38. B—K 3, to create by P—Kt 5 a supported point for the Bishop on Q B 6. White parries this threat at the cost of advancing the Q Kt P to a black square.

37. P—Kt 4   P—R 3
38. K—R 2   *12*

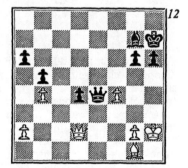

12

38. ...   P—Kt 4
39. P—Kt 3

Obviously the pawn cannot be taken because of the mate. But now a handy route on the white squares to K B 4 has been opened up for the Black King.

39. ...   P × P
40. P × P   K—Kt 3
41. B—B 2   B—B 3

Preparing to advance the K R P and so increase the efficacy of the manœuvre K—B 4. Next Black combines an attack on the weak B P with threats against the White King.

42. P—R 4

White seeks counterplay on the Q-side.

42. ...	P × P
43. Q—R 2	P—Q 6

There are various possible ways of converting the advantage into victory. Black chooses a plan based on the most rapid advance of the passed pawns. If 44. Q—Kt 8 ch, Black plays 44. ... B—Kt 2 and there are no more checks.

44. Q × P	Q—K 7
45. K—Kt 3	P—K R 4

Threatening 46. ... B—R 5 ch!

46. Q × P	P—R 5 ch
47. K—Kt 2	Q—K 5 ch
48. K—B 1	Q—R 8 ch
49. B—Kt 1	Q—B 6 ch
50. B—B 2	P—Q 7
51. P—B 5 ch	K—R 4

White resigned.

No. 5. Ruy Lopez

V. SMYSLOV   I. RABINOVITCH

(Telephone Match, Moscow–Leningrad, 1941)

1. P—K 4	P—K 4
2. Kt—K B 3	Kt—Q B 3
3. B—Kt 5	P—Q R 3
4. B—R 4	Kt—B 3
5. O—O	B—K 2
6. R—K 1	P—Q Kt 4
7. B—Kt 3	P Q 3
8. P—B 3	O—O
9. P—Q 4	

This move is more often played after the preliminary 9. P—K R 3, which prevents the following pin.

9. ...	B—Kt 5
10. B—K 3	

If 10. P—Q 5, then 10. ... Kt—Q R 4; 11. B—B 2, P—B 3 opening the Q B-file for counterplay. Black could answer the text move by 10. ... P × P; 11. P × P, Kt—Q R 4 ; 12. B—B 2, Kt—B 5; 13. B—B 1, P—B 4 with sufficient initiative on the Q-side. However, he chooses a more difficult course for the struggle.

10. ...	R—K 1	
11. Q Kt—Q 2	P—Q 4	*13*

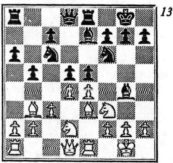

13

12. P—K R 3!

An important strengthening of White's opening system. Usually White plays either 12. Q P × P, Q Kt × P or 12. K P × P, K Kt × P when in both cases Black equalizes without difficulty. After 12. P—K R 3! it is not easy to find a plan of defence.

12. ...   B—R 4

The best line was: 12. ... K P × P; 13. B P × P, B × Kt (if 13. ... B—R 4, then 14. P—K 5, Kt—K 5; 15. Kt × Kt, P × Kt; 16. Q—B 2! P × Kt; 17. Q × Kt, P × P; 18. K × P); 14. Q × B, P × P; 15. Kt ×

P, Kt—Q R 4, although after
16. Kt × Kt ch, B × Kt; 17. B—
Q 5, White preserves a positional
advantage. The move played by
Black loses a pawn.

13. P—Kt 4   B—Kt 3

Here 13. ... K P × P; 14. Kt × P,
Kt × Kt; 15. B × Kt, B—Kt 3;
16. B × Kt, B × B; 17. B × P
leads to loss of material.

14. Q P × P   K Kt × K P
15. Kt—B 1!

The Q P is attacked and must be
lost.

15. ...   Kt—R 4
16. B × P   P—B 3
17. B × Kt   B × B
18. Q × Q   B × Q
19. Kt (B 3)—Q 2 B—Q 6

Not 19. ... R × P; 20. B—Q 4!
An ending has been reached where
Black's two Bishops cannot be
considered sufficient compensation
for the lost pawn.

20. B—Q 4   B—Kt 4

20. ... Kt—B 5 led to a more
complicated struggle, although
after, for example, 21. Kt × Kt,
P × Kt; 22. Kt—Q 2, R—Kt 1;
23. P—Kt 4, P—Q R 4; 24. P—R 3,
B—Kt 4; 25. Kt—K 4, the extra
pawn guarantees victory.

21. Kt—K 4   B—K B 5
22. Kt—B 5   B—Kt 3   *14*

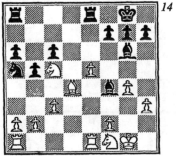

14

23. P—Kt 3!

By shutting the enemy Kt out of
play White increases his superiority.

23. ...   K R—Kt 1
24. Kt—K 3   Kt—Kt 2
25. Kt × Kt   B × Kt

A necessary exchange, otherwise
after 25. ... R × Kt; 26. Kt—Kt 2,
B—R 3; 27. P—K B 4, Black would
risk losing a piece.

26. R × B   R × Kt
27. P—K B 4

The avalanche of pawns rushes
forward. The presence of Bishops
of opposite colours in this position
does not increase Black's drawing
chances, as Black's Bishop soon
becomes locked up on the K-side
and remains there to the end of the
game a silent onlooker.

27. ...   P—R 3
28. P—B 5   B—R 2
29. P—K 6!

White opens the long diagonal
for his Bishop and prevents Black
from playing P—Kt 3, which would
be possible against other moves.

29. ...   P × P
30. R × P   R—Q B 1
31. P—Kt 4   K—B 2
32. Q R—K 1   R (1)—B 2
33. K—B 2

The King is making for K B 4
where it will support the further
advance of the white pawns. Black
can do nothing against this plan.

33. ...   P—Q R 4
34. P—R 3   P × P
35. R P × P   R—B 1
36. K—Kt 3   R—Q 2
37. K—B 4   K—B 1
38. B—B 5 ch   K—B 2
39. R—K 7 ch   R × R
40. R × R ch   K—B 3

Or 40. ... K—Kt 1; 41. B—Q 4
and White wins.

41. P—R 4   B × P
42. P × B   Black
                   resigned.

No. 6.   French Defence

V. SMYSLOV   I. BOLESLAVSKY

*(Tournament for the Absolute Championship of the U.S.S.R.,
Moscow–Leningrad, 1941)*

1. P—K 4	P—K 3
2. P—Q 4	P—Q 4
3. Kt—Q B 3	B—Kt 5
4. P—K 5	P—Q B 4
5. P—Q R 3	B × Kt ch
6. P × B	Kt—K 2
7. P—Q R 4	*15*

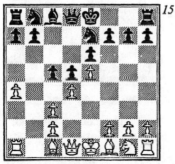

15

The starting-point of innumerable investigations. The doubled pawns on the Q B-file make cooperation between both flanks difficult for White; however the pawn centre is strengthened and there is the possibility of exploiting the weaknesses on the black squares in the opponent's camp. With this aim in view White makes an outlet for his black-squared Bishop.

7. ...	Q—R 4
8. Q—Q 2	

Another plan here is 8. B—Q 2, P—B 5; 9. Q—Kt 4 with active play on the K-side.

8. ...	Q Kt—B 3
9. Kt—B 3	P—B 5

After this move White need never fear any complications in the centre. True, the exchange 9. ... P × P; 10. P × P, Q × Q ch; 11. B × Q, stopping 11. ... Kt—R 4, also left White the better chances. Preferable was 9. ... B—Q 2.

10. P—Kt 3	O—O
11. B—K Kt 2	P—B 3
12. P × P	R × P
13. O—O	

The opening has resulted in White's favour: he controls more space and can build up an attack on the backward K P.

13. ...	B—Q 2
14. B—Q R 3	R—K 1
15. Kt—R 4	Kt—B 1

He would have done better to have exchanged the Kt by 15. ... Kt—B 4

16. P—B 4	Q Kt—K 2
17. K R—Kt 1	

White takes measures to strengthen his Q-side position before beginning a systematic siege of the K P.

17. ...	Q—B 2
18. P—R 5	B—B 3
19. Kt—B 3	Kt—K Kt 3

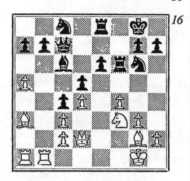

20. Kt—K 5!

Now the Kt occupies a beautiful position in the centre. Black cannot exchange it, as then the K B-file becomes an avenue for attack. For example, 20. ... Kt × Kt; 21. B P × Kt, R—B 2; 22. R—K B 1, R × R ch; 23. R × R, Q × R P; 24. B—Kt 4, Q—B 2; 25. Q—B 4, with the threat of 26. Q—B 8 ch! If then 25. ... P—K R 3, White continues with 26. B—B 3 threatening B—R 5 with a decisive attack.

20. ...	Kt (B 1)—K2
21. B—B 5	P—Q R 3
22. Kt—Kt 4	

White has stabilized the Q-side, where his black-squared Bishop has found a strong position at Q B 5. His advantage in space is obvious. Now he intends to attack on the K-side, but first pressure is brought to bear on the backward K P.

22. ...	R—B 2
23. R—K 1	Kt—B 4
24. R—K 2	P—R 3
25. Q R—K 1	Q—B 1

25. ... B—Q 2 was impossible because of 26. B × P, while 25. ... Q × R P; 26. R × P, R × R; 27. R × R only increased White's initiative.

26. B—B 3

This move has the double purpose of freeing K Kt 2 for a Rook and preparing either B—R 5 or P—R 4—R 5 increasing still further his advantage in space.

26. ...	K—R 2
27. R—K B 1	Q—B 2

28. Q—K 1

White has concentrated all his forces on the K-side. As before, it is bad for Black to play 28. ... Q × R P; 29. R × P, R × R; 30. Q × R, as the white pieces invade his position. If 28. ... Q—Q 2; 29. Kt—B 2, Kt—B 1; 30. B—R 5, P—K Kt 3; 31. B—B 3, White then threatens Kt—Kt 4—K 5, and should Black try to prevent this manœuvre by 31. ... P—R 4, White can take advantage of this new weakness in Black's pawn formation by 32. Kt—R 3.

28. ...	Kt—B 1
29. Kt—K 5	R—B 3
30. P—Kt 4	Kt—Q 3
31. Q—Kt 3	Kt—B 2

The danger of a pawn storm looms over Black's position. If 31. ... Kt—K 5, White simply plays 32. B × Kt ch, P × B; 33. Kt × P, not fearing 33. ... B—Kt 4, because of 34. Kt—Q 6. After other moves Black's position remains difficult since White always has the possibility of a pawn breakthrough.

32. P—Kt 5   Kt × Kt

This sacrifice is forced on account of 33. P—Kt 6 ch.

33. P × R   Kt × B ch
34. R × Kt   P × P
35. P—B 5

A thrust which leads to speedy victory.

35. ...   Q × Q ch
36. R × Q   P—K 4
37. R (2)—Kt 2   Kt—Q 2

In defending himself from one mate the King falls into a second mating net.

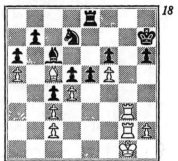

18

18

38. R—Kt 7 ch   K—R 1
39. R (7)—Kt 6   K—R 2
40. B—R 3   P × P
41. B—B 1!   Black
                  resigned.

No. 7.   Queen's Pawn, Grunfeld Defence

V. SMYSLOV   A. LILIENTHAL

(Moscow Championship, 1942)

1. P—Q 4   Kt—K B 3
2. P—Q B 4   P—K Kt 3
3. P—K Kt 3   P—Q 4

The advance of the central pawn reflects the influence of the new ideas, characteristic of the modern understanding of opening strategy. The struggle against the pawn centre by the pieces acting on the centre squares—that is the problem, which is exemplified in reality by the Grunfeld Defence. In recent years Soviet masters have introduced much that is new in the investigation and improvement of this difficult defence.

4. P × P   Kt × P
5. B—Kt 2   B—Kt 2
6. Kt—K B 3   O—O
7. O—O   Kt—Kt 3
8. Kt—B 3   Kt—B 3

A curious manœuvre—by a vigorous sortie the Kt entices the white pawn forward to a square where it will come under further attacks. If 9. P—K 3, Black could play 9. ... P—Q R 4 to blockade White's Q-side by the advance of the Q R P. Black also has the possibility of opening up the game by P—K 4.

9. P—Q 5   Kt—Kt 1
10. Kt—Q 4

Striving to stop 10. ... P—Q B 3, which would be answered by 11. P × P! But the position of the Kt on Q 4 has its darker sides.

10. ...   P—K 3!
11. P—K 4   P × P

Useless! He should have consistently undermined White's pawn wedge by 11. ... P—Q B 3. After 11. ... P—Q B 3; 12. Kt—Kt 3, K P × P; 13. P × P, P × P; 14. Kt × P, Kt—B 3, Black experiences no difficulty in development.

12. P × P

The white Q P is now isolated, and probably Black hoped to take advantage of this. However in this position the isolated pawn is not a weakness at all; on the contrary, it disorganizes the normal development of the opponent's Q-side.

12. ...   Q Kt—Q 2
13. B—B 4   Kt—K 4
14. P—K R 3   Kt (Kt 3)—
15. P—Kt 3   B 5

A certain care is required. The natural-looking 15. Q—B 2 allowed 15. ... P—Q B 4! For example, 15. Q—B 2, P—Q B 4; 16. P × Pe.p., Q × Kt; 17. P × P, B × Kt P; 18. B × B, Q R—Kt 1 and Black has the initiative.

15. ...   Kt—Q 3
16. R—K 1   R—K 1
17. R—Q B 1

Threatening to go over to the attack by 18. Kt (B 3)—Kt 5; if 17. ... B—Q 2, then 18. R—B 2 followed by doubling Rooks on the K-file is possible.

17. ...   P—Q R 3
18. Kt—R 4   Kt—Kt 4 *19*

19

19. Kt—K 6!

A very effective combination: the game is opened up to White's advantage. His pieces are beautifully placed, and now the fianchettoed Bishop, helped by the advanced pawn, becomes a terrible force. If 19. ... P × Kt; 20. B × Kt, P × P; 21. Q × P ch, Black cannot avoid material loss.

19. ...   B × Kt
20. P × B   R × P
21. Kt—B 5   Q × Q

Black was in an embarrassing position. 21. ... R—Q 3 was bad due to the following variation: 22. Q—K 2, Kt—Q 5 (or 22. ... Kt—Q 6; 23. Kt × Kt, R × Kt; 24. B × Kt P) 23. Q—K 4, P—B 4; 24. Q—K 3 and the black Knights are entangled.

22. K R × Q   R—Q 3
23. Kt × Kt P   R × R ch
24. R × R   R—Kt 1

The end game has brought Black no relief as the weak pawns on the Q-side are difficult to defend. White, relying on a strong pair of Bishops, combines chasing a Black Kt and attacking the weak pawns.

25. P—Q R 4	Kt—B 6
26. R—Q 2	R—K 1
27. Kt—B 5	P—Q R 4
28. R—B 2!	

The hunt continues. Black's Bishop cannot help because the Kt blocking the diagonal has no square of retreat.

28. ...	Kt—Q 8
29. B—Q 2	B—B 1!

A resourceful defence. If 30. B × P, then 30. ... Kt × P! with good practical chances, as 31. K × Kt, B × Kt ch; 32. R × B is impossible on account of 32. ... Kt—Q 6 ch. White prefers another plan.

30. Kt—K4	R—Kt 1
31. B × P	R × P
32. B × P	

And so White's toil is crowned with success. But to realize the advantage of the extra pawn is not easy as Black's pieces are actively placed.

32. ...	Kt—Q 6 20

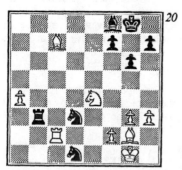

20

33. B—B 1!

An excellent defensive move, which prevents the counterplay based on 33. ... R—Kt 8. Black now constructs a shield with his Knights to cut off the distant passed pawn from its own pieces.

33. ...	Kt(Q8)—Kt7
34. P—R 5	P—B 4
35. Kt—Q 2	R—R 6
36. Kt—B 4!	

Breaking the obstacle formed by the black Knights. Now the crisis must be very near: everything depends on whether Black can take advantage of the defensive positions of White's pieces and recover the pawn. If not, that pawn will quickly decide the battle.

36. ...	Kt × Kt
37. R × Kt	R—R 8
38. B—Kt 6	

Here the Bishop occupies the best position and at the same time leaves the way to the eighth rank clear for the Rook. 38. ... B—Kt 5 is parried by 39. R—Q 4, while if 38. ... Kt—K 8, then 39. R—B 3, B—Kt 5; 40. R—B 8 ch, K—B 2; 41. P—R 6, Kt—B 5 ch; 42. K—Kt 2, Kt—K 8 ch; 43. K—R 1, Kt—Q 6; 44. P—R 7 preserves a winning advantage.

38. ...	Kt—K 4
39. R—B 3	B—Kt 5
40. R—B 8 ch	K—B 2
41. K—Kt 2!	

Black resigned, because the white pawn cannot be taken. After 41. ... B × P; 42. B—Q 4, R—K 8; 43. R—B 5, Black loses a piece; if 41. ... Kt—Q 2, then White wins by 42. B—Kt 5, Kt × B; 43. P × Kt, B—Q 3; 44. P—Kt 7.

No. 8. Ruy Lopez

V. SMYSLOV   M. BOTVINNIK

(Moscow Championship, 1943)

1. P—K 4   P—K 4
2. Kt—K B 3   Kt—Q B 3
3. B—Kt 5   P—Q R 3
4. B—R 4   Kt—B 3
5. O—O   Kt × P

Leading to the Open Variation of the Ruy Lopez, which has enjoyed great popularity in the past.

In spite of the evolution of opening ideas, this system of defence has stood the stern test of time.

In choosing this old method of development in this game, grandmaster Botvinnik intended to put to the test a new continuation, which up to that time had not been met in tournaments in the U.S.S.R.

6. P—Q 4   P—Q Kt 4
7. B—Kt 3   P—Q 4
8. P × P   B—K 3
9. P—B 3

The alternative plan is 9. Q—K 2 in order to become active in the centre after 10. R—Q 1.

9. ...   B—Q B 4

The placing of the Bishop on Q B 4 is usually bound up with a plan of attack on the K-side. 9. ... B—K 2, leaving Q B 4 free for the manœuvre Kt—B 4, puts less responsibility on Black.

10. Q Kt—Q 2   O—O
11. B- -B 2   *21*

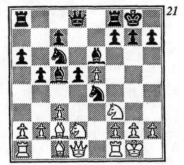

11. ...   Kt×K B P!?

An interesting and courageous idea! Black strives to create a direct attack on his opponent's King. From the point of view of the general laws of opening strategy an attempt to seize the initiative at such an early stage of the game may be open to criticism; but in the practical struggle, where the train of thought is limited by a cruel time control, it is not always easy to find the correct way of solving the problems, which are put in White's way in this opening.

12. R × Kt   P—B 3!

The opening of the K B-file and the rapid mobilization of all the pieces is the point of the previous Kt sacrifice.

13. P × P   Q × P
14. Q—B 1!

By bringing his Queen over to the K-side White strengthens his position. The Kt remains on Q 2 to serve as an extra defence for the other Kt on K B 3.

14. ...   B—K Kt 5
15. K—R 1

White should have given preference to 15. Q—Q 3! which attacks both K R 7 and Q 5. Evidently, Black would have had to consent to the continuation 15. ... Q—B 4; 16. Q × Q, B × Q; 17. B—Kt 3, Q R—Q 1; 18. Kt—B 1, B × R ch; 19. K × B, with an ending favourable for White.

15. ...   B × R
16. Q × B   Q R —K 1
17. Q—Kt 3   Kt—K 4
18. B—Q 1

Methodically defending his K B 3. Black's pieces are beautifully placed, and White must endure their attacks until he can disentangle his pieces on the first rank.

18. ...   Kt—Q 6   22

More active is 18. ... P—K R 4, for if 19. P—K R 4, the black Bishop would remain for a long time on the important square K Kt 5. A possible continuation would be 18. ... P—K R 4; 19. P—K R 4, Kt—Q 6; 20. K—R 2, P—B 4; 21. Kt—B 1 with a tense struggle in prospect. However, even as this complicated game went, great creative effort was demanded of both players.

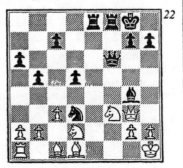

19. P—K R 3

Making an outlet for the King and thus ridding himself of the threats to the first rank.

19. ...   B—R 4
20. B—B 2   Kt—B 5
21. Kt—K Kt 1!

This prevents the entry of the enemy Rook at K 2 and at the same time executes the regrouping of minor pieces, which he was planning.

21. ...   P—B 4
22. Kt (Q 2)—B 3   Kt—K 7
23. Kt × Kt   R × Kt
24. B—Q 1

The Bishop comes back to its old defensive position again. The natural 24. B—Q 3 could be answered by 24. ... B × Kt; 25. P × B, R—K 8 ch; 26. Q × R, Q × P ch; 27. K—R 2, Q × B and Black has a dangerous attack. After the text move White answers 24. ... B × Kt with 25. P × B, R—K 3; 26. B—Q 2 followed by P—K B 4, B—B 3 and the transfer of the Rook to the K-side.

24. ...   R—K 3
25. B—Q 2   P—R 3
26. K—R 2   R—K 5

Black ought to have retreated his Bishop to K Kt 3, so preventing White's tactical threat. After the move played White gains a decisive advantage.

27. Kt—Kt 5!   P × Kt
28. B × B   R—K 4
29. B—B 3   Q—K 2
30. P—Q R 4

The opening of the Q R-file helps White to bring his Rook into action. 30. ... P—Q Kt 5 does not work on account of 31. P × P, P × P; 32. B × Q Kt P!

30. ...	K—R 2
31. P × P	P × P
32. R—R 7	Q—Q 3
33. B—Kt 4	

Now 34. B × P is threatened. 33. B × Kt P did not work at once because of 33. ... R × K B; 34. P × R, R—K 7 ch.

33. ...	R—Q 1
34. K—R 1	

Because of his time-trouble White does not notice the combination which he carries out later.

34. ...	P—Q 5	
35. P × P	P × P	23

36. B—B 4!	R—K 8 ch

36. ... P × B lost to 37. B—B 5 ch.

37. Q × R	Q × B
38. R—Q 7	R × R
39. B × R	P—Q 6
40. B—Kt 4	

40. B × P also wins. Now White's material advantage guarantees him a fairly simple win.

40. ...	P—Q 7
41. Q—K 2	P—Kt 5
42. Q—Q 3 ch	P—Kt 3
43. K—Kt 1	K—R 3
44. P—Q Kt 3	K—Kt 2
45. B—B 3	Q—K B 2
46. K—B 2	Q—K 3
47. Q—K 3	Q—Q 3
48. B—Q 1	Q—Q 4
49. P—Kt 4	K—R 2
50. K—K 2	Black
	resigned.

No. 9.   Sicilian Defence

V. SMYSLOV   A. KOTOV

(Moscow Championship, 1943)

1. P—K 4	P—Q B 4
2. Kt—Q B 3	Kt—Q B 3
3. P—K Kt 3	P—K Kt 3
4. B—Kt 2	B—Kt 2
5. P—Q 3	P—Q 3
6. Kt—B 3	

In the Closed Variation of the Sicilian Defence, which M. I. Tchigorin did much work on, the Kt is usually developed on K 2. In this game White varies a little from known theoretical paths.

6. ...	P—K 3
7. B—Kt 5	K Kt—K 2
8. Q—Q 2	

Intending to exchange the black-squared Bishops by B—R 6. Black prevents this threat, but as a result has difficulty in castling. This circumstance leaves its imprint on the plans of both players.

8. ...	P—K R 3
9. B—K 3	P—K 4

Black hurries to develop his Q B, but this helps White eventually to open the K B-file by P—K B 4.

10. O—O   B—K 3
11. Kt—K 1   Q—Q 2
12. P—Q R 3

This move and R—Q Kt 1, which soon follows, were played to be ready should Black castle Q-side.

12. ...   B—R 6
13. P—B 4   Kt—Q 5
14. R—Kt 1   P × P
15. B × P   B × B
16. Q × B   O—O   24

At last Black has managed to castle, however White by advancing his K Kt P prepares an immediate attack on his opponent's King.

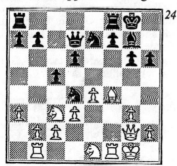

17. P—K Kt 4   Q R—Q 1
18. K—R 1   Kt—K 3
19. B—Q 2   P—Q 4
20. Kt—B 3   P—Q 5

Black blocks the centre, a plan which fits in well with White's intentions: it is well known that when the pawn position in the centre is fixed it is easier to carry out an attack on the wing. He should have played 20. ... P × P; 21. Kt × P, Kt—Q 5.

21. Kt—K 2   Kt—B 3
22. Q—R 3   K—R 2
23. Kt—Kt 3   P—B 3   25

One gets the impression that Black has only to play Kt—K 4 to complete his defensive set-up. But in this critical moment a combination bursts upon his position.

24. Kt—B 5 !

A piece sacrifice typical of such positions. The special characteristic in this case is White's desire not to recover the sacrificed material immediately but to increase systematically the force of his attack. One should not calculate concrete variations here, but rather rely on an appraisal of the position based on general principles.

24. ...   P × Kt
25. Kt P × P   Kt—B 2

If 25. ... Kt—Kt 4, then 26. B × Kt, P × B; 27. Kt × P ch and 28. Kt—K 6 winning the exchange and remaining with Rook and two pawns against two minor pieces. White also retains his attack.

26. R—Kt 1   Kt—K 1

This prepares the King's flight to the Q-side and also avoids the combination 27. R × B ch, K × R; 28. R—Kt 1 ch, K—B 2; 29. Q—

R 5 ch, K—K 2; 30. R—Kt 7 ch.
If Black had tried to defend himself
by 26. ... R—K R 1, the following
continuation would have been
decisive: 27. B × P, B × B (27. ...
K—Kt 1; 28. R × B ch, Q × R;
29. R—Kt 1); 28. R—Kt 6, Q—
Kt 2; 29. R × Q ch, K × R; 30.
Q—Kt 3 ch and 31. Q × Kt.

27. R—Kt 6	R—B 2
28. Q R—Kt 1	K—Kt 1
29. R × R P	K—B 1

Avoiding the threatened mate.

30. R—R 7	K—K 2
31. Q—R 5	K—Q 3

Black continues the King march
in search of a secure haven. The
attempt to free Q 1 for the King
by 31. ... R—Q B 1 was insuffi-
cient on account of 32. Kt—Kt 5!
P × Kt; 33. B × P ch, e.g. (a) 33.
... Kt—B 3; 34. R × B, R × R;
35. B × Kt ch, K × B; 36. Q—
R 6 ch, K—K 4; 37. R × R, Q—
K 1; 38. R—Kt 6 or (b) 33. ... K—
Q 3; 34. B—B 4 ch, K—K 2 (34. ...
Kt—K 4; 35. P—B 6!); 35. P—B 6 ch!
Kt × P; 36. R (1) × B, Kt × Q;
37. R × R ch, K—K 3; 38. R × Q,
Kt × B; 39. R × Kt P with a won
ending.

32. B—B 4 ch	Kt—K 4

Seemingly Black has warded off
the direct threats to his King by
closing the dangerous diagonal.
Now, however, White finds a
manœuvre after which his attack

flares up with new vigour. 32. ...
K—K 2 is followed by 33. Kt—
Kt 5!, P × Kt; 34. B × P ch.

33. B × Kt ch	P × B	26

26

34. P—B 6!

The decisive blow; it is based on
the problem motives of the pinning
of and line-cutting by the Black
pieces. White's attack has reached
its zenith. However Black takes the
pawn he suffers material loss.

34. ...	Kt × P
35. Q × P ch	K—B 3
36. R (7) × B!	K—Kt 4
37. Kt × P ch	K—Kt 3

Or 37. ... Q × Kt; 38. Q × Q,
P × Q; 39. R × R.

38. P—Kt 4	R—Q B 1

38. ... P × Kt is impossible
because of the obvious mate in
two.

39. R × R	Q × R
40. Q—Q 6 ch	R—B 3
41. Kt × R	Kt × P
42. P × P ch	Black
	resigned.

No. 10.   Catalan System
G. RAVINSKY   V. SMYSLOV
(Thirteenth Soviet Championship, Moscow, 1944)

1. P—Q 4	Kt—K B 3
2. P—Q B 4	P—K 3
3. P—K Kt 3	P—Q 4
4. B—Kt 2	P × P

One of the best ways of handling this opening: while White is winning back the pawn, Black mobilizes his Q-side. The alternative system consists in maintaining a pawn at Q 4 and so limiting the activity of White's K B on the long diagonal. Thus after 4. ... B—K 2; 5. Kt—K B 3, O—O; 6. O—O, Q Kt—Q 2; 7. Q—B 2, P—B 3; 8. Q Kt—Q 2, P—Q Kt 3; 9. P—K 4, B—Kt 2, Black maintains his pawn centre. Both systems are frequently met in tournament practice.

5. Q—R 4 ch   B—Q 2

With the intention of playing the bishop to Q B 3. Also possible here is 5. ... Q Kt—Q 2.

6. Q × B P	B—B 3
7. Kt—K B 3	B—K 2

Black first prepares to castle. Another continuation worth attention is 7. ... Q Kt—Q 2; 8. Kt—B 3, Kt—Kt 3; 9. Q—Q 3, B—Kt 5, strengthening his control over K 5; or 7. ... B—Q 4; 8. Q—Q 3, P—K 5; 9. Q—Q 1, P—B 4; 10. Kt—B 3, B—B 3, and Black has carried out the important advance P—Q B 4. Apropos of this last variation, 8. Q—R 4 ch may be answered by 8. ... Q—Q 2; 9. Q—Q 1, P—B 4, and if 10. Kt—K 5, then 10. ... Q—B 2.

8. Kt—B 3	O—O
9. O—O	Q Kt—Q 2
10. B—Kt 5	

10. Q—Q 3 led to a more complicated game. After 10. Q—Q 3, Kt—Q 4; 11. P—K 4, Kt × Kt; 12. P × Kt it would not be good to continue 12. ... Kt—B 4; 13. Q—K 3, Kt × P because of 14. Kt—K 5 and White regains the pawn with the better game. Instead of 12. ... Kt—B 4, it would be interesting to test out 12. ... P—K B 4, stirring up complications in the centre.

10. ...	P—K R 3
11. B × Kt	Kt × B
12. Q R—Q 1	27

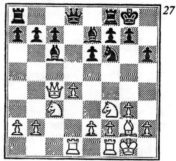
27

12. ...	Q—Q 3

Black's pieces must be regrouped to deal with the advance of White's central pawns. Accordingly he vacates his Q-square to be able to execute the manœuvre K R—Q 1, B—K 1 and P—Q B 3 with a solid position.

13. Q—Q 3	Q—Kt 5
14. Q—B 2	Q—R 4
15. P—K 4	K R—Q 1

Now 16. Kt—K 5 can be answered by 16. ... B—K 1; 17. Kt—B 4, Q—R 3; 18. P—Kt 3, P—B 3 with

the threat of P—Q Kt 4 and Q—
Kt 3: White cannot bring a Kt to
Q 6 by 19. P—K 5, Kt—Q 4;
20. Kt—K 4, for after 20. ... Kt—
Kt 5 White's Q-side pawns are
under attack.

16. K R—K 1   B—K 1

Black is consistent in carrying
out his plans. He is not afraid of
17. P—Q 5, P × P; 18. P × P,
B—Kt 5; 19. Kt—Q 4, B—Q 2;
20. P—Q R 3, as he can play either
20. ... B—Q 3 or 20. ... B × Kt;
21. Q × B, Q × Q; 22. P × Q,
R—K 1 with an equal ending.

With his next move White begins
the advance of his Q-side pawns.
However, relying on the potential
power of his two Bishops, Black has
time to strengthen his position and
unhurriedly prepare counterplay.

17. P—Q R 3   P—B 3
18. Kt—Q R 4   Q R—B 1
19. P—Q Kt 4   Q—B 2
20. Q—Kt 3   P—Q Kt 3
21. R—Q B 1

A position has arisen which is
surprisingly reminiscent of one of
the main variations of the Queen's
Gambit. Such is the interrelation of
ideas in chess! At this moment
White's forces are aimed at preventing the advance of the Q B P.

21. ...   P—B 4!

But Black plays 21. ... P—B 4 all
the same! This break marks the
beginning of the counter-attack.

22. Q P × P   B × Kt
23. Q × B   P × P
24. B—B 1   Q—Kt 3
25. P—Kt 5   28

Hoping to blockade the pawn by
26. B—B 4.

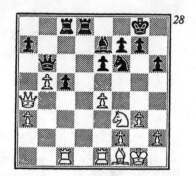

25. ...   P—B 5!

The pawn marches forward,
offering itself as a sacrifice for the
sake of new attacking chances
against the enemy King. White may
take the pawn with either Bishop or
Rook. Let us look at these possibilities.

After 26. B × P, Kt—Kt 5 the
weakness of White's K B 2 is
revealed.

If then 27. R—K 2, Black con-
tinues 27. ... R—Q 6!; 28. B × R,
R × R ch; 29. K—Kt 2, R— B 6
with dangerous threats, e.g. 30. Q—
Q 1, Q × P ch; 31. R × Q, Kt—
K 6 ch; 32. K—Kt 1, Kt × Q; 33.
R—Q 2, B—B 4 ch; 34. K—B 1,
Kt—B 7; 35. K—K 2, R × R P and
Black has an extra pawn in the end-
ing. To 27. R—B 1 the reply could
still be 27. ... R—Q 6!; 28. B × R,
R × R.

In the event of 27. R—B 2 Black
plays 27. ... R—Q 2 with the idea
of doubling Rooks on the Q B-file
and answering 28. P—R 3 with 28.
... Kt × P; 29. R × Kt, B—B 4;
30. R—K 2, Q—B 2 with a double
attack on the Bishop and the
K Kt P. Or 28. B—B 1, R (Q 2)—
B 2; 29. R—Q 2 (if 29. R (1)—B 1,
then 29. ... B × R P!), R—B 6
increasing the pressure.

Finally, let us consider the variations arising out of 26. R × P Kt—Kt 5!

Now unsatisfactory for White is 27. Q—B 2, R × R; 28. B × R, Kt × P, as 29. Q × Kt loses to 29. ... B—B 4; but by playing 27. R—K 2! R × R (or 27. ... B—B 4; 28. Q—B 2); 28. Q × R, B—B 4; 29. Q—B 2, Q × P; 30. P—R 3, White could have driven off the main attack to his King.

These variations show what dangers were attached to the capture of the pawn. Nevertheless, White should have sought solace where he could and played 26. R × P. By declining this chance the passed pawn is allowed to pass over the attacked square.

26. P—R 3	P—B 6
27. Q—Kt 3	B—B 4
28. R—B 2	

28. R—K 2 is followed by 28. ... B × P ch; 29. R × B, Kt × P; 30. Q—B 2, R—Q 7; 31. Q × Kt, Q × R ch; 32. K—R 1, R—Kt 7 and Black has a strong attack.

28. ...	R—Q 7!

The pressure on the point K B 7 grows all the stronger. It is interesting to notice how Black's counter-attack has grown up around the advance of his Q B P. If now 29. Kt × R, then 29. ... B × P ch; 30. K—Kt 2, B × R; 31. Kt—B 3, Q—K 6; 32. R—K 2, Q × R ch!; 33. B × Q, P—B 7 and the pawn promotes.

29. R × R	P × R
30. R—K 2	B × P ch

The first fruits of the attack. Of course, against 31. R × B, Kt × P is decisive.

31. K—Kt 2	R—B 6!
32. Q—Q 1	B—K 6
33. Kt × P	Q—Q 5

Black's pieces have taken up dominating positions, from which they exert the greatest pressure on White's position.

34. Q—K 1	Kt × P
35. Kt × Kt	Q × Kt ch
36. K—R 2	Q—Q 5
37. R—K Kt 2	R—B 8

Rather than take the R P Black prefers to invade the eighth rank with his heavy pieces. The end of the struggle is close at hand.

38. Q—K 2	Q—R 8	
39. Q × B	R × B	
40. P—Kt 4	R—K 8	29

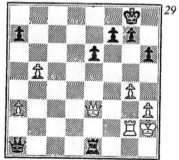

White resigned. After 41. Q × Q R P, Q—K 4 ch; 42. R—Kt 3, R—K 7 ch or 41. R—K 2, R—R 8 ch; 42. K—Kt 3, Q—K B 8; 43. R—K Kt 2, Q × P, Black wins easily.

No. 11.   Caro-Kann Defence
V. SMYSLOV   V. MAKOGONOV
(Thirteenth Soviet Championship, Moscow, 1944)

1. P—K 4	P—Q B 3		6. B—Q 3	P—Q B 4
2. P—Q 4	P—Q 4		7. P—B 3	P—B 5
3. P—K B 3				

This move does not enjoy a wide popularity, although it has its virtues. White strengthens his centre which causes his opponent to be extremely accurate in the choice of replies. As well as this, the system gives to the whole game a sharper and more individual character than in the usual variations of the Caro-Kann, where early on the tension in the centre is removed by pawn exchanges.

3. ...   P—K 3

Considered the most promising continuation. The alternative is 3. ... P × P; 4. P × P, P—K 4; 5. Kt—K B 3, B—K 3!, but not 5. ... P × P; 6. B—Q B 4 and White gets a strong attack.

4. B—K 3   Q—Kt 3

Attacking the Q Kt P and also preparing for P—Q B 4—the thematic advance in such a pawn configuration. In the event of 4. ... P × P; 5. Kt—Q 2, P × P; 6. K Kt × P White has a strong attack for the pawn.

5. Kt—Q 2   Kt—Q 2

Black refrains from taking the offered pawn because he wants to take it several moves later in more favourable circumstances. The immediate 5. ... P—Q B 4 would be answered by 6. K P × P; K P × P; 7. P × P, B × P; 8. B × B, Q × B; 9. Kt—Kt 3 and Black has an isolated Q P.

A major decision: Black closes the position on the Q-side, intending to capture the Q Kt P and castle Q-side.

8. B—Q B 2	Q × Kt P	
9. Kt—K 2	Q—R 6	
10. O—O	Kt—Kt 3	
11. P × P		

Just as Black has managed to stabilize the position on the flank, White opens a line in the centre.

11. ...	P × P	
12. R—K 1	B—Q 2	
13. Kt—K B 1	O—O—O	
		30

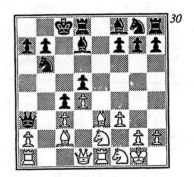

30

14. B—B 1

An excellently timed manœuvre, which forces the Black Queen to abandon its good position at Q R 6 and so frees the way for the advance of the Q R P. Now Black cannot establish a blockade of the Q-side by controlling the critical square Q R 5.

14. ...	Q—R 4
15. P—Q R 4	B—Q 3
16. Kt—K 3	Kt—K 2
17. B—Q 2	Q R—K 1

Black frees Q 1 in case he needs to retreat the Queen and keeps the other Rook on the K-side.

18. Kt—Kt 3

Threatening to provoke the weakening of Black's pawn position by 19. Kt—R5.

18. ...   P—R 4

Limiting the activity of the Kt. Now Black's decision to keep a Rook on K R 1 so as to continue with P—Kt 3 and deprive White of any sort of initiative is justified. The immediate 18. ... P—K Kt 3 was not so accurate on account of 19. Kt—Kt 4; in that case to exchange the Kt would not be good for Black, since White would get new possibilities by pressure on the open file.

19. Kt (K 3)—B 5	Kt × Kt
20. Kt × Kt	B × Kt
21. B × B ch	K—Kt 1
22. P—B 4	

Opening a way for the Queen to start operations on the K-side.

22. ...	P—Kt 3
23. B—B 2	P—B 4

Black is very consistent in his desire to limit the mobility of the enemy Bishop and prevent P—B 5.

24. Q—B 3   R—K 5   *31*

A fine positional idea, which is the logical complement of Black's previous strategy: White's activity after 25. Q—Kt 3 is curtailed. If now 25. B × R, then 25. ... Q P × B; 26. Q—Kt 3, R—Kt 1 followed

by Kt—Q 4 and Black's position is impregnable. Against 24. ... P—R 5 White would probably have continued 25. Q—R 3.

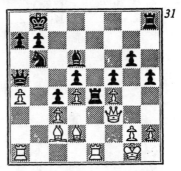

25. Q—Kt 3!

The beginning of an interesting manœuvre: the Queen gradually infiltrates into the enemy's position deflecting his pieces to passive positions.

25. ...	R—Kt 1
26. Q—Kt 5	B—K 2
27. Q—R 6	B—B 3
28. Q—R 7	R—Kt 2
29. Q—R 8 ch	Kt—B 1
30. B × R	

At last White accepts the sacrifice of the exchange, taking advantage of the fact that the Kt cannot immediately occupy the important square Q 4.

30. ...	Q P × B
31. Q—B 8	Q—Q 1

Materially speaking White has a little advantage, but in an ending— after the exchange of Queens— Black would transfer his Kt to Q 4 and preserve a strong position. So White decides to keep the Queens on and by continual threats make a systematic re-grouping difficult for Black.

32. Q—Kt 4	R—Q B 2
33. P—R 5	P—R 3
34. Q R—Kt 1	B—K 2
35. Q—R 4	Q—Q 2
36. Q—R 2	Q—Q 4
37. R—Kt 2	Kt—R 2 *32*

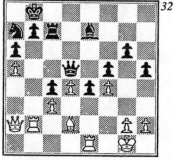

A complex and tense position has been reached. Black tries to bring his pieces into active play, but White's position contains sufficient resources to neutralize the threats of his opponent.

38. R—Kt 6   Kt—B 3

Clearly Black has overestimated his chances. True, now he wins the Q R P, but White is allowed to bring his heavy pieces into action and remove the base of the pawn chain—K 5—B 4—Kt 3—R 4—the K Kt P. So 38. ... R—B 3 was preferable, offering the exchange of Rooks, after which Black would have had no worries about the solidity of his position.

| 39. R (1)—Kt 1 | K—B 1 |
| 40. Q—Kt 2 | Kt × R P |

This is forced on account of the triple attack on the Q Kt P. Now, however, White wins an important pawn on the K-side.

| 41. R × K Kt P | Kt—Kt 6 |
| 42. B—K 3 | P—R 4 |

This is what Black had counted on: the white Rook has been diverted to the other side and in the meantime the Q R P moves forward.

| 43. Q—K 2 | P—Q R 5 |
| 44. R—Kt 2 | |

This move and R—R 2, which soon follows, brings to a standstill the dangerous advance of the passed Q R P. At the same time the White Queen is left free to start aggressive action.

44. ...	Q—R 4
45. R—Kt 8 ch	B—Q 1
46. R—R 2!	P—Kt 4
47. Q × R P	Q × P
48. Q × P ch	R—Q 2 *33*

49. K—B 2

And now it is clear that while Black's operations on the Q-side may have created for him most threatening passed pawns they have not guaranteed the security of his King. The second invasion of the enemy camp by the White Queen decides the outcome of this tense struggle. The open position of the Black King allows White to build up an attack which cannot be warded off.

49. ...	Q—R 4
50. Q—K 6!	Q—B 2
51. P—B 5	K—Kt 2
52. R—Kt 6	K—B 1
53. Q × KP	

This capture threatens 54. R—Q B 6 with a further strengthening of the attack.

53. ...   Q—Kt 2
54. R—B 6 ch   K—Kt 1
55. P—Q 5

At last the black-squared Bishop enters the game—and very forcefully.

55. ...   Kt—R 4
56. Q—K 5 ch   K— R 1
57. Q—K 6   K—Kt 1
58. R—Kt 2!

An important link in the final manœuvre planned by White. If 58. ... P—R 6, then 59. R × Kt P!, Q × R (Kt 4); 60. Q × R, Kt × R; 61. P × Kt and White wins.

58. ...   Kt—Kt 6
59. B—B 4 ch   K—R 2
60. R—R 6 ch   Black
                     resigned

After 60. ... Q × R; 61. Q × R ch he loses a piece. Now the idea behind 58. R—Kt 2 becomes apparent: the Black Kt is diverted from the defence of its position.

No. 12.   Sicilian Defence

V. SMYSLOV   A. KONSTANTINOPOLSKY

(*Moscow Championship, 1944*)

1. P—K 4   P—Q B 4
2. Kt—K B 3   Kt—Q B 3
3. P—Q 4   P × P
4. Kt × P   Kt—B 3
5. Kt—Q B 3   P—Q 3
6. B—K 2   P—K Kt 3

Black employs the most active system of development, known by theory as the Dragon Variation. It usually leads to sharp play.

7. B—K 3   B—Kt 2
8. Q—Q 2   O—O
9. O—O—O

Castling on opposite sides in this position determines the character of the play for the rest of the game: White has chances in the centre and on the K-side based on the advance of the K R P, while Black has counterplay along the open Q B-file. Now it would hardly be correct to play 9. ... P—Q 4; 10. Kt × Kt, P × Kt; 11. P × P, P × P; 12. Kt × P, Kt × Kt;

13. Q × Kt, Q—B 2 (13. ... R—Kt 1; 14. P—Q Kt 3!); 14. Q × R, B—B 4; 15. Q × R ch, K × Q; 16. B—Q 3! But he could play 9. ... Kt—K Kt 5; 10. B × Kt, B × B; 11. P—B 3, B—Q 2 with a perfectly satisfactory position. However, he chooses a more complex defence.

9. ...   Kt × Kt
10. B × Kt   B—K 3
11. K—Kt 1   R—B 1
12. P—K R 4!

The signal for the attack. The advance of the K R P threatens to open the way to the Black King.

12. ...   B—B 5
13. B—B 3   R—K 1

This prophylactic move, preparing a Queen sortie to Q R 4 (13. ... Q—R 4 would be bad because of 14. P—Q Kt 3, B—K 3; 15. Kt—Q 5, attacking the K P), is unsatisfactory in this position. He should have played 13. ... P—K R 4 keeping the K R-file closed. After 13. ... P—K R 4; 14. K R—K 1, R—K 1; 15. P—Q Kt 3, B—K 3; 16. Kt—K 2 and 17. B—Kt 2 White has a strong position in the centre, but there is a long and difficult struggle still ahead.

14. P—R 5

Of course! The opening of the K R-file ensures White a powerful attack. Black's counterplay on the Q-side is obviously slow.

14. ...   **Q—R 4**
15. P—R 3

A quiet reply which prevents possible threats to the White King.

15. ...   **Q—R 3**

15. ... Kt × R P could be answered by 16. B × B, Kt × B (or 16. ... K × B; 17. P—K Kt 4, Kt—B 3; 18. Q—R 6 ch, K—Kt 1; 19. P—Kt 5 etc.); 17. Q—R 6, P—B 3; 18. B—Kt 4 and 19. P—B 4 with a strong attack.

16. P × P   **R P × P**   *34*

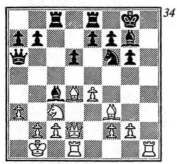

34

17. Kt—Q 5!

The Kt hurries to take an active part in the battle. If 17. ... B × Kt; 18. P × B, the threat of P—K Kt 4 —Kt 5 gains momentum.

17. ...   **P—K 4**
18. Kt × Kt ch   **B × Kt**
19. B—B 3

Thanks to the central pawn thrust —P—K 4—Black has managed to 'conceal' his chief defender—his fianchettoed Bishop. But a new weakness—on Q 3—has appeared in his position. By combining attack on the King with pressure on the Q-file White methodically builds up a general assault.

19. ...   **R—B 3**
20. B—K Kt 4   **R—Q 1**
21. P—B 4!   **Q—Kt 4**
22. P—B 5

The attack grows with every move. The advance of the K B P finally smashes the enemy King's pawn cover. If 22. ... P—Kt 4, then 23. R—R 6, K—Kt 2; 24. Q R—R 1 threatening 25. R × B, followed by R—R 6 ch. If then 24. ... R—K Kt 1, Black has no saving move after 25. P—Q Kt 3!

22. ...   **P × P**
23. B × B P   **K—B 1**
24. B—Q Kt 4   **P—Kt 3**   *35*

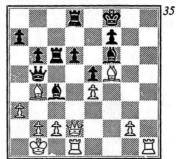

35

25. R—R6

All White's pieces have taken up excellent positions. The dénouement cannot be far off. If 25. ...

K—K2, then 26. P—Kt 4, P—R 4;   27. Q—R 6 ch   K—K 1
27. P—Kt 5 is decisive.   28. Q—R 8 ch   K—K 2
  25. ...   P—R 4   29. Q—R 4!   R—K R 1
  26. R × B   P × B   30. R—R 6 ch   Black
                                             resigned.

No. 13. Sicilian Defence
V. SMYSLOV   I. RUDAKOVSKY
(Fourteenth Soviet Championship, Moscow, 1945)

1. P—K 4   P—Q B 4
2. Kt—K B 3   P—K 3
3. P—Q 4   P × P
4. Kt × P   Kt—K B 3
5. Kt—Q B 3   P—Q 3

Black's central pawn set-up is characteristic of the so-called Scheveningen Variation, one of the most popular systems of development in the Sicilian Defence. White's chances are usually based on an attack on the K-side.

6. B—K 2   B—K 2
7. O—O   O—O
8. B—K 3   Kt—B 3
9. P—B 4   Q—B 2
10. Q K 1

This move has a twofold aim: to transfer the Queen to K Kt 3, where it will be in a good attacking position, and to vacate Q 1 for the manœuvre Q R—Q 1.

10. ...   Kt × Kt
11. B × Kt   P—K 4

This central pawn thrust is the point of the previous exchange. Now it is better for White to retreat his Bishop from Q 4, as after 12. P × P, P × P; 13. Q—Kt 3, B—Q B 4 the black-squared Bishops are exchanged, which, in

my opinion, lessens White's chances of attack.

12. B—K 3   B—K 3

It was better to develop the Bishop on B 3 by B—Q 2—B 3. The text move has the defect that it allows White to start a pawn advance on the K-side with a gain of tempo.

13. P—B 5   B—B 5

Black executes a plan, which from the positional point of view is incorrect: P—K 4 weakened the centre point Q 4, so he should preserve his white-squared Bishop to defend that important square. It is true that after 13. ... B—Q 2, White could continue 14. P—K Kt 4, B—B 3; 15. B—B 3 with the threat of P—Kt 5. Then 15. ... P—K R 3 would not help on account of 16. P—Kt 5, P × P; 17. B × Kt P and White has opened the K Kt-file for attack. Instead of 15. ... P—K R 3, it would be interesting to try 15. ... P—Q 4; 16. P × P, P—K 5; 17. Kt × P, Kt × Q P with sharp play, although even then by 18. B—Q 4 White would seem to preserve the better chances.

14. B × B   Q × B   *36*

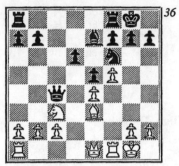

36

15. B—Kt 5!

An instructive example of how to take advantage of the weakness at Q 5 in such positions. The exchange on K B 6 is unavoidable whereupon the white Kt becomes firmly entrenched on Q 5. This gives White good prospects of a direct attack on the King.

15. ...	K R—K 1
16. B × Kt	B × B
17. Kt—Q 5	B—Q 1

In answer to 17. ... Q × B P White could play 18. R—B 2 and if 18. ... Q—B 4, then 19. R—B 1 and 20. Kt—B 7 winning the exchange.

18. P—B 3	P—Q Kt 4
19. P—Q Kt 3	Q—B 4 ch
20. K—R 1	R—Q B 1
21. R—B 3	K—R 1 *37*

Here and on the previous move Black might have played P—B 3, but by doing so he would have condemned himself to passive defence; White would only have to transfer his heavy pieces to the K-side to start a decisive storming of Black's King position.

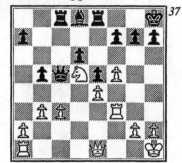

37

22. P—B 6!

A typical thrust—the pawn cover around Black's King is broken up.

22. ...   P × P

If 22. ... P—Kt 3, one has only to play 23. Q—Q 2 threatening Q—R 6.

23. Q—R 4	R—K Kt 1
24. Kt × P	R—Kt 2
25. R—Kt 3	

Threatening mate by both 26. Q × P ch, R × Q; 27. R—Kt 8 and 26. R × R, K × R; 27. Q × P ch, K × Kt; 28. R—B 1 ch, K—K 2; 29. Q × P.

25. ...	B × Kt
26. Q × B	R—K Kt 1
27. R—Q 1	P—Q 4
28. R × R!	Black resigned.

No. 14. Ruy Lopez
V. SMYSLOV   S. RESHEVSKY
(*Radio Match, U.S.S.R.–U.S.A., 1945*)

1. P—K 4	P—K 4		5. O—O	Kt × P
2. Kt—K B 3	Kt—Q B 3			
3. B—Kt 5	P—Q R 3			
4. B—R 4	Kt—B 3			

In playing the Open Defence Reshevsky evidently hoped that the old plan of attack, which he had prepared for this encounter, would not be sufficiently familiar to his opponent.

6. P—Q 4	P—Q Kt 4
7. B—Kt 3	P—Q 4
8. P × P	B—K 3
9. P—B 3	B—Q B 4
10. Q Kt—Q 2	O—O
11. B—B 2	P—B 4

For 11. ... Kt × K B P?! see game No. 8, Smyslov–Botvinnik. If 11. ... Kt × Kt, then 12. Q × Kt! and White has good prospects of a K-side attack. By the text move Black strengthens the Kt in its active position, which I believe to be the best plan here.

12. Kt—Kt 3	B—Kt 3
13. K Kt—Q 4	Kt × Kt
14. Kt × Kt	B × Kt

Black goes straight for complications, having in mind the forced variation which until very recently was considered to give him the initiative. 14. ... Q—K 2 deserved attention, as there need be no hurry to declare one's intentions.

| 15. P × B | P—B 5 |
| 16. P—B 3 | Kt—Kt 6 |

The logical completion of Black's opening idea. Of course, 16. ... Kt Kt 4; 17. P—K R 4, Kt—B 2; 18. B × P, Q × P; 19. Q—Q 2 gives White the better game. This variation (16. ... Kt—Kt 6) has been known for a long time: in the game Duras-Maroczy (Ostend, 1906) there followed 17. P × Kt, P × P; 18. R—K 1, Q—R 5; 19. B —K 3, B—Kt 5 and black has a fine attack. Not long before the Radio Match, U.S.S.R.-U.S.A., this position occurred in two of Boleslavsky's games against Ragosin (Moscow,

1942) and Botvinnik (Sverdlovsk, 1943) and it aroused great interest among Soviet chessplayers.

17. P × Kt   P × P   *38*

18. Q—Q 3

The beginning of an interesting manœuvre, which leads to a peculiar distribution of forces on both sides. If now 18. ... Q—R 5, then 19. Q × P ch, Q × Q; 20. B × Q ch, K × B; 21. B—Q 2 with a good ending for White, while if 18. ... P—Kt 3; 19. Q—K 3, Q—R 5; 20. Q—R 6, the mate is defended. Therefore Black's reply is practically forced.

18. ...	B—B 4
19. Q × B!	R × Q
20. B × R	Q—R 5
21. B—R 3	Q × P ch
22. K—R 1	Q × K P
23. B—Q 2	

A very interesting position has arisen: in exchange for the Bishops and Rook Black has a Queen and will quickly get an avalanche of pawns on the Q-side. Who has the better chances in the sharp struggle about to commence? This question awaits a conclusive answer in further analysis. In the above-

mentioned game Botvinnik continued here 23. ... P—B 4; 24. Q R
—K 1, Q × P; 25. B—B 4, P—Q 5;
26. B × P, P—Q 6 with a complicated game. Evidently White's
attacking possibilities are more
real than the dangerous threat of
the advance of Black's passed
pawns. However, Reshevsky
chooses another continuation.

23. ...   Q × P
24. B—B 4   P—B 4

Afterwards 24. ... P—Q 5! was
considered preferable; the intention is to cut down the mobility
of White's pieces by rapidly advancing the Q P. But even then I think
White retains attacking chances.
After the text move White could,
if he wished, transpose into well-
known paths by 25. Q R—K 1,
but there is a more energetic
manœuvre at his disposal.

25. B—K 6 ch   K—R 1
26. B × Q P

Annihilating the dangerous
passed pawn. Against the reply
26. ... Q—Q 5 White had prepared
27. B—K 4 followed by 28. B ×
Kt P.

26. ...   R—Q 1
27. Q R—Q 1   P—B 5
28. B × Kt P   P—B 6   39

28. ... Q × P was impossible
because of 29. B × P!, R × R;
30. R × R. Black advances his
passed pawns without wasting
any time. If Black had transferred his Queen to the defence of
his K-side by 28. ... Q—B 3, then
after 29. B—K 4, P—B 6; 30. R ×
R ch, Q × R; 31. B—B 2 his
pawns would have been blockaded.

29. B—K 5!

The Bishops have taken up a
dominating position in the centre of
the board. Now there is no danger
from 29. ... Q—K 7; 30. B × P,
R × B because of 31. Q R—K 1!,
R—R 4 ch; 32. K—Kt 1 and
thanks to the mating threats on
the back rank White has a decisive
advantage.

29. ...   P—Kt 5
30. B—Q Kt 3   R—Q 7!

Preventing a White Rook from
reaching the seventh rank. After
30. ... R × R; 31. R × R, P—K R
4; 32. R—Q 7, Q—Kt 8 ch; 33. K—
R 2, P—B 7; 34 R × P, Q—K 8;
35. R—Kt 8 ch, K—R 2; 36. R—
R 8 ch, K—Kt 3; 37. B × P ch,
K—B 2; 38. B—Kt 3 further
resistance would be useless.

31. P—B 4!

White intends to break open
Black's King position by the
advance of this pawn; there is also
the direct threat of 32. R × R,
Q × R; 33. R—Q 1, as the pawn on
K B 4 prevents the Queen from
interpolating a check at K R 3.

31. ...   P—K R 4
32. R—Q Kt 1   R—K B 7! 40

33. K R—K 1!   Q—Q 7

If 33. ... R—K 7; 34. K R—Q 1, R—Q 7; 35. R × Q, for the Rook is defended on Q 1. If 33. ... Q—R 6 then 34. B—Q 4, R × B P; 35. R—K 8 ch, K—R 2; 36. B—B 2 ch, K—R 3; 37. B—K 3, P—Kt 4; 38. R—K 7.

34. Q R—Q 1   Q—Kt 7

34. ... R—K 7 does not help matters on account of 35. R—K Kt 1, Q—K 6; 36. R—Q 8 ch, K—R 2; 37. B—Kt 8 ch, K—Kt 3; 38. R—Q 6 ch, K—B 4; 39. B—R 7 ch with a winning attack.

35. R—Q 8 ch

At last a Rook has broken into Black's position. Now the white pieces bear down on Black's King. There is an energetic finish to this exciting game.

35. ...	K—R 2
36. B—Kt 8 ch	K—Kt 3
37. R—Q 6 ch	K—B 4
38. B—K 6 ch	K—Kt 3
39. B—Q 5 ch	K—R 2
40. B—K 4 ch	K—Kt 1
41. B—Kt 6	Black resigned.

No. 15.   Queen's Gambit Declined, Slav Defence
S. RESHEVSKY   V. SMYSLOV
(*Radio Match, U.S.S.R.–U.S.A., 1945*)

1. P—Q 4	P—Q 4
2. P—Q B 4	P—Q B 3
3. Kt—K B 3	Kt—K B 3
4. Kt—B 3	P × P
5. P—K 3	

In search of revenge in the second game of the Radio Match, Reshevsky chooses a line, which leads to a complicated positional struggle without early exchanges. Such an approach to the choice of opening is psychologically understandable. The continuation 5. P—Q R 4, B—B 4; 6. P—K 3, P—K 3; 7. B × P is more often met in practice; White then has the slightly better prospects because of his well-centralized position.

5. ...	P—Q Kt 4
6. P—Q R 4	P—Kt 5
7. Kt—R 2	

Thus White re-establishes the material balance, but the Kt now stands on an unsatisfactory square, and more time is needed to bring it into play again.

| 7. ... | P—K 3 |
| 8. B × P | B—K 2 |

Black intends to castle rather than hurry on with counterplay on the Q-side, as in that case White gets attacking chances from the insecure position of the Black King in the centre.

As will be seen, the plan of development used by Black in this game allows him a more favourable position for effecting the freeing manœuvre P—Q B 4.

9.	O—O	O—O
10.	Q—K 2	B—Kt 2
11.	K R—Q 1	*41*

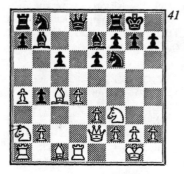
41

11. ...   P—Q R 4!

Strengthening the pawn bastion on the flank and intending to answer 12. P—K 4 with 12. ... P—B 4. In the game Kotov–Smyslov (from the Soviet Teams' Championship, Moscow, 1945) there followed: 12. P—K 4, P—B 4; 13. P × P, Q—B 2; 14. P—K 5, Kt.—K 5; 15. B—K 3, Q Kt—Q 2 and Black had an excellent game. Also if in this variation White tries 13. P—Q 5, then 13. ... P × P; 14. P × P, B—Q 3; 15. B—K Kt 5, Q Kt—Q 2; 16. Kt—B 1, Q—B 2 gives equal chances.

12.	B—Q 2	Q Kt—Q 2
13.	Kt—B 1	Q—Kt 3
14.	Kt—Kt 3	

In the game Fridstein–Smyslov (Moscow Championship, 1944) 14. Kt—Q 3 was played, but Black was still able to play the freeing

move 14. ... P—B 4, after which he had excellent prospects. The text move attacks the Q R P and strengthens Q 4.

14. ...   P—B 4

A characteristic manœuvre for this type of position and one which completes the opening system chosen by Black.

15.	B—K 1	K R—Q 1
16.	B—Kt 5	*42*

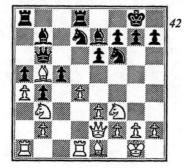
42

16. ...   B—Q 4!

The Bishop takes up an active position in the centre, and at the same time Q Kt 2 is freed for the Queen so that pressure may be exerted along the diagonal Q R 1—K R 8.

17.	Q Kt—Q 2	Q—Kt 2
18.	Kt—B 4	Kt—Kt 3
19.	Q Kt—K 5	Kt—K 5
20.	P × P	Kt × Q B P
21.	Kt—Q 4!	

An interesting plan: White concentrates his minor pieces on Q B 6, leaving his K Kt P en prise. The sacrifice is a sham, for if 21. ... B × P, then 22. P—B 3, B—R 6; 23. B—B 6 and White wins the exchange. In addition White prepares to eliminate his opponent's pressure along the long diagonal by P—B 3 and P—K 4. Black bases his plan on counterplay on the Q-side, where White has pawn weaknesses (the square Q Kt 3).

21. ...	K R—Q B 1!
22. P—B 3	Kt—Kt 6
23. Kt × Kt	B × Kt

And so the Bishop reaches the important square Q Kt 6, and the Q R P is additionally attacked. As a result of this manœuvre the freedom of White's Rooks is considerably restricted. Now 24. R (Q 1)—B 1 cannot be played because of 24. ... R × R; 25. R × R, B × P. If 24. R—Q 2, Black could continue 24. ... P—B 3; 25. Kt—Kt 4 (25. Kt—Q 3, Kt—B 5), R—Q 1 so as to play for control of the Q-file.

24. R—Q 3	B—B 7
25. R—Q 2	P—Kt 6!

Now the position of the Bishop at Q B 7 is consolidated. At the same time an object of attack—the Q Kt P—is fixed.

26. B—B 2	B—Kt 5

By this move Black commences a direct attack on the Q-side; he intends to create combinational threats based on the sacrifice of a piece on Q B 6.

27. R—Q 4	Kt—Q 4

27. ... B—B 6 would be premature, as after 28. P × B, P—Kt 7; 29. R—K B 1, P—Kt 8=Q; 30. R × Q, B × R; 31. Q—Q 1, B—Kt 3; 32. B—B 6 White wins the exchange back.

28. Kt—Q 3	*43*

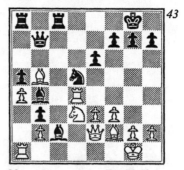

43

28. ...	P—K 4!

Black diverts the White Kt from the defence of its Q Kt 2 by a pawn sacrifice and so makes the ground favourable for combinations. Of course, White could reply 29. R—Q B 4, but after 29. ... B—Q 3; 30. P—K 4, Kt—Kt 5 Black has the initiative. However, Reshevsky accepts the challenge.

29. Kt × P	B—B 6!
30. Kt—B 4	

White gives up the exchange; otherwise after 30. P × B, Kt × B P; 31. Q—Q 2, Kt × B; 32. P × Kt, P—Kt 7 he would have to surrender the Rook for the pawn.

30. ...	B × R
31. P × B	Q—B 2

Although Black has won the exchange for a pawn, it is not easy to convert this advantage into a win because White is left with two active Bishops.

32. B—Kt 3	Q—R 2
33. Q—K 5	Kt—Kt 5
34. Kt—Q 6	R—B 1
35. Q—K 3	Q R—Q 1
36. Q—B 3	Q—K 2
37. R—K 1	Q—Kt 4
38. Q—K 3	Q—Kt 3 *44*

Black does not exchange Queens because he wants to be able to keep the possibility of exchanging minor pieces on Q 6 and to drive the Kt away from Q 3.

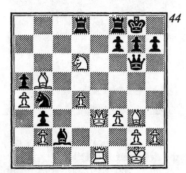

44

39. Kt—K4

This leads to the loss of the centre pawn, after which the outcome of the game is decided. The only way to continue the struggle was by 39. Kt—Kt 7. For instance: 39. Kt—Kt 7, R—B 1; 40. Kt × P, B—Q 6; 41. R—Q 1, B × B; 42. P × B, Q—Kt 3; 43. Kt × P, Q × Kt P or 40. Kt—B 5, B—B 4; 41. Q × P, Kt—B 7; 42. R—Q 1, Kt × P; 43. R × Kt, R × Kt.

If 40. B—Q 6, Black may continue 40. ... B—B 4; 41. B × Kt, P × B; 42. Kt—B 5, Q—Q 3; 43. Kt × P, R—B 7; 44. R—K 2, R × R; 45. B × R, B—K 3; 46. Kt —B 5, R—Q 1 and Black wins the Q P.

So even after 39. Kt—Kt 7 Black would have preserved his advantage.

39. ... B × Kt
40. Q × B Kt—B 7

Now the Q P is lost, and an ending is reached which to be won only requires the necessary accuracy.

41. Q × Q R P × Q
42. R—Q B 1 Kt × P
43. B—B 7 R—Q 4
44. B—Q B 4 R—B 1!
45. B—R 6

And not 45. B × R on account of 45. ... Kt—K 7 ch. For example, 46. K—B 1, Kt × R; 47. B × R P, R—B 4 or 46. K—B 2, Kt × R; 47. B × R P, R—B 4; 48. B—Q 2, Kt—Q 6 ch, and in both cases Black wins.

45. ... R—K 1
46. K—B 1 Kt—B 7
47. K—Kt 1 R—K 8 ch

The exchange of Rooks simplifies the winning process.

48. R × R Kt × R
49. K—B 2 Kt—B 7
50. K—K 2 R—Q B 4
51. B—Kt 3 Kt—Kt 5
52. B—Q 3 P—Kt 4

Black does not hurry to exchange minor pieces while his King is away from the centre of the board.

53. B—K 4 R—B 5
54. B—K 1 K—B 1
55. B—B 3 P—B 3
56. P—Kt 4 K—K 2
57. K—Q 2 K—Q 3
58. K—K2

45

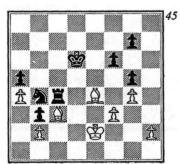

45

58. ...	Kt—Q 4
59. B × R P	R × P
60. B—K 1	R—R 7
61. K—Q 3	R × P
62. K—B 4	R—K 7
63. B—Kt 3 ch	Kt—B 5
64. K × P	R × B!

The simplest road to victory.

65. P × R	K—K 4
66. P—R 4	K × P
67. P × P	P × P
68. K—B 4	K—B 6
69. B—K 1	K × P
70. K—Q 4	K—B 6
71. K—K 5	P—Kt 5

White resigned.

No. 16.   Sicilian Defence
V. SMYSLOV   A. KOTOV
(Moscow Championship, 1946)

1. P—K 4	P—Q B 4
2. Kt—Q B 3	Kt—Q B 3
3. P—K Kt 3	P—K Kt 3
4. B—Kt 2	B—Kt 2
5. P—Q 3	P—Kt 3
6. B—K 3	B—Kt 2
7. Kt—R 3	

An original method of development. White avoided the usual continuation 7. K Kt—K 2, believing that the position of the Kt on K R 3 would leave him in a more favourable situation to parry Black's blockading manœuvre—Kt—Q 5—with Kt—Q 1 and P—Q B 3.

7. ...	P—K 3
8. O—O	K Kt—K 2
9. Q—Q 2	Kt—Q 5 46

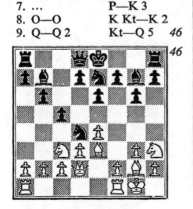

46

Black hopes to prevent the positional threat—the exchange of the black-squared Bishops—by pressure on Q B 7. But this manœuvre does not achieve the desired result. Better was 9. ... O—O with 10. ... P—Q 4 to follow.

10. B—R 6!

Forcing the exchange of Bishops and thus weakening the black squares in his opponent's position. In the event of 10. ... B × B; 11. Q × B, Kt × P; 12. Q R—B 1, Kt—Q 5; 13. Q—Kt 7, R—K Kt 1; 14. Q × R P, White gets an attacking game.

10. ...	O—O
11. B × B	K × B
12. Kt—K 2	Kt × Kt ch
13. Q × Kt	P—Q 4
14. P—K 5	R—Q Kt 1
15. P—Q B 3	P—Q Kt 4
16. Kt—B 4	Kt—B 3

A mistaken manœuvre: the Kt is needed for the defence of the castled position. Black starts counterplay on the Q-side, underestimating the attacking possibilities of his opponent. As becomes clear from what follows, White's attack is more real than the chances that Black gets after the opening of the Q Kt-file. He should have given preference to 16. ... P—Q 5, exchanging the Bishops. After 17. B × B, R × B; 18. P—B 4, P × P; 19. P × P, Kt—B 3; 20. Kt—Q 3, Q—K 2, Black could try to remove the blockading Kt by Kt—Kt 5.

17. K R—K 1   P—Kt 5
18. Q R—B 1   P × P
19. P × P   B—R 3
20. Q—Kt 4

Going over to a direct attack on the enemy King. If 20. ... R—Kt 7, then White replies 21. P—B 4! undermining Black's pawn centre.

20. ...   Kt—K 2   47

Thus the Kt returns to its former position to defend the King, but not without loss of time.

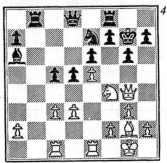

47

21. P—B 4!   P × P

A little better was 21. ... P—Q 5, preventing the opening of the Q-file, although after 22. P—K R 4 with the threats of P—R 5 and Kt—R 5 —B 6 White preserved a strong attacking position.

22. P × P   Kt—Kt 1
23. K R—Q 1   Q—K 2
24. R—Q 6   R—Kt 3
25. Q R—Q 1

White has seized control of the open Q-file with both Rooks,

and now 26. R—Q 7 is threatened. The Q B P is indirectly protected on account of Kt—R 5 ch.

25. ...   B—B 1
26. P—K R 4   R × R
27. P × R   Q—Q 1   47a

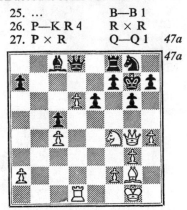

47a

28. Q—K 2!

By bringing the Queen to the centre square K 5, White wins the Q B P. Black cannot play 28. ... Q—B 3 because of the loss of a piece after 29. P—Q 7, B—R 3; 30. R—Q 6.

28. ...   Kt—B 3
29. Q—K 5   B—R 3
30. Q × B P   K—Kt 1
31. P—Q 7

White has several ways of winning. By giving up his passed pawn he throws the black pieces on to unfavourable squares.

31. ...   Kt × P
32. Q × P   B—B 1
33. P—B 5   Q—B 3
34. P—B 6   Kt—K 4
35. P—B 7   Kt—Kt 5

Black is quite lost.

36. Q—Kt 6   Q—B 4
37. R—Q 8   Q—B 7
38. Kt—Q 3   Q—Q 8 ch
39. B—B 1   Kt—R 7
40. K × Kt   Q × B
41. Q—Q 6   Black
                     resigned.

No. 17. Ruy Lopez

I. BONDAREVSKY   V. SMYSLOV

(Moscow Championship, 1946)

1. P—K 4	P—K 4
2. Kt—K B 3	Kt—Q B 3
3. B—Kt 5	P—Q R 3
4. B—R 4	Kt—B 3
5. O—O	B—K 2
6. B × Kt	

White avoids well-studied continuations and directs the game along paths similar in ideas to the Exchange Variation.

6. ...	Q P × B
7. R—K 1	Kt—Q 2
8. P—Q 4	P × P
9. Q × P	O—O
10. B—B 4	Kt—B 4
11. Q × Q	B × Q
12. Kt—B 3	48

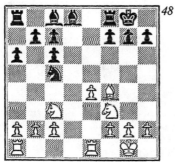

48

12. ...   P—B 4!

White's extra pawn on the K-side has little real significance while a sufficient number of pieces remains on the board. With the text move Black pursues the aim of opening the position and so increasing the activity of his Bishops.

13. P—K 5

This advance does not answer the demands of the position, since it gives the black Kt an excellent blockading square at K 3. He should have played 13. B—Kt 5, bringing about further simplification. After 13. ... B × B; 14. Kt × B, P—R 3; 15. P—Q Kt 4, Kt × P; 16. K Kt × Kt, P × Kt; 17. Kt × P, B—B 4 the position is approximately equal.

13. ...	Kt—K 3
14. B—Q 2	P—K Kt 4

The pawns start moving. In addition to the conquest of space, Black stops the threat of Kt—K 2 followed by Kt—B 4 or Q 4, exchanging the Kt, which is so important for the attack. White's difficulties stem from the fact that he has no strong points in the centre for his minor pieces.

15. Kt—K 2	P—B 4
16. B—B 3	P—Kt 4

Black works up a pawn advance across the whole board. Already White is threatened with the loss of a piece after 17. ... P—K Kt 5; 18. Kt—Q 2, P—Kt 5. Soon the terrible Bishops, still dozing on the first rank, must take an active part in the struggle.

17. P—Q Kt 3	B—Kt 2
18. Kt—Kt 3	P—K Kt 5
19. Kt—Q 2	B—K 2
20. Kt—R 5	*49*

49

20. ...   K—B 2!

The King is aimed for Kt 3 so as to strengthen the K B P and embarrass the White Kt.

21. Kt—B 1   K—Kt 3
22. Kt—B 6   Q R—Q 1
23. Q R—Q 1   R × R
24. R × R   R—Q 1
25. R × R   B × R

With the exchange of Rooks the position has become simpler, but no easier for White. After Black's Kt—Q 5 the position of the White Kt on K B 6 would appear to be hopeless; Black also threatens Kt—B 5 with a double attack on K Kt P and Bishop. White's best here is 26. B—Kt 2.

26. Kt—K 3   50

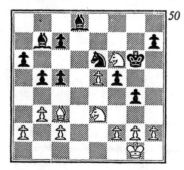

50

26. ...   P—K B 5!

A reply which White had not foreseen. The attacked Kt can neither take the K Kt P because of 27. ... P—K R 4 nor advance to Q 5 because of 27. ... P—B 3, and a piece is lost in both cases. The sad retreat to the first rank is all that remains.

27. Kt—Q 1   B × Kt
28. P × B   B—K 5
29. B—Kt 2   P—Kt 5

Depriving the white Kt of its Q B 3 and threatening to win a piece by 30. ... B—B 7 should White play 30. P—Q B 3.

30. P—K B 3   B × Q B P
31. Kt—B 2   P × P
32. P × P   B—Kt 8
33. Kt—K 4   B × P
34. Kt—Q 2   P—Q R 4

Black has won two pawns and at any moment threatens to free his trapped Bishop by P—Q R 5.

35. K—B 2   Kt—Q 5
36. B × Kt   P × B
37. K—E 2   K × P
38. K—Q 3   K—K 4
39. K—B 2

After 39. K—B 4, P—R 5; 40. K × P, B × P the Bishop is free again, while if 39. Kt—B 4 ch, K—Q 4; 40. Kt × P, B—Kt 8 ch, Black wins easily.

39. ...   P—R 5
40. P × P   P—B 4
41. P—R 5   P—B 5
42. P—R 6   P—Q 6 ch

White resigned. If 43. K—Q 1, then 43. ... P—B 6; 44. P—R 7, B—Q 4 or if 43. K—Kt 2, then 43. ... P—B 6 ch; 44. K × B, P × Kt; 45. P—R 7, P—Q 8=Q; 46. P—R 8=Q, P—Kt 6 ch and wins.

No. 18. Queen's Pawn, Grunfeld Defence
J. SAJTAR   V. SMYSLOV
(*Match-Tournament, Moscow–Prague, 1946*)

1. P—Q 4   Kt—K B 3
2. P—Q B 4   P—K Kt 3
3. Kt—Q B 3   P—Q 4
4. Kt—B 3   B—Kt 2
5. Q—R 4 ch

The idea of this check is to make it difficult for Black to play P—Q B 4 after, for example, 5. ... P—B 3; 6. P × P, Kt × P; 7. P—K 4, Kt × Kt; 8. P × Kt. But, in my opinion, Black's reply guarantees him full equality.

5. ...   B—Q 2
6. Q—Kt 3   B—B 3

This move is something of an experiment and needs further practical tests. Quite playable is 6. ... P × P luring the Queen to Q B 4, for 7. Q × Kt P, Kt—B 3; 8. B—B 4, R—Q Kt 1; 9. Q × B P, Q × Q; 10. B × Q, R × P is not dangerous for Black.

7. B—B 4   P × P
8. Q × B P   O—O
9. R Q 1   *51*

White prepares P—Q 5, aiming for an advantage in space; at the same time Black must look to the defence of his Q B P. However, this threat is not powerful, and it seems that his delay in castling is the reason for White's later difficulties. 9. Kt—K 5, making difficult the normal development of Black's Q-side, was more active. After 9. ... K Kt—Q 2, a possibility would be 10. R—Q 1, Kt × Kt; 11. B × Kt, exchanging the black-squared Bishops. Evidently Black would do best to choose a line connected with the move 9. ... P—K 3, followed

by either Kt—Q 4 or B—Q 4 as the situation demands.

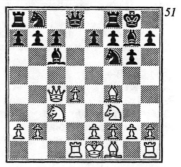
51

9. ...   Q Kt—Q 2

Black has prepared an interesting combination in reply to the obvious P—Q 5, e.g. 10. P—Q 5, Kt—Kt 3; 11. Q—Kt 3, K Kt × P; 12. P—K 4, B × Kt ch; 13. P × B, Kt × B; 14. R × Q, Q R × R. For the sacrificed Queen Black has a sufficient equivalent in the shape of Rook, Kt and pawn. As well as this the threats of B—R 5 and B × P make White's defence a difficult problem. If in this variation the Queen had retreated to Q B 5 instead of Q Kt 3, interesting complications would have arisen: after 11. Q—B 5, Q Kt × P; 12. P—K 4 does not achieve its aim because of 12. ... Kt—Q 2!, while 12. Kt × Kt, B × Kt; 13. P—K 4, P—Kt 3 is favourable for Black.

10. Kt—K 5   Kt × Kt
11. B × Kt

11. P × Kt led to sharp and intricate play: 11. P × Kt, Kt—Q 2; 12. P—K 6, P × P; 13. Q × P ch, K—R 1; 14. P—K 3, Q—K 1

and White is troubled by the development of his K B.

It would then be dangerous to take the Q B P, e.g. 15. B × P, R—B 1; 16. B—Kt 3, Kt—B 4; 17. Q—Kt 4, Kt—R 5; 18. Kt × Kt, B × Kt and now 19. P—Kt 3 is impossible on account of 19. ... B—B 6 ch.

If 15. Q—R 3, Black could play 15. ... Kt—B 4 with the following variations:

(1) 16. B—K 2, Kt—R 5!; 17. Kt × Kt, B × Kt; 18. R—Q 2, R—Q 1; 19. R × R, Q × R and if 20. O—O, then 20. ... B × P and Black has excellent play.

(2) 16. B—K R 6, B × B; 17. Q × B, Q—B 2; 18. Q—R 4, Q R—Q 1; 19. B—B 4, R × R ch; 20. Kt × R, Q—B 3; 21. Q × Q ch, R × Q with an equal ending.

| 11. ... | P—K 3 |
| 12. Q—Q 3 | Q—K 2 |

The struggle revolves around the advance P—K 4, to which Black would now reply 13. ... Q—Kt 5; 14. R—Q 2, K R—Q 1, intending to answer either 15. B × P or 15. B—K 2 with 15. ... Kt × P! and the complications are in Black's favour.

An interesting variation would by 15. B—K 2, Kt × P!; 16. B × B, Kt × R; 17. B—B 6, Kt—K 5; 18. P—Q R 3, Q—R 4 and 19. P—Q Kt 4 is bad because of 19. ... Q—K B 4.

| 13. Q—B 2 | B—R 3 |
| 14. P—B 3 | |

Irreparably weakening his K 3 square. However, the immediate 14. P—K 4 entailed considerable risk after 14. ... Kt—Q 2; 15. B—Kt 3 (or 15. B—Kt 5, Kt × B; 16. P × Kt, B × B; 17. Kt × B,

Q—Kt 5 ch; 18. Kt—B 3, B—B 5 winning a pawn), P—B 4; 16. P—B 3, P × P; 17. Kt × P, B × Kt; 18. Q × B, Q—Kt 5 ch; 19. K—B 2, Q × Kt P ch; 20. B—K 2, Kt—B 3; 21. Q × P ch, R—B 2 to be followed by R—K 1 with the threats of Kt—K 5 ch and Kt—Kt 5 ch. It must be admitted that White's whole plan to force P—K 4 seems unfavourable for him.

| 14. ... | Kt—Q 4 |

This obvious move increases his advantage, as if 15. Kt × Kt, then 15. ... P × Kt! and the K P remains at K 2. All the same White should have played this, as now his K-side is shut up for ever.

| 15. Q—Kt 3 | P—R 4 |
| 16. P—Q R 4 | |

Forced, otherwise 16. ... Kt—K 6 and 17. ... P—R 5 is decisive.

| 16. ... | Kt—K 6 |
| 17. R—Q 3 | 52 |

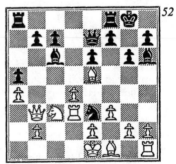

52

| 17. ... | Q—Kt 5! |

Forcing the transition to an ending in which the Q R-file is opened for a Rook. This manœuvre, prepared by the advance of the Q R P , is the quickest way to force the issue.

18. Q × Q	P × Q
19. Kt—K 4	B × Kt
20. P × B	R × P
21. B × P	P—B 4!

An important detail in Black's attacking set-up: by threatening to open the K B-file, Black strengthens his position. One variation is curious: 22. B—Q 6, R—R 8 ch; 23. K—B 2, P × P ch; 24. B × R, P × R; 25. B × B, P—Q 7 and the pawn promotes.

22. P—K 5	R—B 1
23. B—Q 6	Kt—Kt 5
24. P—K 3	

If 24. R—Q 1, then 24. ... B—K 6 and 25. ... Kt—B 7. After the text move the invasion of the opponent's position by the black Rooks is immediately decisive.

24. ...	R—R 8 ch
25. K—K2	R—B 7 ch
26. R—Q 2	P—Kt 6!

White resigned.

No. 19. Ruy Lopez
V. SMYSLOV   I. KONIG
(Radio Match, U.S.S.R.–Great Britain, 1946)

1. P—K 4	P—K 4
2. Kt—K B 3	Kt—Q B 3
3. B—Kt 5	P—Q R 3
4. B—R 4	Kt—B 3
5. O—O	B—K 2
6. R—K 1	P—Q Kt 4
7. B—Kt 3	P—Q 3
8. P—B 3	Kt—Q R 4
9. B—B 2	P—B 4
10. P—Q 4	Q—B 2
11. Q Kt—Q 2	B P × P
12. P × P	B—Kt 5!

An interesting continuation, leading to sharp play. Here 12. ... Kt—B 3 is a mistake: in the game Smyslov–Gerstenfeld (Twelfth Soviet Championship) there followed 13. P—Q 5, Kt—Q Kt 5; 14. B—Kt 1, P—Q R 4; 15. P—Q R 3, Kt—R 3; 16. P—Q Kt 4, O—O; 17. Kt—Kt 3 with advantage to White.

| 13. P—K R 3 | B—R 4 |
| 14. P—Q R 4 | |

White wishes to maintain the tension in the centre, otherwise he would have been content with a

plan connected with 14. P—Q 5. The pressure on the Q-side, which White has just initiated, is intended to embarrass the pawns, weakened by the removal of the Q B to the K-side.

14. ...	O—O
15. B—Q 3	P—Kt 5
16. P—Kt 4	B—Kt 3
17. Q—K 2	P—K R 4! 53

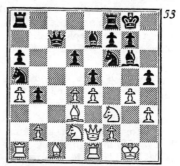

53

A double-edged position has arisen, in which both sides have their weaknesses. The threat to the Q R P is not real because White's K P is also under fire. However, in some variations the weakness of the Q R P is of significance, and for this reason Black is right to go in for counterplay on the K-side. Otherwise, White closes the centre by 18. P—Q 5 and keeps up pressure on both wings.

18.   Q P × P   Q P × P

18. ... R P × P; 19. Kt—R 4 simply involved a transposition of moves.

19. Kt—R 4   P × P
20. P × P   B—R 2

The most prudent course. If not, Black must always be considering the threat of Kt × B, which would be dangerous for him.

21. Kt—B 5   B—B 4
22. P—Kt 5   Kt—Q 2

Up to now Black had conducted a complicated and tense struggle excellently, but now he allows himself to be seriously cramped. He should have decided on the sharp line 22. ... B × Kt; 23. P × B, P—K 5; 24. Kt × P, Kt × Kt; 25. B × Kt, Q—Kt 6 ch; 26. K —B 1, Q—R 6 ch; 27. B—Kt 2, Q × P. Then it would be risky for White to take the exchange, on account of the open position of his King; the best reply would probably be 28. Q—B 3 with about equal chances.

23. Kt—B 1   Kt—Kt 6
24. R—Kt 1   Kt—Q 5
25. Q—Kt 4   K R—Q 1

Black defends cleverly, freeing K B 1 for his Kt. Now a promising line for White is 26. B—K 3, Kt— B 1; 27. Q R—B 1, Kt—Kt 6; 28. Q R—Q 1, when he has finished his development and preserves his attacking position.

However White preferred a move which led to still sharper play.

26. Kt (1)—Kt 3   Kt—B 1   54
                                               54

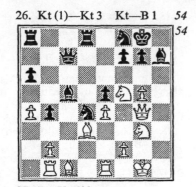

27. P—Kt 6!?

A positional pawn sacrifice, the consequences of which are difficult to assess. It is based on the consideration that the K Kt P occupied a square which was needed for the Q B, while it also blocked the way to Black's King. So White decided to put some life into his attack and stir up complications at the expense of a pawn.

27. ...   B × P

The most natural. 27. ... P × P, which covers the vulnerable K Kt 2 square, is also worth attention. A possible continuation is then 27. ... P × P; 28. B—B 4 ch, K—R 1, 29. Kt—K 3, Q—Q 2; 30. K—Kt 2, Kt (1)—K 3; 31. R— K R 1, or 30. ... Kt (5)—K 3; 31. Kt—K 2 with an intricate position. To give an exhaustive analysis of the complex situation that has arisen would be hardly possible.

28. B—Q B 4!   Kt—B 7

White's quiet move following the sacrifice has provoked a counter reaction from Black, who embarks upon the dangerous path of further complications. 28. ... Kt (5)—K 3 was better; White would have replied 29. P—Kt 3.

29. R—B 1   R—R 2

One might reproach Black with being inconsistent, but it is hard to recommend the acceptance of the second pawn by 29. ... B × P ch; 30. R × B, Q × B, because of 31. Kt—K 7 ch, K—R 1; 32. R—R 2 ch, Kt—R 2 (or 32. ... B—R 2; 33. Kt (3)—B 5, P—Kt 3; 34. B—Kt 5!); 33. Kt (3)—B 5, Q—B 4 ch; 34. B—K 3!, Kt × B; 35. R × Kt ch! K × R; 36. Q—R 4 ch and mate next move.

30. B—K Kt 5   R—Q 2   55

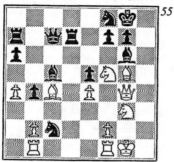
55

31. Kt × P!

The steadily increasing tension reaches a peak in this move. The distribution of pieces on the K Kt-file presents a curious picture. Black can take the proffered Kt, but to do so would result in a desperate position: e.g. 31. ... K × Kt; 32. Kt—B 5 ch, B × Kt (32. ... K—Kt 1; 33. B—B 6, R—Q 3; 34. Kt—R 6 ch! K—R 2; 35.

Q—R 4, R × B; 36. Kt—Kt 4 ch, K—Kt 1; 37. Kt × R ch, K—Kt 2; 38. Kt—K 8 ch and wins); 33. P × B, R—Q 5 (33. ... Kt—Kt 3; 34. Q—R 5!); 34. P—B 6 ch!, K—R 2; 35. B—B 4!, Kt—K 3 (35. ... Kt—Kt 3; 36. Q—R 5 ch, K—Kt 1; 37. Q × Kt ch); 36. Q—R 5 ch, K—Kt 1; 37. K—R 2 with a decisive attack.

In search of counterchances Black resolves to answer sacrifice with sacrifice. However, it does not alter the situation: White still has a very strong attack.

31. ...	B × P ch
32. R × B	Q × B
33. Kt—K 8	Kt—R 2
34. Kt—B 6 ch	K—Kt 2

A mistake. It is true that after 34. ... Kt × Kt; 35. B × Kt to avoid a mating attack Black must play 35. ... R—Q 3; 36. Q—R 4, R × B; 37. Q × R, still with a very difficult position, but it did give him a chance to continue the struggle further. Now the end is sudden.

35. B—R 6 ch!

A little finesse, leading to the win of a whole Rook. If 35. ... K × B, then 36. Kt—B 5 ch, B × Kt; 37. Kt—Kt 8 or R—R 2 mate.

35. ...	K—R 1
36. Kt × R	Q—Q 5
37. Kt × P	Black resigned.

No. 20. Queen's Pawn, Budapest Defence
V. SMYSLOV   H. STEINER
(Groningen, 1946)

1. P—Q 4	Kt—K B 3
2. P—Q B 4	P—K 4
3. P × P	Kt—K 5

More often 3. ... Kt—Kt 5 is played here. After the text move

White develops easily and aims to hold the gambit pawn.

4. Kt—K B 3

A possible alternative is 4. P—Q R 3.

4. …	B—Kt 5 ch
5. B—Q 2	Kt × B
6. Q Kt × Kt	Kt—B 3
7. P—Q R 3	B × Kt ch
8. Q × B	Q—K 2
9. Q—B 3	O—O
10. R—Q 1	R—K 1
11. R—Q 5!	

The Rook is placed in a very advanced position so that the strong pawn on K 5 may be preserved; hereafter a lively struggle, in which White has the initiative, develops around this pawn.

11. …	P—Q Kt 3
12. P—K 3	B—Kt 2
13. B—K 2	Q R—Q 1
14. O—O	Kt—Kt 1! 56

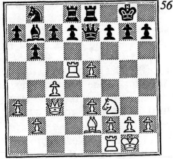

56

15. R—B 1!

Brave, but consistent. Not even a sacrifice of the exchange is too big a price to pay to maintain the key to his position—the advanced K P. If 15. R—Q 2, Black equalized by 15. … B ×Kt; 16. B × B, Q × K P.

| 15. … | B × R |
| 16. P × B | P—Q 3 |

The alternative 16. … P—Q B 4 led to a complicated game. After 17. B—Kt 5, P—Q R 3; 18. P—Q 6, Q—K 3; 19. B—B 4, Q—B 4; 20. B—Q 5, Kt—B 3; 21. B × Kt, P × B; 22. P—R 3! Black has weak pawns on the Q-side, which makes the fight against the White pawns difficult.

17. B—Kt 5	R—K B 1
18. P—K 4!	P—Q R 3
19. B—Q 3	P × P

After this move Black's position is difficult to defend: the Kt is out of play and the Q B P is weak. 19. … K R—K 1 deserved consideration. In the variation 20. P—K 6, P × P; 21. P × P, P—B 4; 22. B—B 4 White still has complex problems to solve.

20. Kt × P   R—Q 3

Black transfers his Rook to the K-side, but this only speeds his defeat. A more tenacious defence was 20. … P—K B 3, although even then after 21. Kt—Kt 4 (intending to bring the Kt to K B 5) White retains the advantage.

21. Kt—B 4	R—R 3
22. Kt—K 3	Q—R 5
23. Q × P	

With the win of a second pawn White obtains a decisive advantage. Black's remaining attacking moves are easily parried, and White quickly goes over to the attack himself.

23. …	R—K B 3
24. P—K Kt 3	Q—R 4
25. P—K 5	R—R 3
26. P—K R 4	Q—B 6 57

57

27. R—B 4!

The final manœuvre: the Rook is brought over to the K-side, where Black's Queen and Rook are a little tied up. The finish is vigorous.

27. ...   P—Q Kt 4

28. R—B 4	Q—R 4
29. Kt—Kt 4	R—K Kt 3
30. B × R	Q × B
31. P—K 6	Q—Kt 8 ch
32. K—R 2	P—B 4
33. P—K 7	R—K 1
34. Q—Q 8	Black resigned.

No. 21   Ruy Lopez
V. SMYSLOV   M. EUWE
(Groningen, 1946)

1. P—K 4	P—K 4
2. Kt—K B 3	Kt—Q B 3
3. B—Kt 5	P—Q R 3
4. B—R 4	Kt—B 3
5. P—Q 3	

An old move, which holds out no promise of any sort of advantage; however, it does exclude transposition into the Open Variation (5. O—O, Kt × P). Meeting Euwe for the first time, I did not wish to allow the Open Variation, which has been deeply studied by the Dutch Champion.

5. ...	P—Q 3
6. P—B 3	P—K Kt 3
7. O—O	B—Kt 2
8. R—K 1	P—Q Kt 4

This advance, which seriously weakens his pawn formation, puts an onus on Black. Usually 8. ... P—Q Kt 4 is connected with the two following ideas:

(1) After 9. B—Kt 3 to transpose into a line characterized by the well-known Tchigorin formations, continuing 9. ... Kt—Q R 4; 10. B—B 2, P—B 4.

(2) After 9. B—B 2 to carry out the central advance P—Q 4.

9. B—B2	O—O
10. B—Kt 5	P—R 3
11. B—R 4	Q—K 1

Black unpins the Kt, planning the manœuvre Kt—K R 4—B 5. Under the cover of the powerful outpost on K B 5 Black is able to prepare an attack on the King. Also possible was 11. ... P—Q 4, but even then after 12. Q Kt—Q 2, P × P; 13. Q Kt × P, P—Kt 4; 14. Kt × Kt ch, B × Kt; 15. B—K Kt 3 or 12. ... P—Kt 4; 13. B—K Kt 3, P × P; 14. P × P! White has a good game.

12. Q Kt—Q 2	Kt—K R 4
13. Kt—B 1	P—Kt 4
14. B—K Kt 3	Kt—K 2 58

Black brings the Kt over to the scene of coming events, but in doing so underestimates the tactical possibilities arising, after White's reply, out of the undefended state of his Kt on K R 4. More expedient was 14. ... Kt—B 5, establishing the Kt in a strong position.

Now by a manœuvre on the Q-side White crosses his opponent's plans on the opposite wing.

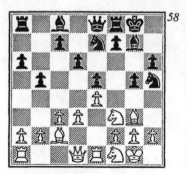

58

15. P—Q R 4!

The right moment! White creates tension on the Q-side and threatens to seize the Q R-file after P × P. Black can neither reply 15. ... B—Q 2 on account of 16. Kt × K P nor 15. ... B—K 3 because of 16. Kt × Kt P. In both cases it is the undefended Kt on K R 4 that tells on Black. Therefore he simplifies, resigning himself to the loss of the initiative on the K-side.

15. ...	Kt × B
16. R P × Kt	

Basically it is capturing with a pawn plus the transfer of a Kt to K B 5 that kills Black's initiative. The Kt on K B 1 still has an excellent square at K 3.

16. ...	B—K 3
17. P—Q 4	P—K B 3
18. B—Kt 3	B × B
19. Q × B ch	Q—B 2
20. Q × Q ch	K × Q
21. Kt—K 3	

The ending is in White's favour: he has more freedom, and Black has a 'bad' Bishop, blocked by his own pawns. White's immediate threat is to double Rooks on the Q R-file, but this danger is easily removed.

21. ...	K R—Q Kt 1!
22. P × P	P × P
23. P—Q 5	

White closes the centre, placing his pawns on white squares. Now 24. P—K Kt 4 is threatened, and the grip on the position is complete.

23. ...	P—R 4
24. K—B 1	P—K Kt 5
25. Kt—R 4	B—R 3
26. Kt (K 3)—B 5!	

And there is the Kt! Otherwise Black, by exchanging his Bishop, would considerably improve his game.

26. ...	Kt—Kt 1
27. K—K2	R—R 5

27. ... B—Kt 4, aiming to exchange minor pieces, was worth considering. In a Rook and pawn ending the defence would be easier. After the text move White forces the exchange of Rooks, and his advantage takes on a definite shape.

28. R × R	P × R
29. R—Q Kt 1	R—Kt 6

This is forced, since White threatened to bring his King to Q B 2, freeing the Rook to attack the Q R P. Of course, 29. ... P—R 6 does not help because of 30. P—Kt 4, and the lone pawn is doomed to death.

30. K—Q 3	P—R 6
31. K—B 2	R × Kt P ch
32. R × R	P × R
33. K × P	*59*

The position has been simplified. Black has managed to liquidate the danger on the Q-side, but as before the Bishop is 'bad', and the Kt is stalemated. 33. ... B—Kt 4 gave practical chances of a draw here. The main variation runs: 33. ... B—Kt 4; 34. K—Kt 3, B × Kt;

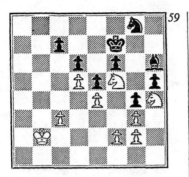

35. P × B, Kt—K 2; 36. Kt × Kt, K × Kt; 37. K—B 4. Now 37. ... P—K B 4! is possible (passive defence by 37. ... K—Q 2 does not give Black serious chances of saving the game with correct play by White: he wins by advancing his Q B P to B 5 ,and using his reserve tempo —P—Kt 3—to put Black in zugzwang), followed by 38. P × P, K—B 3; 39. K—Kt 5, K × P; 40. K—B 6.   60

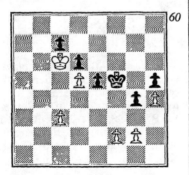

In this ending White retains the advantage, for example: 40. ... K—K 5; 41. P—Q B 4, P—Kt 6; 42. P—B 3 ch, K—K 6; 43. K × P, K—B 7; 44. P—B 5, K × P; 45. P × P, K × P; 46. P—Q 7, P—Kt 7; 47. P—Q 8=Q, P—Kt 8= Q; 48. Q—B 6 ch, K—K 5; 49. P— Q 6 and the advanced passed pawn gives White winning chances.

The alternative is 40. ... P—Kt 6; 41. P—B 3, K—B 5; 42. K × P, K—K 6; 43. K × P, K—B 7; 44. K × P, K × P; 45. P—Q 6, leading to a Queen and pawn ending; 45. ... K × P is impossible because White will later force the exchange of the new Queens by Q—Q 3 ch; if 45. ... K—R 6; 46. P—Q 7, P—Kt 7; 47. P—Q 8=Q, P—Kt 8 =Q; 48. Q—B 6!, Black's position is also very dubious. Scarcely any better chances are given by 41. ... P— K 5; 42. P × P ch, K × P; 43. P— B 4, K—K 6; 44. K × P, K—B 7; 45. P—B 5, K × P; 46. P × P, K—B 6; 47. P—Q 7 etc.

The manœuvre, employed by Black in the game, is intended to bring the Bishop into play.

33. ...   B—Q 7
34. K—B 2   B—K 8
35. P—B 3   Kt—K 2
36. Kt × Kt   K × Kt
37. P × P

This exchange fixes the pawn formation on the K-side, but at the same time Black is relieved of the trouble of defending his R P. Simply 37. Kt—B 5 ch was more appropriate.

37. ...   P × P
38. Kt—B 5 ch   K—B 2
39. P—B 4   K—Kt 3
40. K—Kt 3   K—Kt 4   61

Black intends to sacrifice his Bishop to clear a path into the enemy rear. Passive defence would prolong, but not save, the game, for example: 40. ... K—B 2; 41. K—R 4, K—K 1; 42. K—Kt 5, K—Q 2; 43. Kt—R 6, B × P; 44. Kt × P, B—R 5; 45. Kt—R 6, B—Kt 4; 46. Kt—B 5, B any; 47. K—R 6, K—B 1; 48. K—R 7, B any; 49. K—R 8; then White plays 50. P—Kt 4, freeing the Kt for the manœuvre: 51. Kt—K 7 ch, K—Q 2; 52. Kt—B 6, K—B 1; 53. Kt—R 7 ch, K any; 54. K—Kt 7; if the Bishop stands on K B 7, White wins by 51. Kt—K 7 ch, K—Q 2; 52. Kt—Kt 8, B—R 5; 53. K—Kt 8!, B—Kt 4; 54. K—Kt 7!, and Black is in zugzwang.

41. K—R 4	B × P
42. Kt × B	K—B 5
43. Kt—R 5 ch	K × P
44. Kt × P ch	K —B 4

Or 44. ... K—B 5; 45. K—Kt 5, P—K 5; 46. Kt × K P, K × Kt; 47. K—B 6. If 45. ... K— B 4, then 46. Kt—R 5, K—Kt 4; 47. Kt—Kt 3, K—B 5; 48. Kt—B 1, P—K 5; 49. K—B 6, P—K 6; 50. Kt × P and wins.

45. Kt—K 8!	P—K 5
46. Kt × B P!	P—K 6
47. Kt—Kt 5	

The point of White's manœuvre 47. ... P—K 7 is answered by 48. Kt—Q 4 ch.

47. ...	K—B 5
48. Kt—B 3	K—Kt 6
49. P—B 5	Black resigned.

No. 22.　Ruy Lopez

I. BOLESLAVSKY　　　V. SMYSLOV

(Groningen, 1946)

1. P—K 4	P—K 4
2. Kt—K B 3	Kt—Q B 3
3. B—Kt 5	P—Q R 3
4. B—R 4	Kt—B 3
5. O—O	B—K 2
6. R—K 1	P—Q Kt 4
7. B—Kt 3	P—Q 3
8. P—B 3	O—O
9. P—K R 3	Kt—Q R 4
10. B—B 2	P—B 4
11. P—Q 4	Q—B 2

Here we have the classical position in the Tchigorin System. The wealth of possibilities afforded by the active placing of Black's pieces guarantees this system a wide popularity and a long life.

| 12. Q Kt—Q 2 | B—Q 2 |

12. ... Kt—B 3 is also played here to clarify the position in the centre. In that case Black must reckon with the plan of V. Rauser: 13. P × K P, P × P; 14. Kt—B 1, when the white Kt threatens to occupy the weak squares Q 5 or K B 5.

The text move completes Black's development and reserves the manœuvre Kt—B 5—Kt 3. The Kt is well placed on Q Kt 3 for the defence of Q 4.

13. P × K P	P × P
14. Kt—B 1	Kt—B 5
15. P—Q Kt 3	Kt—Kt 3
16. P—Q R 4	62

A more solid continuation is 16. Q—K 2. In the light of the following counter-blow White's activity on the Q-side seems premature.

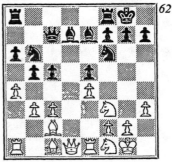

16. ...   P—B 5!
17. P—R 5   P × P
18. P × Kt   Q × B P

This move with its double attack stirs up great complications. A quieter line was 18. ... P × B; 19. P × Q, P × Q=Q; 20. R × Q, K R—B 1; 21. Kt × P, R × P; 22. B—B 4, R—Kt 2, and Black has a good ending.

19. B × P!

The best solution in the circumstances. By sacrificing the exchange White hopes to take advantage of the dangerous position of the Queen on Q R 8. Now the play becomes very double-edged in character.

19. ...   Q × R
20. Q—Q 2   *63*

20. ...   B—R 6

Saving himself from the terrible threat of 21. B—Kt 2 and avoiding the risks connected with 20. ... P—Kt 5; 21. B—Kt 2, Q—R 4; 22. Kt × P, when White has a strong attacking position. For example: 22. ... B—K 3; 23. Kt—B 6, Q—B 4; 24. R—B 1, Q—Q 3; 25. Q × Q, B × Q; 26. B × B, P × B; 27. P—K 5 or 22. ... B—Kt 4; 23. Kt × P! R × Kt; 24. P—K 5 and White's attack is very dangerous.

21. P—Kt 7

A rash advance. White prepares an attacking manœuvre with his Queen, which, however, has its refutation. 21. B—R 2 was better; after 21. B—R 2, B—K 3; 22. Q B × B, Q × B; 23. Q × Q, B × Q; 24. B × R, K × B; 25. Kt × P, R—K 1, the chances are approximately equal, e.g. 26. R—R 1, R × Kt; 27. R × B, P—Kt 5; 28. R × P, R—Q Kt 4. If 26. Kt—B 6, then after 26. ... B—Q 4! the complications are not unfavourable for Black.

21. ...   Q R—Kt 1
22. B—R 2   B—K 3
23. K B × B   P × B
24. Q—R 5   B—Kt 7!

It is a rare sight to see pieces co-operating so excellently in the very heart of the opponent's position.

25. Q—B 7   B × B
26. R × B   *64*

The attack starting with 26. Kt—Kt 5 is insufficient on account of 26. ... Q—Q 5; 27. Kt × K P, Q—Q 2! or 27. R × B, Q—R 2, and Black preserves his material advantage.

26. ... R × P!

That is all there is to it; with the loss of the passed pawn White's attack loses its force. Black is left with a great material advantage and so tries to exchange the Rooks to simplify the struggle.

27. Q—B 6	R—Kt 3
28. Q—B 7	Q—R 6
29. Q × R	Q × R
30. Q × R P	

White liquidates the pawns on the Q-side, keeping in hand the threat of 31. Q × P ch. After the immediate 30. Q × P ch, K—R 1; 31. Q × R P Black can reply 31. ... Q—B 4, while if 30. Q × P ch, K—R 1; 31. Kt × P, then 31. ... Q—B 2 and in both cases the advance of the Q Kt P decides the issue.

| 30. ... | Kt × P |
| 31. Q × P | Kt × P! |

Now the King's covering of pawns is destroyed. If 32. K × Kt, then 32. ... P—K 5 recovers the piece.

32. Kt × P	Q—Kt 4
33. K—R 2	Q—B 5 ch
34. K—Kt 1	Kt × P ch

White resigned.

No. 23. Sicilian Defence

V. SMYSLOV   C. KOTTNAUER

(Groningen, 1946)

1. P—K 4	P—Q B 4
2. Kt—K B 3	P—Q 3
3. P—Q 4	P × P
4. Kt × P	Kt—K B 3
5. Kt—Q B 3	P—Q R 3
6. B—K 2	P—K 3
7. O—O	P—Q Kt 4

This move—a typical one in the Sicilian Defence—is premature at this stage. Black is starting an attack on the Q-side before completing his development. Such tactics can bring success only if White plays passively.

| 8. B—B 3 | R—R 2 |

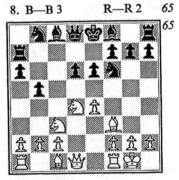

9. Q—K 2!

Much stronger than 9. B—K 3. In that case Black could still have completed the development of his Q-side by first R—Q 2 and then B—Kt 2. After the text move 9. ... R—Q 2 would be answered by 10. P—K 5, P × P; 11. Kt—B 6, Q—B 2; 12. Kt × Kt, Q × Kt; 13. B—B 6, winning the exchange. So Black is forced to put the Rook on a less satisfactory square.

9. ...	R—B 2
10. R—Q 1	Q Kt—Q 2
11. P—Q R 4	

The pawns, weakened by the early Q-side advance, are easily exposed to attack. 11. ... P—Kt 5 is bad on account of 12. Kt—R 2, P—Q R 4; 13. Kt—Kt 5. It is obvious now that Black's opening idea has suffered a reversal.

11. ...	P × P
12. Kt × R P	B—Kt 2　*66*

12. ... B—K 2; 13. B—Q 2 is no better.

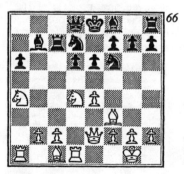
66

13. P—K 5!

A break-through in the centre which guarantees White a great positional superiority. After 13. ... P × P; 14. B × B, P × Kt; 15. B

× P Black experiences great difficulties. However, the continuation chosen in the game is no better.

13. ...	Kt × P
14. B × B	R × B
15. Q × P	Q—Kt 1
16. Kt—B 6	Kt × Kt
17. Q × Kt ch	Kt—Q 2　*67*

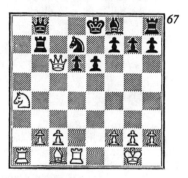
67

18. Kt—B 5!!

A beautiful combination. White opens all the lines for the attack.
If now 18. ... R—B 2, than 19. Kt × Kt, R × Kt; 20. R—R 8 and wins; therefore the piece sacrifice must be accepted.

18. ...	P × Kt
19. B—B 4	

The point of the combination. Against 19. ... Q × B White had prepared the following variation: 20. Q—B 8 ch, K—K 2; 21. Q × R, K—B 3; 22. R × Kt, K—Kt 3; 23. P—K Kt 3, Q—B 4; 24. R—R 7 and White's heavy pieces invade the enemy position with decisive effect.

19. ...	B—Q 3
20. B × B	R—Kt 3
21. Q × Kt ch!	Black
	resigned.

No. 24.　Sicilian Defence

V. SMYSLOV　　A. DENKER

(*Match, U.S.S.R.–U.S.A., Moscow, 1946*)

1. P—K 4	P—Q B 4
2. Kt—Q B 3	Kt—Q B 3
3. P—K Kt 3	P—K Kt 3
4. B—Kt 2	B—Kt 2
5. P—Q 3	P—K 3
6. B—K 3	Kt—Q 5

It is too early to occupy this centre square. 6. ... P—Q 3 is better.

7. Q Kt—K 2 !

Preparing to build up a strong pawn centre by P—Q B 3 and P—Q 4 and so limit the activity of Black's Bishop on the long diagonal I first used this manœuvre against J. Sajtar in the Moscow-Prague Match, 1946. In the event of 7. ... Kt × Kt; 8. Kt × Kt, B × P; 9. R—Q Kt 1 White recovers the pawn on Q B 5, since Black cannot continue 9. ... Q—R 4 ch; 10. B—Q 2, Q × P on account of 11. R × B!, Q × R; 12. B—Q B 3 with advantage to White.

7. ...	P—Q 3
8. P—Q B 3	Kt—Q B 3

Here it seems more natural to play 8. ... Kt × Kt; 9. Kt × Kt, Kt—K 2; 10. P—Q 4, Q—B 2.

9. P—Q 4	P × P
10. Kt × P	Kt × Kt
11. B × Kt	P—K 4

It stands to reason that it is bad to exchange the K B, which is needed for the defence of the K-side. So Black decides on the thrust P—K 4, wishing to gain time to complete the development of his pieces. But he is left with a backward Q P, which is the source of his future troubles. 11. ... Kt—B 3 was less demanding.

12. B—K 3	Kt—K 2

Now 12. ... Kt—B 3, recommended in the magazine *Chess in the U.S.S.R.*, No. 11-12, 1946, is hardly good. For example: 13. Kt—K 2, B—K 3; 14. O—O, P—Q 4; 15. P × P, and if 15. ... Kt × P, then 16. B—B 5. 15. ... B × P is met by 16. Q—R 4 ch, Q—Q 2; 17. Q × Q ch, K × Q; 18. Q R—Q 1, K—K 3 (18. ... K—B 3; 19. R × B! Kt × R; 20. P—Q B 4); 19. B—R 3 ch, K—K 2; 20. B—B 5 ch, K—K 1; 21. P—K B 4! with a strong attack.

13. Kt—K 2	O—O
14. O—O	B—K 3
15. Q—Q 2	

Obviously 15. ... P—Q 4 cannot be played now because of 16. B—B 5. Black is therefore forced to carry on the struggle with the handicap of a backward pawn.

15. ...	Q—B 2　　*68*

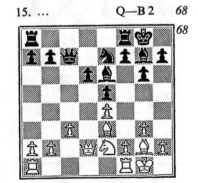

68

16. K R—B 1 !

White's main task is to establish control over Q 5, and for this P—Q B 4 is most suited. The attempt to prevent this by 16. ... P—Q Kt 4 leads to an unsatisfactory position after 17. P—Q R 4, P—Q R 3; 18. R—Q 1, e.g. 18. ... Q R—Q 1; 19. P × P, P × P; 20. R—R 7! or 18. ... K R—Q 1; 19. P × P, P × P; 20. R × R, R × R; 21. Q × P. If 18. ... B—Kt 6, then 19. Q × P, Q × Q; 20. R × Q, B × P; 21. Kt—B 1 with the threat of P—Kt 3. Also insufficient is 16. ... P—Q Kt 4; 17. P—Q R 4, P × P; 18. R × P, P—Q R 4; 19. K R—R 1 threatening P—Q Kt 4.

Black is unwilling to defend passively and instead strives to take the initiative on the K-side with his next move.

16. ...	P—B 4
17. P—Q B 4	P × P
18. Kt—B 3	Kt—B 4

After 18. ... B × P White could continue with 19. Kt × P, P—Q 4; 20. Kt—Kt 5 with complications in his favour. For example: 20. ... P—Q 5; 21. Kt—K 6, P × B; 22. Q × P, Q—Q 3; 23. Kt × R, B—B 2 (23. ... B—Q 4; 24. B × B ch, Kt × B; 25. Q—B 5, B × Kt; 26. Q × Q, B × Q; 27. R—Q 1!); 24. R—Q 1, Kt—Q 4; 25. Q—Kt 3, R—Q 1; 26. Kt × Kt P!, P × Kt; 27. B × Kt, B × B; 28. R × B, Q × R; 29. R—Q 1! and wins.

19. Kt × P

Thus White has built up a strong position in the centre. In addition, the long diagonal has been opened for his K B. If now 19. ... Kt—Q 5, then 20. P—B 5! P—Q 4; 21. Kt—

Kt 5, B—B 2; 22. P—B 4 with an attack.

19. ...	Kt × B
20. Q × Kt	P—K R 3
21. R—Q 1	

21. ... B × P would be answered by 22. Q R—B 1, setting up a dangerous pin on the Bishop.

21. ...	K R—Q 1
22. Q R—B 1	Q R—B 1
23. P—Kt 3	P—Kt 3 69

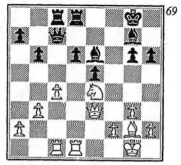

69

24. Kt—B 3!

White aims to exchange the white-squared Bishops and leave himself with a centralized Kt against a Bishop which is blocked by its own pawns. From the point of view of strategic principles Black could, of course, play 24. ... K—R 2, avoiding the exchange. But after 25. B—K 4! with P—K R 4—R 5 to follow or 26. Kt—Kt 5 and 27. Q—Q 3 White would exert very strong pressure on his opponent's position.

24. ...	Q—K 2
25. B—Q 5	K—R 2
26. B × B	Q × B
27. R—Q 3	R—B 2
28. R (1)—Q 1	R—B 2

As a counter to White's attack on the Q P Black tries to get some play by doubling Rooks on the

K B-file. However the systematic occupation of the white squares leads to the complete dominance of the centre by White.

29. Kt—K 4	B—B1
30. R—Q 5	Q—Kt 5
31. R (1)—Q 3	

Avoiding the immediate 31. Kt × P on account of 31. ... B × Kt; 32. R × B, Q × R ch!; 33. R × Q, R × R ch. If Black answers the text move by 31. ... Q—K 3, then White continues 32. Q—Q 2, R (2) —Q 2; 33. P—B 5, Kt P × P; 34. Kt × B P.

31. ...	B—K 2
32. Kt × P	B × Kt
33. R × B	R (1)—K B 1
34. Q × K P	R × P
35. R—Q 7 ch	R (7)—B 2
36. R × R ch	R × R 70

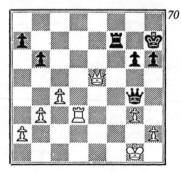

70

37. R—Q 8!

It was this invasion of Black's position that White had counted on when he gave up the K B P. The Queen on K 5 is in a strong position in the centre of the board,

and Black is threatened by a mating attack along the back rank. It is curious to note that although the White King is seemingly in an open position there is not even one saving check at Black's disposal.

37. ...	R—K Kt 2
38. Q—K 8	P—K Kt 4
39. Q—R 8 ch	K—Kt 3
40. R—Q 6 ch	K—B 2
41. Q × P	

The game was adjourned in this position. Play continued:

41. ...	Q—B 4
42. R—Q 1!	Q—B 4 ch
43. K—Kt 2	Q—K 2
44. R—B 1 ch	K—Kt 1
45. Q—K B 6	Q—K 1
46. Q—B 5	

White must regroup his forces for the final attack: the Rook must seize the open K-file, standing on K 2, while the Queen occupies K 4.

46. ...	P—Kt 5
47. R—B 2	Q—K 2
48. Q—Q 3	R—Kt 4

After 48. ... Q—Kt 2 ch White could by 49. Q—Q 5 ch bring about a Rook and pawn ending, in which he has two extra pawns.

49. R—K 2	Q—B 1
50. Q—K 4	

Completing the regrouping. Now the end comes quickly.

50. ...	R—Kt 2
51. Q—Q 5 ch	Q—B 2
52. R—K 6!	Black
	resigned.

Black has not one useful move.

No. 25. Queen's Gambit Declined, Slav Defence
A. TOLUSH   V. SMYSLOV
(Fifteenth Soviet Championship, Leningrad, 1947)

1. P—Q 4	P—Q 4	11. P—K 6!	P × P
2. P—Q B 4	P—Q B 3	12. Q—Kt 4	71
3. Kt—K B 3	Kt—K B 3		
4. Kt—B 3	P × P		
5. P—K 4			

White embarks on a gambit line, allowing Black to defend his Q B P. In exchange for this White gets an active position in the centre and good attacking chances.

5. ...	P—Q Kt 4
6. P—K 5	Kt—Q 4
7. P—Q R 4	B—K 3!

The idea behind this manœuvre —paradoxical at first glance— consists in transferring the Bishop to Q 4 after the exchange of Knights. A very sharp struggle now develops. Black proposed to answer 8. Kt—K 4 with 8. ... Kt— B 2 followed by B—Q 4 and P— K 3. If 8. Kt—Kt 5, then 8. ... Kt × Kt; 9. P × Kt, B—Q 4; if here 9. Kt × B, then 9. ... Kt × Q; 10. Kt × Q, Kt × Kt P! and Black has the initiative in the ending.

Another promising plan is 7. ... P—K 3 followed simply by B—K 2.

8. P × P	Kt × Kt
9. P × Kt	P × P
10. Kt—Kt 5	B—Q 4

The Bishop has taken up an active position in the centre. Black has only to play P—K 3 to have a solid position.

White is, therefore, forced to sacrifice a second pawn to disorganize the normal development of his opponent's K-side.

Having the double threat of Kt × R P and Kt × K P. It would appear that White's attack must meet with success, but this conclusion is far from clear. Very interesting for the theory of the opening is the game Tolush-Levenfish (Leningrad Championship, 1947), in which White evidently hoped to strengthen the attack by playing 12. B—B 4. Nevertheless, after 12. ... Kt—B 3; 13. B—K 2, P—K 4!; 14. P × P, P—K 3; 15. Q—Kt 1, B—B 4, Black by giving back the pawn had taken the initiative.

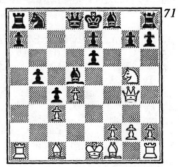

71

12. ...   P—K R 4!

A vigorous reply. In sharp positions, where intensive and resolute actions are called for, it is very important to 'feel' the rhythm of the struggle and estimate the time factor.

13. Q—B 4   Q—Q 3

Black decides to lure the white Queen to K B 7 and retreat the

King to the Q-side. At the same time the threat of Kt—B 7 is parried.

14. Q—B 7 ch   K—Q 2
15. B—R 3

The alternative here is 15. B—B 4, to which Black could reply 15. .... P—K 4; 16. P × P (16. Q—B 5 ch, P—K 3; 17. Q—B 7 ch, Q—K 2; 18. B × K P, Kt—B 3), B × Q; 17. P × Q, B—Kt 3!; 18. P × P, B × P, e.g. 19. O—O—O ch, K—B 1; 20. P—Kt 3, B—R 6 ch; 21. K—Q 2, R—Q 1 ch; 22. K—K 1, R—K 1 ch; 23. K—Q 2, Kt—B 3 and Black has the better chances.

15. ...   Q—B 2
16. B—K 2   Kt—B 3
17. B × R P   72

In this complicated and tense position Tolush overlooks an interesting counter by Black. Correct was 17. B—B 3, trying to undermine the bulwark of Black's defence—the Bishop at Q 4. A possible continuation would be 17. ... Kt—Q 1; 18. Q—Kt 6 (interesting is 18. B × B, Kt × Q; 19. B × P ch, K—B 3; 20. Kt × Kt, R—R 3!; 21. Kt—K 5 ch, Q × Kt ch!; 22. P × Q, R × B, and Black has an extra pawn), R—R 3; 19. Q—Kt 1, Q—B 3; 20. Kt—K 4, Kt—Kt 2, and Black still has a number of difficult problems to solve before he can realize his material advantage.

17. ...   Kt—K 4!

An unexpected riposte. The Queen is trapped and has not one satisfactory retreat (18. Q—B 4, Kt—Q 6 ch); White must take the Kt.

18. P × Kt   Q × P ch
19. K—B 1   Q × Kt
20. B—B 3   Q—B 3
21. B × B

A last attempt to prolong the resistance, but White's game is hopeless.

21. ...   Q × Q
22. B × R   P—R 4
23. P—Kt 3   Q—B 4
24. K—Kt 2   P—Kt 4
25. P—R 3   B—Kt 2
26. Q R—Q 1 ch   K—B 2
27. P—Kt 4   Q—B 2

White resigned.

A short but stormy skirmish.

No. 26.   Queen's Gambit Declined, Half Slav Defence
V. SMYSLOV   V. RAGOSIN
(Fifteenth Soviet Championship, Leningrad, 1947)

1. P—Q 4   P—Q 4
2. P—Q B 4   P—K 3
3. Kt—Q B 3   P—Q B 3
4. Kt—B 3

The gambit line 4. P—K 4, P × P; 5. Kt × P, B—Kt 5 ch; 6. B—Q 2, Q × P; 7. B × B, Q × Kt ch; 8. B—K 2 leads to sharp play, in which White has a strong attack in return for the pawn.

4. ...   Kt—B 3
5. B—Kt 5   P × P

In destroying the equilibrium in the centre Black embarks upon a difficult and complicated struggle. He sets up a pawn majority on the Q-side but allows White an initiative based on the advance of the K P.

6. P—K 4   P—Kt 4
7. P—K 5   P—K R 3
8. B—R 4   P—Kt 4
9. K Kt × P   Kt—Q 4   *73*

Black chooses a variation involving the sacrifice of the exchange. In this position great popularity is enjoyed by 9. ... P × Kt; 10. B × Kt P, Q Kt—Q 2, leading to Botvinnik's system (see game No. 40).

73

10. Kt × B P!   Q × B
11. Kt × R   B—Kt 5
12. R—B 1

The most logical move. Another possibility is 12. Q—Q 2, P—Q B 4; 13. O—O—O, Kt—Q B 3 with chances for both sides.

12. ...   P—Q B 4

Starting a counter-attack based on rapid development for his pieces. However, in this game the attempt

suffers a decisive defeat. In his book on the openings A. Sokolsky suggested the following defensive plan for Black: 12. ... Q—K 5 ch; 13. B—K 2, Kt—B 5 and if 14. P—B 3, then 14. ... Q—R 2 regaining the Kt. But instead of 14. P—B 3, White can play 14. Q—Q 2!, e.g. 14. ... Kt—Q 6 ch; 15. K—B 1, Kt × R; 16. Kt × Q, B × Q; 17. Kt × B, P—Q R 4! and it is difficult to assess the chances.

13. P × P   Kt—Q 2
14. B—K 2   B—Kt 2   *74*

14. ... Kt—K 6 is bad on account of 15. B—R 5 ch, K—Q 1; 16. Kt—B 7 ch, K—K 1; 17. Q—B 3 with advantage to White.

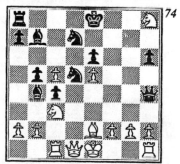

74

15. B—R 5 ch!

This check ruins Black's plans for castling Q-side. The Bishop comes to the aid of the Kt, which has been standing aside from the general conflict for some time.

15. ...   K—Q 1
16. O—O   B × Kt
17. R × B!

Now the Rook enters the game with decisive effect. If 17. ... Kt × R, then 18. Kt—B 7 ch, K—B 2; 19. Q—Q 6 ch, K—B 1; 20. P—B 6, and there is no answer to White's threats.

Therefore Black cannot establish material equality and must allow the Rook to go over to the K-side.

17. ...	K—B 2
18. Kt—Kt 6	Q—K 5
19. R—K Kt 3	Kt × B P
20. B—B 3	

The game is really already over: White's K-side has been well fortified, and his great material superiority guarantees him quite an easy victory.

| 20. ... | Q—B 4 |
| 21. Q—Q 4! | |

The Queen has occupied an attacking position in the centre. The remaining moves were:

21. ...	K—Kt 3
22. P—Kt 4	P × P e.p.
23. P × P	Q—B 7
24. B × Kt	R—Q 1
25. Kt—B 4	B × B
26. R—Q B 3	Black
	resigned.

A valuable game from the theoretical point of view.

27. Ending

V. SMYSLOV   H. GOLOMBEK

(*Match, Great Britain–U.S.S.R., London, 1947*)

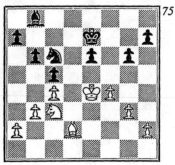

75
75

In this position White has a minimal advantage: it consists in the strong position occupied by the White King in the centre and the fact that his Bishop is more active than Black's, which is a little restricted in its movements. The slight disarray of Black's pawns on the K-side complicates the defence.

33. Kt—Q 1

Now Q B 3 is freed so that the Bishop can occupy the important long diagonal, while the Kt is destined for K Kt 4, where it will threaten to attack the enemy pawns. White does not fear the reply P—K 4 because after P—B 5 the possibility of creating a passed pawn on the wing would be enhanced and Black's position in the centre (his Q 4 square) would be weakened.

| 33. ... | B—Q 3 |
| 34. Kt—B 2 | Kt—Q 1 |

34. ... Kt—Q 5 achieved nothing on account of 35. B—B 3. Black transfers his Kt to K B 2, where it will occupy an excellent defensive position.

| 35. B—B 3 | Kt—B 2 |
| 36. Kt—Kt 4 | |

From here the Kt threatens to attack the K R P and provoke its advance, thus creating a new weakness in Black's pawn formation. With his next move Black goes to meet White's plans.

36. ...	P—K R 4
37. B—B 6 ch!	

An important intermediate check. To take advantage of the pawn weakness, it must first of all be fixed. With this aim White established his Bishop on K B 6, where it prevents any possible activity based on P—K Kt 4.

37. ...	K—Q 2
38. Kt—B 2	B—B 2

Black pursues waiting tactics. 38. ... B—K 2, to drive the Bishop from B 6, was better. It is true that after 38. ... B—K 2; 39. B—B 3, the attempt to free himself by 39. ... P—K Kt 4; 40. P × P, Kt × P ch; 41. K—K 3 leads to a position where White's advantage is incontestable.

39. Kt—Q 3	K—B 3

Evidently, moving the King to Q B 3 is explained by a desire to prepare P—Q Kt 4. If 40. Kt—K 5 ch, Black replies 40. ... B × Kt, and the Kt on K B 2 prevents any further activity by White on the K-side.

40. Kt—K 1!	

White is aiming to get his Kt to K R 4, where it will attack the weak K Kt P. This threat forces Black to reorganize his defence.

40. ...	Kt—Q 3 ch
41. K—Q 3	Kt—B 4
42. Kt—B 3	K—Q 2

He cannot play 42. ... P—Q Kt 4 on account of 43. P × P ch, K × P; 44. Kt—Kt 5 and the K P is lost.

43. K—K 4	

This move threatens 44. Kt—K 5 ch, B × Kt; 45. K × B, and, after moving the Bishop, to march the King to the K Kt P.

43. ...	Kt—Q 3 ch
44. K—K 3	Kt—B 4 ch
45. K—B 2	B—Q 3
46. P—K R 3!	

The position has been defined: the weak K P and K Kt P have been fixed. Now White starts a pawn advance on the K-side.

46. ...	B—B 2
47. P—K Kt 4	P × P
48. P × P	Kt—R 3
49. K—Kt 3	Kt—B 2

The Kt returns to its old defensive position, covering here the entry squares K 4 and K Kt 4. But 49. ... K—K 1 was preferable; White could then continue 50. B—K 5, B—Q 1; 51. B—Kt 8, P—R 3; 52. Kt—K 5, P—K Kt 4; 53. Kt—B 6, B—B 3; 54. B—K 5, B × B; 55. Kt × B, P × P ch; 56. K × P, and White has an outside passed pawn in the Kt ending.

50. P—Kt 5	

In this way White renews the threat of Kt—R 4. Now 50. ... Kt—Q 3 is impossible because of 51. Kt—K 5 ch. Black's position has become critical.

50. ...	B—Q 1
51. K—Kt 4	B × B
52. P × B	K—Q 3
53. Kt—K 5!	Black resigned.

No. 28. Ruy Lopez

V. SMYSLOV   A. SOKOLSKY

(Tchigorin Memorial Tournament, Moscow, 1947)

1. P—K 4	P—K 4
2. Kt—K B 3	Kt—Q B 3
3. B—Kt 5	P—Q R 3
4. B—R 4	Kt—B 3
5. O—O	Kt × P
6. P—Q 4	P—Q Kt 4
7. B—Kt 3	P—Q 4
8. P × P	B—K 3
9. Q—K 2	

After P. Keres' games against V. Alatortsev (Fifteenth Soviet Championship, 1947) and C. H. O'D. Alexander (Match, Great Britain–U.S.S.R., London, 1947) this move acquired great popularity. The usual continuation here is 9. P—B 3, which preserves the white-squared Bishop from exchange. By 9. Q—K 2 White frees the square Q 1 for a Rook and begins active play in the centre.

9. ...	Kt—B 4
10. R—Q 1	Kt × B

In the position reached there are the following interesting variations:

(1) 10. ... Kt × B; 11. R P ×Kt, B—K 2; 12. P—B 4, O—O; 13. Kt —B 3, Kt—Kt 5; 14. B—K 3, P— Q B 3; 15. Q R—B 1, Q—Kt 1; 16. B—Kt 5! with good play on the black squares (Keres – Alexander, Match, Great Britain– U.S.S.R., London, 1947).

(2) 10. ... Kt × B; 11. R P × Kt, Q—B 1; 12. P—B 4!, Q P × P; 13. P × P, B × P; 14. Q—K 4 with a strong attack for the pawn (Smyslov–Euwe, World Championship Tournament, 1948).

(3) 10. ... P—Kt 5; 11. B—K 3, Kt × B; 12. R P × Kt, Q—B 1; 13. P—B 4, Q P × P; 14. P × P, P—R 3; 15. Q Kt—Q 2, B—K 2; 16. Kt—Kt 3, O—O; 17. B—B 5! with the same idea of play on the black squares as in the first variation (Smyslov–Reshevsky, World Championship Tournament, 1948).

(4) The most active plan of defence was met in the game Boleslavsky–Tolush (Eighteenth Soviet Championship, 1950): 10. ... B—K 2; 11. P—B 4, P—Q 5!; 12. Q Kt—Q 2, B—B 4; 13. Kt— B 1, P—Kt 5; 14. Kt—Kt 3, B—Kt 3; 15. B—K 3, P—Q 6!, and Black has a positional advantage.

However, the attacking and defensive possibilities in these variations do not present a full picture but only give the reader an idea of the direction of modern theoretical ideas.

11. R P × Kt	B—Q B 4
12. B—K 3!	

Intending to answer 12. ... P— Q 5 with 13. B—Kt 5, Q—Q 2; 14. Q × P!, P × Q; 15. R × R ch.

12. ...	B × B
13. Q × B	Q—K 2
14. Q—B 3	Kt—Q 1

This retreat is forced. 14. ... Kt— Kt 5 canot be played because of 15. R—Q 4, P—Q B 4; 16. R × Kt, P—Q 5; 17. R × Q P winning a piece. The opening has developed in White's favour. By his next move he fixes the weak squares in Black's position, preventing P—Q B 4.

15. P—Q Kt 4!　O—O
16. Q Kt—Q 2

Not the most accurate. More correct was 16. Kt—Q 4, which does not allow the pin which follows now. Sokolsky rids himself of his 'bad' Bishop.

16. ...　　　　B—Kt 5!
17. P—K R 3　B × Kt
18. Kt × B　　P—Q B 3
19. R—Q 2　　P—R 3
20. P—Q Kt 3　R—K 1
21. Kt—Q 4!

The beginning of an interestingly conceived attack. The pawn cannot be taken because of 22. R—K 2; at the same time White threatens 22. P—B 4. A sharp struggle develops around this advance.

21. ...　　　　Q—Kt 4
22. R—K B 1　Kt—K 3　76

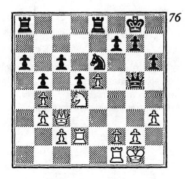
76

23. P—B 4!

White does not stop at a pawn sacrifice to open up lines for attack.

23. ...　　　　Kt × P
24. R (2)—B 2　Kt—K 3

An unsatisfactory reply. Better prospects were given by 24. ... Kt—

Kt 3, after which it is not easy to find a clear way to attack. Possibly White would have to be content with 25. Kt × B P, Q R—B 1; 26. Q—B 3, Kt × P; 27. Kt × Kt, Q × Kt; 28. Q × P ch, K—R 2. After the text move White's attack becomes unstoppable.

25. Kt—B 5　　K R—Q B 1
26. P—R 4!　　Q—Q 1
27. Q—Kt 3　　K—R 2　77

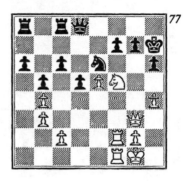
77

28. Kt—Q 6

Another good continuation is 28. Kt × Kt P, Kt × Kt; 29. R × P, Q—R 1; 30. P—R 5, and Black's position is very difficult. White preferred the simplest way.

28. ...　　　　R—B 2
29. Kt × B P　Q—K 2
30. Kt—Q 6　　R—K Kt 1

Loses at once. Nevertheless, other continuations do not save the game. For example: 30. ... R—K B 1; 31. R × R, Kt × R; 32. R—B 7, and Black must give up his Queen.

31. Q—Q 3 ch　Black
　　　　　　　　resigned.

No. 29. Ending
A. TSVETKOV   V. SMYSLOV
(Tchigorin Memorial Tournament, Moscow, 1947)

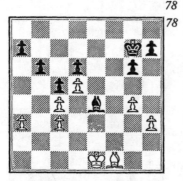

78
78

In this Bishop ending Black has an incontestable positional advantage, which consists in a better pawn formation: the white pawns on the K-side—K R 3 and K Kt 4—and also those in the centre—Q B 4 and Q 5—are on squares of the same colour as the Bishop and have to be defended; the weakness of the doubled Q B Ps in this position does not play a real part, as the pawn at Q B 3 helps to control the important square Q 4.

42. ...   P—K Kt 4!

The pawns on the K-side must be fixed on favourable squares. Otherwise, White on his move would play P—Kt 5.

43. K—B 2   K—B 3
44. K—K 3   K—K 4
45. B—K 2   B—B 7

The King has been centralized, and now Black begins a manœuvre to prepare the pawn break on the Q-side—P—Q R 3 and P—Q Kt 4 —in the most favourable situation.

Complicated play resulted from 45. ... B—Kt 7; 46. K—B 2, B × P; 47. K—Kt 3, K—K5, giving up a piece to break through with the King and attack the enemy pawns.

46. K—Q 2   B—Kt 8
47. K—K 3   P—K R 3!

Black is in no hurry. He puts his pawns on black squares to prevent later on even the slightest chance of counterplay connected with B—Q 3 (attacking the K R P) and B—B 5—Q 7 or B 8.

48. B—B 3

If 48. B—Q 1, then 48. ... B— K 5; 49. B—K 2, B—B 7, and Black transfers his Bishop to Q R 5 in accordance with the overall plan.

48. ...   B—B 7
49. B—K 2   P—R 3
50. K—Q 2   B—R 5
51. K—K 3   P—Kt 4!

The long-prepared break, which denotes the beginning of the decisive action. Black threatens to attack the weak pawns after 52. ... P × P; 53. B × P, B—Kt 4.

52. P × P   P × P
53. B—B 3   ·

If 53. P—B 4, then 53. ... P × P; 54. B × P, B—B 7 and then 55. ... B—K 5, obtaining two connected passed pawns in the centre.

53. ...   B—Kt 6
54. B—K 2   B—B 5!

An excellent manœuvre, forcing a pawn ending. All the finesses of the following interesting ending were already calculated by Black.

55. B × B	P × B
56. P—Q R 4	K × P
57. P—R 5	K—B 3
58. K—K 4	P—Q 4 ch
59. K—K 5	P—Q 5
60. P × P	P—B 6
61. P—Q 5 ch	K—Q 2!

Drawing the mating net round the White King.

62. P—R 6	P—B 7
63. P—R 7	P—B 8=Q
64. P—R 8=Q	Q—B 5 mate.

No. 30. Ending
V. SMYSLOV   M. EUWE
(*World Championship Tournament, 1948*)

79

79

The game was adjourned in this position.

In this minor piece ending White's pieces are much more active, especially if you consider the unfortunate position of the black Bishop on Q R 1. However, to profit from these circumstances presents a very difficult problem, in so far as there are no serious weaknesses in Black's pawn formation and his pieces may be transferred to better positions. On resumption play continued:

41. P—Kt 4!

The sealed move. Now capture on K R 5 followed by Kt—Kt 3 is threatened; or even P—Kt 5, shutting the black-squared Bishop out of play.

41. ...   P × P

This exchange was not compulsory; it even enhances White's chances of gaining the initiative on the K-side. Black could put his Bishop in an active position by 41. ... B—B 5. True, after 41. ... B—B 5; 42. P—Kt 5, Kt—B 1; 43. B—R 5, B—B 8; 44. P—R 4, P × P; 45. P × P, B—Kt 2; 46. K—Kt 2, White threatens to play the Kt to Q B 4 to increase the positional pressure or gain what in this position would be an advantage—the two Bishops.

42. P × P   B—B 8!

An integral part of Black's defensive plan. In the event of 42. ... P—B 4; 43. P—Kt 5, B—K Kt 2; 44. Kt—K 3 Black's pieces are shut in; on the other hand White's threat of P—Kt 5 cannot be prevented by 42. ... P—B 3 because of 43. P—Kt 5, P × P; 44. B—Q 2! It should also be observed that instead of the text move the continuation 42. ... B—B 5; 43. P—Kt 5, Kt—Kt 1, preparing P—B 3, seems dubious. The following plan of attack is then possible: 44. P—R 4, P × P; 45. P × P, B—Kt 2; 46. Kt—Q 2, P—B 3; 47. Kt—B 4, P × P;

48. P × P, followed by capture of the Q P. This variation discloses the vulnerability of the point Q 3 in the opponent's position.

43. P—Kt 5

Advancing the pawn deprives Black of counterchances and dooms him to passive defence.

43. ...   B—Kt 2
44. K—B 2   Kt—B 1

Black plans the manœuvre Kt—Kt 3 and later Kt—Q 2. A line recommended by several analysts—44. ... Kt—Kt 1 to be followed by P—B 3—would be unsatisfactory on account of the variation 44. ... Kt—Kt 1; 45. Kt—Kt 3!, P—B 3; 46. Kt—K 2, B—Kt 7; 47. K—K 3, threatening to pursue the enemy Bishop to Q 4. After the exchange on Q 4 Black loses a central pawn. In addition to this the position of the Kt on K Kt 1 makes a desolate impression.

45. Kt—K 3   K—K 2
46. B—R 5

Of course, the manœuvre Kt—Kt 3—Q 2 must be prevented. On the other hand Black gets the chance to establish his Bishop on Q R 6 and so strengthen his Q P. To increase his initiative further White must transfer his white-squared Bishop to the diagonal K R 3—Q B 8.

46. ...   B—R 6
47. K—Kt 3   B—B 4
48. B—Q 2

White changes his tactics. Since Black has managed to strengthen his position on the Q-side, White prepares the thrust P—K R 5 to create play on the other wing. For example: if 48. ... Kt—Kt 3, then

49. P—R 5! P × P; 50. Kt—B 5 ch, K—Q 2; 51. B—K 2 etc.

It is scarcely worth considering defence by 48. ... B—Q 5; 49. Kt—B 2, Kt—Kt 3 because of 50. Kt × B, P × Kt; 51. B—Q B 1, Kt—Q 2; 52. B—Kt 2, Kt—K 4; 53. B—K B 1, P—Q 6; 54. B × Kt, P × B; 55. B × P, and White has an extra passed pawn in the Bishop ending.

48. ...   K—B 1
49. Kt—B 2   K—K 2

There was nothing to be gained by 49. ... Kt—K 2; 50. B—R 5, B—B 1 (or 50. ... Kt—Kt 1; 51. Kt—Kt 4, P—B 3; 52. Kt—B 6); 51. P—Kt 4 and 52. B—B 7.

50. B—K 2   Kt—R 2

Better was 50. ... Kt—Kt 3! Having missed this opportunity, Black is left with only passive defence. After 50. ... Kt—Kt 3 White would probably have to content himself with 51. P—R 5, P × P; 52. K—R 4, Kt—Q 2; 53. K × P, beginning a flanking manœuvre on the K-side.

51. B—R 5!

Preventing the move 51. ... B—B 1 by 52. P—Kt 4, B—Kt 8; 53. K—Kt 2, B—Q 5; 54. Kt × B, P × Kt; 55. B—Kt 6, and White wins a piece.

51. ...   Kt—B 1
52. B—K Kt 4!

Now that the Bishop has occupied this diagonal White's pieces are ideally placed. In spite of the material equality the struggle is really already over.

52. ...   P—B 3

Waiting tactics—52. ... K—K 1; 53. B—B 7, K—K 2—were insufficient, for after 54. K—Kt 2!

Black has no useful moves at his disposal. For example: 54. ... K— K 1; 55. P—Kt 4, B—R 2; 56. B × Kt and 57. B × P; or 54. ... Kt—R 2; 55. P—Kt 4, B—Q 5; 56. Kt × B, P × Kt; 57. B— Kt 6; or finally 54. ... B—R 2; 55. Kt— Kt 4, threatening 56. Kt—B 6 ch.

| 53. B—K 6 | P × P |
| 54. P × P | Kt—Kt 3 |

In the event of 54. ... K—K 1; 55. B—B 7, K—K 2; 56. K—B 3 Black finds himself in zugzwang: if 56. ... B—R 2, then 57. Kt—Kt 4.

55. P—Kt 4

White now wins a pawn, as Black cannot play 55. ... B—Kt 8 on account of 56. K—Kt 2.

55. ...	Kt—B 5
56. P × B	Kt × B
57. P × P ch	K × P
58. B—B 7	

As a result of a forced series of moves the Black K Kt P perishes and with it Black's game.

58. ...	Kt—B 5
59. B × P	P—R 4
60. K—Kt 4	P—Kt 5
61. B—B 5	K—K 2
62. B—K 6	Kt—Q 3
63. Kt—K 3!	Kt × P

If 63. ... P—R 5, then 64. Kt— B 5 ch, Kt × Kt; 65. P × Kt, P—Kt 6; 66. P—B 6 ch, K—Q 3; 67. P—B 7, K—K 2; 68. P—Q 6 ch and White wins.

64. K—B 5	Kt—Q 3 ch
65. K × P	Kt—B 2 ch
66. K —B 4	Kt—Q 1
67. Kt—B 5 ch	K—B 1
68. P—Kt 6	Kt × B
69. P × Kt	P—R 5
70. K—K 5!	Black
	resigned.

No. 31. Ruy Lopez

V. SMYSLOV   S. RESHEVSKY

(World Championship Tournament, 1948)

1. P—K 4	P—K 4
2. Kt—K B 3	Kt—Q B 3
3. B—Kt 5	P—Q R 3
4. B—R 4	P—Q 3

In this game Reshevsky selects a variation, which had already been met in the first rounds of the World Championship.

| 5. P—B 3 | Kt—K 2 |

Behind the development of the Kt on K 2 is the intention to transfer it later to K Kt 3, where it strengthens the important point K 4.

| 6. P—Q 4 | B—Q 2 |
| 7. B—Kt 3 | P—R 3 |

The threat was 8. Kt—Kt 5

8. Q Kt—Q 2	Kt—Kt 3
9. Kt—B 4	B—K 2
10. O—O	O—O
11. Kt—K 3	B—B 3

Having completed their development, both sides are aiming at the most fitting deployment of pieces. Black could also play 11. ... R—K 1 to answer 12. Kt—Q 5 with 12. ... B—K B 1.

| 12. Kt—Q 5 | R—K 1 |

In the game Euwe-Keres, played in the first round of the World Championship Tournament, Black continued 12. ... P × P; 13, Kt ×

P (13. P × P, B—Kt 5!), R—K 1. In choosing the text move Reshevsky thought that he was strengthening the whole variation, but White by his simple reply gains a positional advantage.

13. P × P!

Black is now forced to recapture with a piece, as if 13. ... P × P, then 14. Kt × B ch, and Black's Bishop on Q 2 is hanging.

13. ...   B × P

If 13. ... K Kt × P; 14. Kt × Kt, Kt × Kt; 15. P—K B 4, Kt—B 3; 16. P—K 5!, White has a strong attack.

14. Kt × B   P × Kt
15. Q—B 3

White's advantage is determined: his Kt on Q 5 dominates the centre and this is still further increased by the open Q-file. As well as this White has two active Bishops.

15. ...   B—K 3

He wishes to rid himself of the strong Kt at Q 5. Scarcely any better was 15. ... Kt—Q R 4; 16. B—B 2, P—Q B 3; 17. Kt—K 3, B—K 3; 18. Kt—B 5, Q—B 2; 19. Q—Kt 4, K—R 2; 20. P—K R 4! P—B 3; 21. P—R 5, Kt—B 1; 22. P—Q Kt 3 with excellent prospects in the coming positional struggle.

16. R—Q 1   B × Kt
17. R × B

White's initiative increases all the time. Now the Rook occupies an active position in the centre of the board. 17. P × B was weaker on account of 17. ... P—K 5.

17. ...   Q—K 2   80

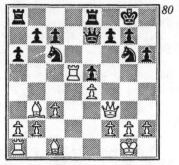

18. Q—B 5!

With the threat of 19. R—Q 7, but also indirectly attacking the Kt on K Kt 3. For example: 18. ... Q R—Q 1; 19. B × P!, P × B; 20. R × R and 21. Q × Kt ch. In this variation 19. ... R × R is answered by 20. B × R, of course. Therefore Black's reply is forced.

18. ...   Kt—B 1
19. B—K 3   Kt—K 3
20. Q R—Q 1   K R—Q 1
21. P—Kt 3

White takes advantage of the immobility of Black's pieces to strengthen his position and limit the activity of the enemy Knights. Black has no counterplay; he decides to neutralize the pressure on the open file even at the cost of a backward Q P.

21. ...   R—Q 3
22. R × R   P × R
23. Q—Kt 4   K—R 1

Retreating the King to B 1 (24. B × P was threatened) also had its inconveniences. For example: 23. ... K—B 1; 24. B—Kt 6, threatening 25. B × Kt, P × B; 26. Q—B 3 ch, K—Kt 1; 27. Q—Q 3, attacking the Q P with gain of tempo. Or 23. ... K—B 1; 24. B—Kt 6, Kt—B 2; 25. Q—B 5 (with the threats of Q × P ch and R × P),

Kt—K 1; 26. Q—R 7, Kt—B 3; 27. Q—R 8 ch, Kt—Kt 1; 28. R—Q 3 with the idea of transferring the Rook to K B 3.

Therefore the move played by Reshevsky cannot be considered less appropriate than 23. ... K—B 1, which was suggested by several commentators.

24. B—Kt 6!

Depriving the Black Rook of the Square Q 1 and preparing to double the heavy pieces on the Q-file (R—Q 3 and Q—Q 1). If 24. ... Kt—B 2, White intended 25. Q—B 3, R—K B 1, 26. Q—Q 3, Kt—K 1; 27. B—R 4, and Black cannot avoid loss of material.

24. ...   Kt—Kt 1

This move has a surprising refutation, based on the fact that the back rank is undefended. However, the preliminary 24. ... R—Q B 1 was also insufficient because of the variation; 25. R—Q 2, Kt—Kt 1; 26. Q—Q1, R—B 3; 27. B—R 7, Kt—Q 2; 28. B—Q 5, R—B 2; 29. B × Kt, Q × B; 30. R × P, winning a pawn.

25. B × Kt   P × B   81

26. Q—R 4!

An effective manœuvre, which leads to the win of a pawn. If 26. ...

Q × Q; 27. P × Q, Black cannot defend the Q P.

26. ...   Q—Q 2
27. Q—Q 8 ch

The harmonious co-operation of pieces behind the enemy lines, resulting logically from systematic strategy, is rare in practice.

27. ...	Q × Q
28. B × Q	Kt—Q 2
29. B—B7	Kt—B 4
30. R × P	

With the win of the pawn White gets a won ending. If 30. ... Kt × P, then, of course, 31. R × P, and Black loses yet another pawn.

30. ...	R—Q B 1
31. B—Kt 6	Kt—R 5
32. R × P	Kt × Kt P
33. R × P	Kt—B 5

Black forces a Rook and pawn ending; otherwise, after 33. ... R × P; 34. B—Q 4 White builds up an attack on K Kt 7.

34. R—K 6	Kt × B
35. R × Kt	R × P
36. R × Kt P	R—B 7
	82

Black wins back one of the pawns, but White's pawn majority on the K-side guarantees him victory.

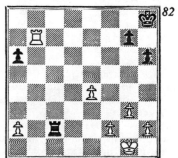

37. P—K R 4	R × R P
38. K—Kt 2	P—Q R 4
39. P—R 5	P—R 5
40. R—R 7	K—Kt 1
41. P—Kt 4	P—R 6
42. K—Kt 3	R—K 7
43. K—B 3	R—R 7
44. K—K 3	K—B 1
45. P—B 3	R—R 8
46. K—B 4	

The White King advances towards

K Kt 6 under cover of the pawn chain. Already 47. K—B 5 and 48. P—B 4 is threatened.

46. ...	P—R 7
47. P—K 5	K—Kt 1
48. K—B 5	R—K B 8
49. R × P	R × P ch
50. K—Kt 6	K—B 1
51. R—R 8 ch	K—K 2
52. R—R 7 ch	Black
	resigned.

No. 32.   Queen's Gambit Declined

V. SMYSLOV   P. KERES

(*World Championship Tournament, 1948*)

1. P—Q 4	P—Q 4
2. P—Q B 4	P—K 3
3. Kt—Q B 3	Kt—K B 3
4. B—Kt 5	P—B 3
5. P—K 3	Q Kt—Q 2
6. P × P	K P × P

The exchange of centre pawns defines the further course of the opening struggle: now White must aim for active play on the Q-side, where he has an half-open Q B-file, while Black's chances are based on the use of the K-file for operations on the K-side.

In my opinion this variation gives White a very slight positional advantage.

7. B—Q 3	B—K 2
8. Kt—B 3	

An alternative plan of development may foreshadow castling Q-side. In that case after 8. Q—B 2, O—O; 9. K Kt—K 2, R—K 1; 10. O—O—O double-edged play, usually accompanied by pawn storms on both wings, commences.

8. ...	O—O
9. Q—B 2	R—K 1
10. O—O	Kt—B 1
11. Q R—Kt 1	

In accordance with his projected strategic plan White intends to advance his Q Kt P so as to shatter his opponent's position on the flank.

11. ...	Kt—Kt 3
12. P—Q Kt 4	B—Q 3

As the further course of the game shows, Black here makes a small inaccuracy. Better was 12. ... P—Q R 3, and if 13. P—Q R 4, then 13. ... Kt—K 5, ridding himself of the pin.

13. P—Kt 5	B—Q 2	
14. P × P	B × P	*83*

More in keeping with the needs of the position was 14. ... P × P, so as to keep the Bishop to defend the Q B P. Now Black has an isolated pawn on Q 4, which allows White to carry out a manœuvre completely disorganizing the attacking plan of his opponent.

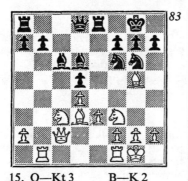
83

15. Q—Kt 3	B—K 2
16. B × Kt!	B × B
17. B—Kt 5	

The logical completion of White's manœuvre. After the exchange of the white-squared Bishops Black is doomed to passive defence. His minor pieces, situated on the K-side, now have no good prospects at all.

17. ...	Q—Q 3
18. K R—B 1	P—K R 4
19. Kt—K 2	P—R 5
20. B × B	P × B
21. Q—R 4	

White is in firm control of the open files and exerts strong pressure on the weak points Q R 7 and Q B 6. Black's diversion with the K R P is not dangerous.

| 21. ... | Kt—K 2   84 |

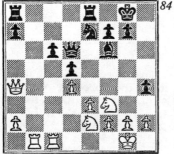
84

22. R—Kt 7!

Control of the seventh rank underlines White's advantage.

In the event of 22. Q—R 6 Black could get some counterplay by 22. ... Q R—Kt 1, with the idea of exchanging Rooks on the open file. Then 23. Q × R P is not dangerous on account of 23. ... R—R 1, winning back the pawn; 23. R—Kt 7 is answered by 23. ... R × R; 24. Q × R, Q—R 6 with some counterchances.

22. ...	P—R 4
23. P—K R 3	K R—Kt 1
24. K R—Kt 1	R × R
25. R × R	P—B 4 85

All the same Black has managed to carry out this advance, which does put some life into his game; however, a number of new weaknesses are created in his pawn formation and these later become the objects of attack for White's pieces. The attempt to exchange Rooks by, for example, 25. ... R—Kt 1; 26. R × R ch, Q × R; 27. Q × R P, Q—Kt 8 ch; 28. Kt—K 1, Kt—B 4; 29. K—B 1, Kt—Q 3 does not achieve anything because of 30. Q—R 8 ch, K—R 2; 31. Q × P, Kt—B 5; 32. Kt—B 4, Q—Q 8; 33. Kt—Q 3, and White is left two pawns up, for which loss of material his opponent has no real compensation.
85

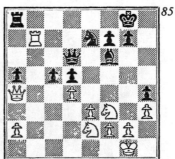
85

26. R—Kt 5!   P × P

26. ... P—B 5 is answered simply by 27. R × R P, and Black's passed pawn is blockaded by Kt—B 3.

27. Kt (K 2) × P   R—Q B 1

If 27. ... Q—B 2; 28. Kt—Kt 3, Q—B 3, White can increase the pressure on his opponent's loose pawns by 29. Kt—B 5 (the threat is R × R P). It would be difficult to maintain that Black could in this position support all his weak pawns —Q R, Q and K R pawns. For example: 29. ... B—B 6; 30. Kt × K R P, P—Q 5; 31. Kt—B 5! (31. ...-Kt × Kt; 32. R—Kt 8 ch, winning the Queen). If 29. ... Q—B 2, then 30. Q—K Kt 4 with the idea of playing Kt—Q 7, after which White's attack becomes even more tangible. Against a passive reply P—Q R 4 would be possible.

28. Kt—Kt 3   B—B 6

Otherwise the Q R P is lost; but now the important K R P dies, and with its death Black's troubles, connected with the defence of his King position, increase.

29. Q × K R P   R—B 5   86

86

30. P—Kt 4!

This useful move not only parries the attack on the Queen but also ensures a flight square at Kt 2 for the King in case the Black Rook invades the back rank.

30. ...   P—R 5

If 30. ... R—R 5, it is sufficient to play 31. Kt—Kt 5 with mating threats; 30. ... B—B 3 could be answered in the same way.

31. Kt (Kt 3)—Q 4   B × Kt
32. Kt × B   Q—K 4

Neither does 32. ... Kt—B 3 save the game. The simplest reply is 33. Kt × Kt, R × Kt; 34. R—R 5, Q—Q 2; 35. Q—Kt 5, and White wins yet another pawn.

33. Kt—B 3   Q—Q 3

He cannot play 23. ... R—B 8 ch; 34. K—Kt 2, Q—K 5 on account of 35. R—Kt 8 ch, winning a piece.

34. R—R 5   R—B 1
35. R × R P

Now the game is easily won. The remaining moves were:

35. ...	Kt—Kt 3
36. Q—R 5	Q—K B 3
37. Q—B 5	Q—B 3
38. R—R 7	R—B 1
39. R—Q 7	P—Q 5
40. R × Q P	R—R 1
41. P—Q R 4!	

The sealed move. White had in mind the following variation if 41. ... R × P: 42. R—Q 8 ch, Kt—B 1 (42. ... K—R 2; 43. Q—R 5 mate); 43. Q × P ch! K × Q; 44. Kt—K 5 ch.

Black resigned without resuming.

No. 33. Ruy Lopez
V. SMYSLOV   M. EUWE
(*World Championship Tournament, 1948*)

1. P—K 4	P—K 4
2. Kt—K B 3	Kt—Q B 3
3. B—Kt 5	P—Q R 3
4. B—R 4	Kt—B 3
5. O—O	Kt × P

It is not without interest to recall that in the first encounter between these two players—at Groningen, 1946—Smyslov played 5. P—Q 3, which does not allow 5. ... Kt × P. This time the opening follows the lines of the Open Defence, a favourite with grandmaster Euwe.

6. P—Q 4	P—Q Kt 4
7. B—Kt 3	P—Q 4
8. P × P	B—K 3
9. Q—K 2	

This continuation received a thorough testing in the games of the tournament. One of the peculiarities of such a competition, where the struggle takes on the character of a match, is the relatively frequent repetition of definite opening systems. In this game both sides aim for the same position, appraising it differently however.

9. ...	Kt—B 4
10. R—Q 1	Kt × B

Black removes the white-squared Bishop so that on his next move he may take his Queen away from its dangerous position opposite the White Rook on the Q-file. However, there is no need to hurry with the exchange. Serious attention should be given to 10. ... B—K 2; 11. P—B 4, P—Q 5!, which leads to a sharp and complicated game.

11. R P × Kt	Q—B 1	*87*

Up to here the play has followed the game Keres-Reshevsky from the previous round of the tournament; White then continued 12. B—Kt 5, P—R 3; 13. B—R 4 and got into a difficult position. No doubt Euwe, as Black, was not averse to repeating this variation, but now an unpleasant surprise awaits him.

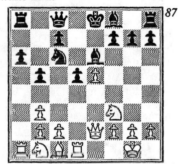
87

12. P—B 4!

An unexpected reply, which bursts Black's position in the centre asunder. While offering a pawn sacrifice White gets excellent attacking chances against the enemy King.

12. ...	Q P × P	
13. P × P	B × P	*88*

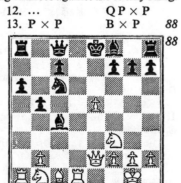
88

14. Q—K 4!

The idea of the previous pawn sacrifice consists in this centralization of the White Queen. Now Black's weak points on the Q-side and his poor development begin to have their say.

14. ...   Kt—K 2

With other replies White also preserved a strong attack, which more than compensates for the pawn. For example.

(1) 14. ... Q—K 3; 15. R—Q 6, B × R; 16. Q × Kt ch, K—K 2; 17. P × B ch, Q × P; 18. Q—K 4 ch, Q—K 3; 19. Q—R 4 ch, P—B 3; 20. Q—Kt 3, attacking both the Q B P and K Kt P at once.

(2) 14. ... Q—Kt 2; 15. Kt—B 3, R—Q Kt 1 (or 15. ... B—B 4; 16. P—K 6, B × P; 17. Kt—K 5); 16. P—K 6!

(a) 16. ... B × P; 17. Kt—Kt 5, Kt—Q 1; 18. R × Kt ch, K × R; 19. Kt × B ch, P × Kt; 20. Q × K P, B—K 2; 21. B—Kt 5!, with the threat of 22. R—Q 1 ch; or

(b) 16. ... P × P; 17. Kt—Kt 5, Kt—Q 1; 18. R × Kt ch, K × R; 19. Kt—B 7 ch, K—K1; 20. Kt × R, with a material advantage.

(3) 14. ... Kt—Kt 5!; 15. B—Kt 5. Now what has been recommended by several analysts—15. ... B—B 4—is bad because of 16. Kt—R 3!, O—O; 17. Kt × B, P × Kt; 18. Q × P, and the Black Bishop has no retreat; or 16. ... B—Kt 6; 17. K R—Q B 1, B—B 1; 18. Kt × P, and Black's position is smashed.

Therefore in variation 3 the correct answer to 15. B—Kt 5 is 15. ... P—Q B 3, resigning oneself to the loss of the Queen after

16. R—Q 8 ch, Q × R; 17. B × Q, R × B.

These variations give a clear impression of the dangers involved in the defence of Black's position.

89

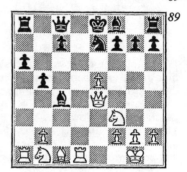

89

15. Kt—R 3!

Evidently a move which escaped M. Euwe's attention. Now if 15. ... B—Kt 6, then 16. R—Q 3, B—K 3; 17. Kt × P, B—B 4; 18. Kt × P ch. So Black is forced to give back the pawn, remaining in a bad position without any material compensation.

15. ...   P—Q B 3
16. Kt × B   P × Kt
17. Q × B P

Thus White has re-established material equality and retained a dangerous attack against the Black King, which is stuck in the centre.

17. ...   Q—Kt 2   90

If 17. ... Q—K 3, the problem can be solved by a combination: 18. R × P!, Q × Q; 19. R × R ch, Kt—B 1; 20. R × Kt ch, K—K 2; 21. R—B 7 ch, K—K 3; 22. R × P ch, Q × R; 23. Kt—Q 4 ch, or 21. ... K—K 1; 22. B—Kt 5 with a mating attack.

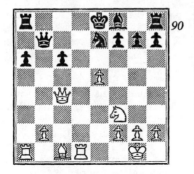

_90_

18. P—K 6!	P—B 3
19. R—Q 7	Q—Kt 4
20. Q × Q	

The simplest plan: after the exchange of Queens, Black cannot defend the weak points on the Q-side.

| 20. ... | B P × Q |
| 21. Kt—Q 4 | |

Threatening 22. Kt × P. The rest is clear without detailed explanation.

21. ...	R—B 1
22. B—K 3	Kt—Kt 3
23. R × R P	Kt—K 4
24. R—Kt 7	B—B 4
25. Kt—B 5	O—O

If 25. ... B × B, then 26. Kt—Q 6 ch.

| 26. P—R 3! | Black |
| | resigned. |

26. ... B × B is answered by 27. Kt—K 7 ch, while if 26. ... P—Kt 3, then 27. Kt—R 6 ch, K—R 1; 28. B × B, R × B; 29. R (R 6)—R 7.

No. 34.   Queen's Pawn, Grunfeld Defence

M. EUWE   V. SMYSLOV

(World Championship Tournament, 1948)

1. P—Q 4	Kt—K B 3
2. P—Q B 4	P—K Kt 3
3. Kt—Q B 3	P—Q 4
4. Kt—B 3	B—Kt 2
5. Q—Kt 3	P × P

This game, my last in the tournament, had a very important bearing on the distribution of the prizes. In the 24th round the games were Botvinnik–Reshevsky and Euwe–Smyslov. Both ended in victory for the Soviet player, and as a result I managed to take second place.

The opening variation chosen by Black was, of course, well known to the ex-World Champion, but I wanted at this most critical moment to test out once again the vitality of the system, which I had often used about that time.

| 6. Q × B P | O—O |
| 7. P—K 4 | B—Kt 5 |

Black puts into effect a plan involving action against the centre by the pieces—one of the most interesting problems of modern chess strategy.

8. B—K 3	K Kt—Q 2
9. Q—Kt 3	Kt—Kt 3
10. P—Q R 4	P—Q R 4
11. P—Q 5	B × Kt
12. P × B	_91_

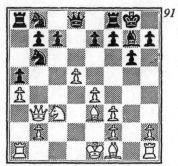

91

12. ...   Q—Q 3 !

An excellent position for the
Queen, whence it can reach Q Kt 5
and increase the pressure on the
Q-side. Euwe thought for a long
time over his reply and found an
active continuation.

13. Kt—Kt 5   Q—Kt 5 ch
14. Q × Q   P × Q
15. Kt × P

Consistently carrying out his
plan. If 15. P—R 5, then 15. ...
B × P; 16. R—Q Kt 1, Kt—R 5,
removing the piece from attack. If
16. R—R 2, Black could continue
16. ... B—K 4; 17. P—B 4, B—Q 3;
18. P—K 5, P—Kt 6! with complications favourable for Black.

15. ...   R × P
16. R—Q Kt 1

Euwe keeps his Rook for the
defence of his Q-side. In the event
of 16. R × R, Kt × R; 17. P—Kt
3, Kt—B 6; 18. B—R 3, B—K 4;
19. B—Kt 6, Kt—R 3; 20. Kt ×
Kt, R—R 1!, Black gains the
initiative.

16. ...   Kt (Kt 3)—
                           Q 2
17. Kt—Kt 5   R—B 1
18. B—K 2

Preference should have been
given to 18. Kt—Q 4, when Black

could continue 18. ... P—Kt 6;
19. Kt × P, R—Kt 5; 20. Kt—Q 2,
R × Kt P with chances for both sides.

18. ...   P—Kt 6
19. Kt—R 3

Defending his Q B 2 from invasion by the enemy Rook. Black
wins a pawn after 19. O—O,
R—B 7; 20. B—Q 1, R × Kt P
because White cannot play 21. B ×
P on account of 21. ... R—Kt 5,
attacking two pieces.

19. ...   B × P

Outwardly simple, but in actual
fact a major decision. Euwe undoubtedly considered this reply, but
hoped with the help of his two
Bishops to win back the pawn on
Q Kt 3 and obtain the better ending. So great is the conviction
nowadays in the advantage of the
two Bishops! Here it is interesting
to recall that M. I. Tchigorin readily
carried on the struggle with two
Knights and obtained repeated
successes. In the art of chess there
are no unalterable laws governing
the struggle, which are appropriate
to every position, otherwise chess
would lose its attractiveness and
eternal character.

20. R × B   R × Kt
21. K—Q 2   *92*

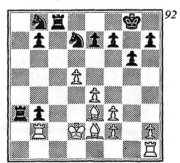

92

Both players were aiming for this position: White has a strong centre and two Bishops, but Black has an extra passed pawn. The question is whether he can keep what he has won. The whole struggle, in which the Knights show great resourcefulness and activity, revolves around Black's passed pawn.

Grandmaster Keres suggests (*The Match-Tournament for the World Championship*, page 312) that instead of 21. K—Q 2 the needs of defence were most simply fulfilled by 21. B—Q 1, which does not allow Black to consolidate his Kt on Q B 4. However, in the variation 21. B—Q 1, Kt—B 4; 22. B × Kt, R × B; 23. R × P, R × R; 24. B × R, R—B 8 ch; 25. B—Q 1, Kt—Q 2, Black preserves an indisputable advantage.

21. ...	Kt—R 3
22. K R—Q Kt 1	Kt (R 3)—
23. B—Q 4	B 4

It seems that it is not so easy to win back the pawn. After 23. B—Q Kt 5, Kt—K 4; 24. B × Kt, R × B; 25. R × P, Kt × P ch; 26. K—K 3, R × B; 27. R × R (R 3), R × R; 28. K × Kt, P—B 3; 29. R—B 3, P—R 4; 30. R—B 7, K—B 1, Black keeps his extra pawn and with it his winning chances.

23. B—Q 1 is now answered by 23. ... R—R 7; 24. R × R, P × R; 25. R—R 1, R—R 1; 26. K—B 3, P—K 3; 27. P × P, P × P; 28. B—B 2, P—Kt 3, and if 29. K—Kt 2, then 29. ... Kt—K 4, and Black once again preserves his positional advantage.

| 23. ... | P—K 4! |
| 24. P × P e.p. | |

One should not reproach White too severely for this exchange. Against 24. B—K 3 Black could continue 24. ... P—B 4; 25. P × P, P × P; 26. P—B 4, P × P; 27. B × P, R—R 5; 28. B—K 3, P—B 5 or 28. B—K R 6, K—B 2; all Black's pieces are in play, while the White Rooks are tied up by the blockade of the enemy pawn.

Keres, in the above-mentioned book, recommends 24. B—K 3 as a satisfactory continuation for White, giving the variation: 24. ... P—B 4; 25. P × P, P × P; 26. P—Q 6; Keres now asserts that "the white Bishops suddenly begin to show great activity".

In fact after the simple 26. ... P—B 5; 27. B—B 4 ch, K—Kt 2; 28. B × Kt, Kt × B White has already had to part with his proud black-squared Bishop. If 29. B × P, then 29. ... R—B 3 wins the Q P in return.

The move 24. B—B 3, which the analysts have examined, also does not give White full equality. After 24. B—B 3, P—B 4; 25. P × P, P × P; 26. B—Kt 5, P—Kt 3 White must still labour under difficulties, and for all that Black preserves his extra pawn. For example: 27. B × Kt, Kt × B; 28. R × P, R × R; 29. R × R, R—B 4.

| 24. ... | Kt × P (K 6) |
| 25. B—K 3 | Kt (Q 2)—B 4 |

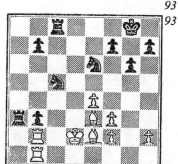

93

26. B × Kt

So White gives up one of his Bishops and goes over completely to passive defence. The White Bishops did not show any superiority in the fight against the Knights, so it is understandable on psychological grounds that Euwe should decide on this exchange, which frees the square K 3 for his King.

Therefore the lengthy discussion by Keres concerning the use of the two Bishops (in his book *The Match-Tournament for the World Championship*, page 314) arouses surprise. Keres criticizes Euwe's move 26. B × Kt (giving it a question mark) and recommends 26. B—Q B 4 (to this he puts an exclamation mark). Among other things, 26. B—Q B 4 (?) may be answered by the immediate 26. ... Kt × P ch! For example: 27. P × Kt, R × B; 28. K—Q 3, R—Kt 5; 29. P—B 3, P—B 4!; 30. K—B 3, R—Kt 4; 31. P × P, P × P; 32. R × P, R (Kt 4) × R ch; 33. R × R, R × R ch; 34. K × R, P—B 5; 35. B—Q 2, K—B 2, followed by advancing the King to K B 4; this ending is won for Black, and it is no more complicated than that which occurred in the game after 26. B × Kt.

| 26. ... | Kt × B |
| 27. K—B 3 | |

Reckoning to answer 27. ... Kt—R 5 ch with 28. K—Kt 4. But Black refrains from unnecessary simplification.

| 27. ... | R—R 5 |
| 28. K—Q 2 | K—Kt 2! |

A fine positional move. Black puts his King on a black square and thus indirectly consolidates his passed pawn. This will become clearer in the further course of the game.

29. K—K 3	R—Q 1
30. R—Q B 1	P—Kt 3
31. B—B 4	R (Q 1)—
	Q R 1

The pawn is invulnerable, for on 32. B × Kt P there follows 32. ... R—Kt 5; 33. R—B 3, R—R 6. In this variation we see disclosed the idea behind Black's 28th move; for thanks to that the Bishop cannot give check.

32. B—Q 5	R—R 7
33. R (B 1)—	R (R 1)—R 5
Q Kt 1	
34. K—Q 2	94

After this move Black forces the win by a small but elegant combination.

94

34. ...	R—Q 5 ch
35. K—K 2	Kt—R 5!
36. R × R	P × R
37. R—Q R 1	

If 37. B × R P, then 37. ... Kt—B 6 ch; 38. K—K 3, R—R 5; 39. B—Kt 3, R—R 6, winning a piece.

| 37. ... | Kt—B 6 ch |
| 38. K—K 3 | R—Q 8 |

White resigned.

No. 35.   Ruy Lopez
I. BOLESLAVSKY   V. SMYSLOV
(Soviet Team Championship, Leningrad, 1948)

1. P—K 4	P—K 4
2. Kt—K B 3	Kt—Q B 3
3. B—Kt 5	P—Q R 3
4. B—R 4	P—Q 3
5. P—B 4	

This move is associated with the name of the Czech grandmaster, O. Duras. White proposes to develop his Q Kt on Q B 3 and build up a dominating position in the centre after P—Q 4. The struggle which revolves round Q 4 forms the basis of the opening strategy in this system.

5. ...	B—Kt 5
6. Kt—B 3	Kt—B 3
7. P—K R 3	B × Kt
8. Q × B	B—K 2
9. Kt—K 2	O—O
10. B × Kt	P × B
11. P—Q 4	95

White has succeeded in advancing his Q P, but he is behind in development and has not castled yet. He would have done better to remove the King to a safe place by 11. O—O. It is true that then Black could gain a firm control over his Q 5 square by 11. ... P—B 4.

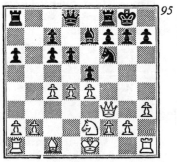

95

11. ...	P—Q 4!

An unexpected counter. Black takes advantage of his better development to provoke a sharp clash; at the same time he opens the way for his Bishop to give a dangerous check at Kt 5. An interesting position has arisen with a typical collision of pawns in the centre. Now 12. K P × P can be answered by 12. ... P—K 5; 13. Q—B 3, P × P, and Black has the freer game. Because of this Boleslavsky chooses another continuation, but the initiative is already in Black's hands.

12. Q P × P	B—Kt 5 ch
13. Kt—B 3	Kt × P
14. O—O	B × Kt
15. P × B	Q—K 2

Beginning an attack on the enemy pawns. The position is clearly in Black's favour, since the Kt occupies a strong position in the centre.

16. P × P	P × P
17. P—B 4!	

The best continuation. 17. B—B 4 was weaker on account of 17.... P—Kt 4! with the following variations: 18. B—K 3, Q × P or 18. B—Kt 3, Kt—Q 7 or finally 18. Q—Kt 4, P—K R 4! Also 17. Q—K 3, Q × P; 18. P—B 3 does not achieve anything because of 18. ... Q × P, attacking the Rook. After the text move White manages to exchange his weak pawns.

17. ...	Q × P
18. B—B 4	Q—B 6!

Forcing a favourable ending.
Since 19. Q × Q, Kt × Q leaves
White a pawn down, he is forced
to make the best of it and allow his
K-side pawns to be doubled.

19. P × P	Q × Q
20. P × Q	Kt—B 6
21. B × P	Kt × Q P
22. B—Kt 3	K R—B 1 *96*

96

At first sight the position is
simple: most of the pieces have
already been exchanged, only a
limited number of pieces and
pawns being left.

23. K R—Q 1	R—B 4
24. R—Q 2	P—R 3

Black avoids playing 24. ... P—
B 3 lest he weaken the second rank.
While the opponent has two Rooks
one must consider the security of
one's position.

25. R—K 1	Q R—Q B I
26. B—Q 6	

White provokes an exchange of
Rooks. Preferable was 26. K—Kt 2,
keeping both Rooks for active
counterplay.

26. ...	R—B 8
27. R × R	R × R ch
28. K—Kt 2	Kt—Kt 3
29. B—Kt 3	*97*

97

29. ...	R—B 3

Defending the third rank. The
exchange of one pair of Rooks has
made the correlation of forces—
Rook and Knight versus Rook and
Bishop—more favourable for Black
in this position. Now Black can
bring his King into action and
start to play on the weaknesses in
the opponent's pawn formation.
The correct solution for White here
is 30. R—Q 6, to exchange the
remaining Rooks and in this way
lessen the attacking possibilities
of the Black pieces. After 30. R—
Q 6, R × R, 31. B × R, P—B 4;
32. P—B 4, K—B 2; 33. K—B 3
White would have a passive, but,
evidently, sufficiently solid, position with drawing chances.

30. K—B 1	P—B 3
31. K—K 2	K—B 2
32. K—Q 3	R—B 4

Planning to transfer the Rook to
Q R 4, where it will be more
aggressively placed.

33. R—Kt 2	Kt—Q 2
34. K—Q 4	R—Q R 4
35. R—B 2	K—K 3
36. R—B 6 ch	K—B 4
37. R—B 7	Kt—K 4
38. R—B 5	*98*

After 38. R × P, Kt × P ch;
39. K—K 3, R—R 6 ch; 40. K—

K 2, Kt—Q 5 ch; 41. K—B 1,
R × P Black is left a pawn up.
Therefore White seeks counterchances, threatening to either win a
piece or, if the Rooks are exchanged,
march the King over to the Black
Q R P. If now 38. ... R—R 5 ch,
then 39. K—B 3, R—R 6 ch;
40. K—Kt 4, R × B P; 41. P—Q R
4, P—Kt 4; 42. K—R 5, and White
has counterplay on the Q-side.
42. ... P—R 4 could then be
answered by 43. P—R 4.   98

98

38. ...	R—R 6!

A strong move, which ruins
White's plan by the threat of mate
at Q 6. Now White has nothing
better than to go into a difficult
Rook and pawn ending.

| 39. B × Kt | R—R 5 ch |
| 40. R—B 4 | |

An unsatisfactory reply. The
fight could only be continued by
40. K—K 3, P × B; 41. R—B 2,
R—R 6 ch; 42. K—K 2. True, in
that case after 42. ... P—Q R 4;
43. R—Q 2, P—Kt 3; 44. R—B 2,
P—R 4; 45. R—Kt 2, R—B 6
Black threatens 46. ... K—B 5 and
so wins a pawn, which in the
end must prove decisive.

40. ...	P × B ch
41. K—Q 5	R × P
42. R—K Kt 4	P—Kt 4

White resigned.

No. 36.   Sicilian Defence
T. PETROSIAN   V. SMYSLOV
(*Seventeenth Soviet Championship, Moscow, 1949*)

1. P—K 4	P—Q B 4
2. Kt—K B 3	P—Q 3
3. P—Q 4	P × P
4. Kt × P	Kt—K B 3
5. Kt—Q B 3	P—Q R 3
6. B—K 2	P—K 3

The set-up of pawns at K 3 and
Q 3 is characteristic of the Scheveningen Variation. It guarantees
Black a solid but slightly cramped
game.

7. O—O	B—K 2
8. B—K 3	O—O
9. P—B 4	Q—B 2
10. P—B 5	

In advancing this pawn White
takes upon himself a definite
obligation to attack on the K-side.
He must also reckon with a
weakening of his position in the
centre, where the K P becomes
vulnerable. A manœuvre more
often met is Q—K 1—Kt 3,
developing the Queen in an active
position and for the moment not
declaring his plans.

10. ...	P—K 4
11. Kt—Kt 3	P—Q Kt 4
12. P—Q R 3	B—Kt 2
13. B—B 3	99

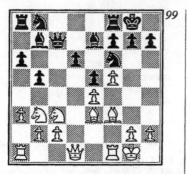

99

13. ...   K R—Q 1

Black prepares a counter in the centre as an answer to any aggression of White's with P—K Kt 4. Thus 14. P—Kt 4, P—Q 4; 15. P × P, P—K 5; 16. Kt × K P, Kt × Q P; 17. Q—K 2, Kt—Q 2 leads to a sharp struggle. In return for the pawn Black has good attacking chances against White's weakened K-side.

14. Kt—Q 2	Q Kt—Q 2
15. K—R 1	Q R—B 1
16. Q—K 2	Kt—Kt 3
17. Q—B 2	Kt—B 5
18. Kt × Kt	Q × Kt
19. B—Kt 5	P—R 3
20. B × Kt	B × B

White exchanged Bishop for Knight in order to take advantage of the weakness at Q 5. However, Black's pressure on the Q B-file and his two Bishops give him excellent prospects. The backward Q P is easily defended.

21. Q R—Q 1   Q—B 4

Intending after 22. Q × Q, R × Q to start a pawn attack on the Q-side. As well as this, by exchanging Queens Black ensures the security of his King position, should the game be opened up.

22. B—K 2   Q × Q
23. R × Q   100

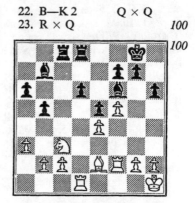

100

23. ...   P—Q 4!

At last the break in the centre. Now White ought to have chosen the variation: 24. P × P, P—K 5; 25. Kt × K P, B × Kt P; 26. B—B 3, B × R P; 27. R—Q 3, and continue the fight with the aid of his passed Q P.

24. Kt × Q P

White counts on simplifying the position, but this allows his second rank to be invaded by a Rook.

24. ...	B × Kt
25. P × B	R × B P
26. P—Q Kt 3	P—K 5!

The pawn rushes forward and at once threatens the win of a piece by 27. ... P—K 6.

| 27. P—K Kt 4 | P—K 6 |
| 28. R—Kt 2 | R—Q 7 |

The decisive manœuvre: Black wins a pawn and himself remains with a strong passed pawn. The presence on the board of Bishops of opposite colour does not ease the defence, for with Rooks on it is hard to fight against a far advanced pawn.

29. R × R	P × R
30. B—Q 1	R × P
31. K—Kt 1	K—B 1
32. K—B 1	B—Kt 4
33. P—Q R 4	P—K R 4
34. P—R 3	P—R 5

The K R P fixes White's K-side pawn formation and deprives his Rook of play on the third rank.

35. P × P	P × P
36. R—B 2	K—K 2
37. R—B 3	R—K 4
38. B—K 2	R—Q 4

Repeating moves to gain time. 38. ... B—K 6 was not sufficient on account of 39. P—B 6 ch, P × P; 40. R—B 5.

39. B—Q 1	K—B 3
40. R—B 3	B—B 5
41. K—K 2	K Kt 4
42. R—B 3	*101*

101

42. ...   P—Kt 5!

Drawing the noose of blockade round the White pieces. If 43. R—Q 3, then 43. ... R—K 4 ch; 44. K—B 2, R—K 8; 45. B—B 3, P—B 3; 46. B—K 2, R—K R 8, and White cannot avoid loss of material.

43. K—B 1	R—K 4
44. B—K 2	B—K 6
45. B—Q 1	K—B 3
46. B—K 2	R—K 5

White resigned. The Black King approaches the passed Q P without any hindrance, which ensures an easy win.

No. 37. Ruy Lopez
V. SMYSLOV   V. LUBLINSKY
(Seventeenth Soviet Championship, Moscow, 1949

1. P—K 4	P—K 4
2. Kt—K B 3	Kt—Q B 3
3. B—Kt 5	P—Q R 3
4. B—R 4	P—Q 3
5. P—B 3	B—Q 2
6. P—Q 4	Kt—B 3

The most natural system of development. In the World Championship Tournament, 1948 the system with 6. ... K Kt—K 2 followed by Kt—Kt 3 was used (see game No. 31).

7. Q Kt—Q 2	B—K 2
8. O—O	O—O
9. R—K 1	B—K 1

Black begins a complicated regrouping of the pieces, known by theory under the name Kecskemet Variation. Another possibility is 9. ... P × P; 10. P × P, Kt—Q Kt 5, starting play on the Q-side.

10. B—Kt 3

A useful move. The Bishop is now in an excellent position,

making it difficult for Black to create counterplay in the centre. After the immediate 10. Kt—B 1 one has to reckon with 10. ... P × P; 11, P × P, P—Q 4; 12. P—K 5, Kt—K 5.

10. ...   Kt—Q 2
11. Kt—B 1   B—B 3

More in keeping with the spirit of the Kecskemet Variation seemed 11. ... K—R 1 and 12. ... P—B 3. The text move leads to a difficult defence.

12. Kt—K 3   Kt—K 2

12. ... P—K Kt 3 is bad on account of 13. Kt—Q 5, B—Kt 2; 14. B—Kt 5.

13. Kt—Kt 4   Kt—K Kt 3
14. P—Kt 3   B—K 2
15. P—K R 4   Kt—B 3
16. Kt—Kt 5

As a result of his opponent's slow manœuvres White goes over to the attack on the King. His Kt has taken up a strong position on K Kt 5, where it remains almost to the end of the game.

16. ...   P—K R 3
17. Kt × Kt ch B × Kt   102

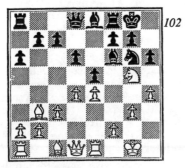

18. Q—R 5!

Intending to answer 18. ... P × Kt with 19. P × P, B—K 2; 20. Q × Kt, regaining the piece. To counter the threat 19. Q × Kt Black puts his Kt into a bad position in the corner, but he does at least strengthen the vulnerable point K B 2 an extra once.

18. ...   Kt—R 1
19. P × P   P × P
20. B—K 3   Q—K 2   103

It is dangerous to accept the Kt sacrifice. After 20. ... P × Kt; 21. P × P, P—K Kt 3; 22. Q—R 4, B—Kt 2; 23. K—Kt 2, B—Q B 3; 24. R—R 1, R—K 1; 25. Q—R 7 ch, K—B 1; 26. B—B 5 ch, R—K 2; 27. Q × Kt ch!, B × Q; 28. R × B ch, K—Kt 2; 29. R × Q, R × R; 30. B × R White wins.

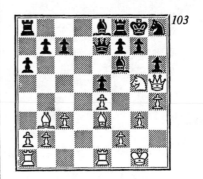

21. B—Q 5!

As before the Kt cannot be taken: if 21. ... P × Kt, then 22. P × P, P—K Kt 3; 23. P × B! If Black does not want to spoil his pawn position, which happens after 21. ... B—B 3; 22. B × B, P × B, then he must play 21. ... P—B 3, depriving his Bishop of the important square Q B 3.

21. ...	P—B 3
22. B—Kt 3	B—Q 2
23. Q R—Q 1	Q R—Q 1
24. R—Q 2	B—B 1
25. K R—Q 1	R × R
26. R × R	Q—B 2

White has seized the open file and preserved his attacking position. With his last move, which renews the threat of 27. ... P × Kt; 28. P × P, P—K Kt 3, Black hopes to drive back the tiresome Kt. However, White has a strong reply to hand.

27. B—B 5!

Now if 27. ... P × Kt, White replies 28. B × R, while if 27. ... B—K 2, then he continues 28. B × B, Q × B; 29. Kt—B 3, R—K 1; 30. Q × K P!, Q × Q; 31. Kt × Q, R × Kt; 32. R—Q 8 ch, K—R 2; 33. R × B, and the K P cannot be taken on account of 34. B—B 2.

27. ...	R—Q 1
28. R × R ch	B × R 104

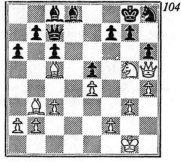

29. Kt × P!	Kt × Kt
30. B—Kt 6!	

This is the point of the combination! White recovers the piece, for if 30. ... Q × B, then 31. Q × Kt ch, K—R 1; 32. P—R 5, creating a mating net.

30. ...	Q—Q 2
31. B × B	K—R 2
32. B × Kt	Q × Q B
33. B—Kt 6 ch	Black
	resigned.

The K P is lost as well.

No. 38.   Queen's Pawn, Grunfeld Defence
V. SMYSLOV   T. FLORIAN
(Match-Tournament, Moscow–Budapest, 1949)

1. P—Q 4	Kt—K B 3
2. P—Q B 4	P—K Kt 3
3. Kt—Q B 3	P—Q 4
4. Kt—B 3	B—Kt 2
5. Q—Kt 3	P × P
6. Q × B P	O—O
7. P—K 4	

White has built up a strong pawn centre. In the struggle against White's centre pawns the following systems have been put forward:

(1) Play with the pieces by 7. ... B—Kt 5; 8. B—K 3, K Kt—Q 2;

(2) A pawn attack on the Q-side

based on 7. ... P—B 3; 8. B—K 2, P—Q Kt 4 etc.

7. ...	Kt—R 3

This move is intended to prepare P—Q B 4 and so shake the firmness of the centre pawns.

8. B—K 2	P—B 4
9. P—Q 5	P—K 3
10. O—O	P × P
11. P × P	Q—R 4

Black carries on with his development and threatens to increase his range of activity by playing his

Queen to Q Kt 5. 11. ... Q—Kt 3, with the same idea, was still better, as the Queen is more favourably placed on Q Kt 3.

12. P—Q R 3

It is necessary to limit the activity of the enemy pieces by depriving them of Q Kt 5.

12. ...   B—B 4
13. Q—K R 4

Both sides have for the most part completed their development. The last move is explained by a desire to attack on the K-side.

13. ...   K R—K I
14. B—R 6   Kt—K 5
15. B × B   K × B   *105*

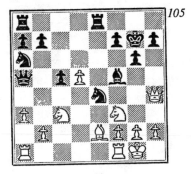

105

16. Kt—K Kt 5!

A sharp attacking manœuvre, based on the sacrifice of a piece. Now the position of the Black King is very seriously threatened; therefore the dangerous Kt ought to be removed by 16. ... Kt × Kt; 17. Q × Kt, Q—Q 1. The alternative continuation 16. ... Kt—B 3 is worse because of 17. P—B 3, creating a strong-point in the centre for a Kt.

16. ...   Kt × Kt
                 (B 6)

Black declines to go over to defence, and instead treads the thorny path of combinational complications.

17. Q × P ch   K—B 3
18. P × Kt

An interesting position has arisen in which Black can take either of the minor pieces. If 18. ... R × B, White could continue 19. P—K B 4! with a very strong attack. For example:
(1) 19. ... Q—B 2; 20. P—Q 6, Q—Q 2; 21. Q R—K 1, R × R; 22. R × R, R—K 1; 23. R—K 7! R × R; 24. Q—R 8 mate.
(2) 19. ... R—K B 1; 20. Q—R 6! R (B 1)—K 1 (20. ... K—K 2; 21. P—Q 6 ch, K—K 1; 22. Kt—R 7 etc.); 21. Q R—K 1, B—Q 6 (21. ... R × R; 22. Kt—R 7 ch; K—K 2; 23. R × R ch, K—Q 1; 24. Q—Kt 5 ch etc.); 22. Q—R 4 with the threat of 23. Kt—K 6 ch. If now 22. ... K—K 2, then 23. Kt—K 4 ch, K—B 1 (or 23. ... P—B 3; 24. R × R, B × R; 25. R—K 1, Q—Kt 4; 26. P—Q 6 ch, K—Q 1; 27. Kt × P, and Black cannot avoid loss of material); 24. P—Q 6, K—Kt 2; 25. P—B 5!, intending to create a mating set-up by 26. P—B 6 ch and 27. Q—R 6.

18. ...   K × Kt
19. Q—Kt 7!

A "quiet" move, threatening a mating attack after 20. P—B 4 ch. Now the Black King has no flight squares and is forced to set off into distant spaces.

19. ...   R—K 5   *106*

Of course, 19. ... R × B is followed by 20. P—B 4 ch, K—Kt 5; 21. P—R 3 ch and mate in two.

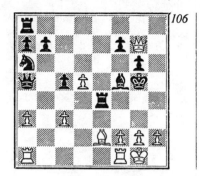

106

20. P—B 4 ch	R × P
21. R × R	K × R
22. R—B 1 ch	K—K 6

22. ... K—Kt 4 does not help on account of 23. P—R 4 ch. If 22. ... K—K 5, then 23. B—B 4 with an irresistible attack.

23. Q—K 5 ch	K—Q 7
24. B—B 4	Q × R P
25. R—B 2 ch	Black resigned.

No. 39.   Queen's Pawn, Grunfeld Defence

E. GEREBEN   V. SMYSLOV

(Match-Tournament, Moscow—Budapest, 1949)

1. P—Q 4	Kt—K B 3
2. Kt—K B 3	P—K Kt 3
3. P—B 4	B—Kt 2
4. Kt—B 3	P—Q 4
5. P—K 3	O—O
6. Q—Kt 3	P—K 3

In this way Black strengthens his Q P and preserves the possibility of opening up the game by P—Q B 4 at the appropriate moment. This is the best way of answering the system chosen by White.

7. B—K 2	P—Kt 3
8. P × P	

Resolving the position of the pawns in the centre before Black has played 8. ... B—Kt 2.

8. ...	P × P
9. O—O	B—Kt 2
10. R—Q 1	Q Kt—Q 2
11. P—Q R 4	

The advance of the Q R P was not necessary. Better was 11. B—Q 2, continuing to mobilize his forces.

| 11. ... | P—B 4 |

Black starts counterplay on the Q-side, not fearing the isolating of his centre pawn in the variation 12. P × P, Kt × P; 13. Q—R 3, because after 13. ... K Kt—K 5 his K B becomes very active.

12. P—R 5	Q—B 2
13. B—Q 2	B—B 3
14. Kt—Q Kt 5	

This Kt sortie only leads in the long run to a loss of time. More expedient was 14. B—Kt 5 to make it difficult for Black to advance his Q-side pawns.

14. ...	Q—Kt 1
15. Kt—B 3	

The Kt comes back to its old square. 15. R P × P, R P × P; 16. R × R, Q × R held no promise of any advantage to White, while 15. P—R 6 had its darker sides— 15. ... Kt—K 5; 16. B—K 1, P—B 5; 17. Q—Kt 4, R—K 1 with the threat of B—B 1. Now Black seizes the initiative and goes over to the attack.

15. ...	P—B 5!
16. Q—R 3	P—Q Kt 4
17. Kt—R 2	P—Q R 3
18. B—Kt 4	R—K 1
19. Kt—B 3	*107*

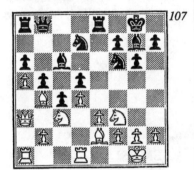

107

| 19. ... | Kt—Kt 5 |

A typical strategic manœuvre: having obtained a space advantage in one part of the board, Black takes up operations in another part—the K-side. The text move frees the way for the advance of the K B P. The White pieces, shut in by the blockading enemy pawns, are now deprived of sufficient mobility to answer the ever-increasing threats.

20. P—R 3	Kt—R 3
21. Kt—K 1	P—B 4
22. Kt—B 2	Kt—B 2

Establishing control over the important square Q 3. However, White now finds an ingenious reply, which threatens to bring the Q P under fire.

| 23. B—K 7! | B—B 3 |

Otherwise White's pressure could become dangerous.

| 24. B × B | Kt × B |
| 25. Kt—Kt 4 | |

The attempt to improve the position of the White Queen by 25. Q—B 5 resulted in favour of Black, e.g. 25. ... B—Kt 2; 26. Kt—Kt 4?, Kt—Q 2 or 26. B—B 3, Kt—Kt 4!; 27. B × P ch, Kt × B; 28. Kt × Kt, Kt—K 5; 29. Kt—K 7 ch, K—B 2.

25. ...	B—Kt 2
26. B—B 3	Q—Q 1
27. P—K Kt 3	Kt—Kt 4
28. B—Kt 2	Kt (Kt 4)—
	K 5
29. Kt × Kt	Kt × Kt

Black's advantage has acquired real proportions. White must now bring his Kt to the defence of the K-side, after which Black's threatening pawns on the other flank gain a new mobility.

| 30. Kt—B 2 | *108* |

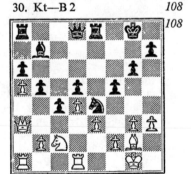

108

30. ...	P—Kt 4!
31. Kt—K 1	Q—B 3
32. Kt—B 3	P—B 5
33. K P × P	P × P
34. P—K Kt 4!	Q R—Q 1
35. R—K 1	P—R 4!

Black consistently develops the attack by opening up the approaches to the White King.

36. Kt—K 5	P × P
37. P × P	Q—R 5
38. Q—K B 3	R—Q 3!
39. Q R—Q 1	

If 39. Q × P, then, of course, 39. ... R—K B 1, winning back the pawn at K B 7.

39. ...	R—K B 1
40. B—B 1	

If 40. K—B 1, then 40. ... Kt— Kt 4; 41. Q—B 3, P—B 6!; 42. Kt × K B P, Kt × Kt; 43. B × Kt, R (Q 3)—K B 3; 44. R—K 3, P— Kt 5! and Black wins.

40. ...	R—R 3
41. B—Kt 2	

41. Q—Kt 2 is impossible because of 41. ... P—K B 6; 42. Kt × K B P, R × Kt.

41. ...	P—Kt 5

Black builds up his attacking position to a maximum and does not hurry to enforce the variation 41. ... Q—R 7 ch; 42. K—B 1, Kt—Kt 6 ch; 43. P × Kt, P × P, after which Black wins material. After the text move White has no useful move at his disposal. If 42. Q—K 2, then 42. ... Q—R 7 ch; 43. K—B 1, Kt—Kt 6 ch; 44. P × Kt, P × P ch; 45. Kt—B 3, R (R 3) —K B 3; 4 6. Q—K 3, R × Kt ch; 47. B × R, P—Kt 7 ch, and Black wins.

42. K—B 1	Kt—Kt 4
43. Q—K 2	*109*

43. ...	P—K B 6!
44. Kt × K B P	Kt × Kt
45. B × Kt	R (R 3)—
	K B 3

Now the loss of a piece is unavoidable: if 46. Q—K 7, then 46. ... Q—R 6 ch. The game continued:

46. K—Kt 2	R × B
47. Q × R	R × Q
48. K × R	B—B 3
49. R—K 5	P—B 6
50. P × P	P × P
51. R—Q B 1	Q—R 6 ch
52. K—B 4	B—Q 2
53. R—K 3	

Or 53. P—B 3, Q—R 7 ch; 54. K—Kt 5, Q—Q 7 ch, etc.

53. ...	Q × P ch
54. K—K 5	Q—K 3 ch
55. K—B 4	Q—B 4 ch
56. K—Kt 3	P—B 7

White resigned.

No. 40. Queen's Gambit Declined, Half Slav Defence
V. SMYSLOV   D. BRONSTEIN
(Candidates' Tournament, Budapest, 1950)

1. P—Q 4	P—Q 4
2. P—Q B 4	P—Q B 3
3. Kt—K B 3	Kt—B 3
4. Kt—B 3	P—K 3
5. B—Kt 5	P × P
6. P—K 4	P—Kt 4

The idea behind Black's counterplay in this variation of the Queen's Gambit—support of the Q B P— was brought into modern tournament practice and worked out by the World Champion, M. Botvinnik. This system is very complicated and for its correct treatment an exact understanding of all the peculiarities of the position is necessary.

7. P—K 5	P—K R 3
8. B—R 4	P—Kt 4
9. Kt × K Kt P	P × Kt

For the continuation 9. ... Kt—Q 4 see game No. 26.

10. B × Kt P	Q Kt—Q 2
11. P—K Kt 3	B—Q Kt 2
12. B—Kt 2	R—K Kt 1

The alternative here is 12. ... Q—Kt 3. The game Lilienthal–Kotov (Sixteenth Soviet Championship, 1949) continued: 12. ... Q—Kt 3; 13. P × Kt, P—B 4; 14. P × P, B × P; 15. O—O, O—O—O; 16. Q—K 2, B—Q 5, with chances for both sides. Bronstein avoids well-known paths, but his novelty did not justify itself in this game.

13. B × Kt	Kt × B
14. P × Kt	Q × B P *110*

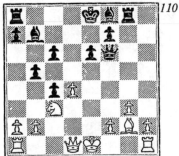

110

15. P—Q R 4!

Probably Black only reckoned on 15. Kt × P, P × Kt; 16. B × B, B—Kt 5 ch; 17. K—B 1, R—Q 1; 18. B—B 6 ch, K—B 1, with good play for Black. The text move exposes the weakness of the Q-side pawns and ensures White some advantage.

15. ...	P—Kt 5
16. Kt—K 4	Q—B 4
17. Q—K 2	O—O—O

The attempt to support the Q B P by 17. ... B—Q R 3 is refuted by 18. Kt—B 6 ch, Q × Kt; 19. B × P ch, winning the exchange.

18. Q × P	B—Kt 2
19. Q × P	B × P

19. ... R × P is answered by 20. Q × R!, B × Q; 21. Kt—Q 6 ch.

20. O—O	Q—K 4!

Defending himself from Kt—Q 6 ch and at the same time preparing P—K B 4 and R—Kt 5.

21. K—R 1

Now both 21. ... P—K B 4 and 21. ... R—Kt 5 are answered by 22. P—B 4, which wards off all the opponent's threats.

21. ...	P—R 4
22. Q—B 4	R—R 1
23. K R—K 1	

Correct was 23. Q R—B 1, which prevents the freeing move P—Q B 4. For example: 23. ... R—Q 4; 24. Kt—B 3, R—B 4; 25. Q—K 2, B × Kt; 26. Q × Q or 24. ... Q—R 4; 25. P—R 4, and White drives off the attack and remains a pawn up.

After the text move the point K B 2 is weakened, and Black could create dangerous complications by sacrificing a piece. For example: 23. ... B × B P; 24. Kt × B, Q × K Kt P; 25. Kt—Kt 4, Q R—Kt 1; 26. B × P, R × Kt; 27. B × B ch, K—Kt 1!; 28. Q—B 8 ch!, R × Q; 29. P × Q, K × B; 30. R—K 3, R—B 7; 31. R

—K B 1, and the ending with all the Rooks still on must be drawn.

| 23. ... | Q—R 4 |

This tempting move is insufficient, as White now removes the danger threatening his King position.

| 24. P—R 4 | Q—Kt 5 *111* |

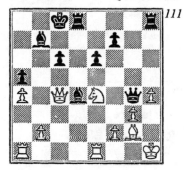

111

25. Q—K 2!

In this way White completely safeguards himself from the assault of the Black pieces and brings about a favourable ending, in which he is a pawn up.

| 25. ... | Q × Q |

This exchange is forced, otherwise White himself builds up a strong K-side attack by 26. Q R—B 1.

26. R × Q	K—B 2
27. R—Q B 1	R—Q 4
28. Kt—B 3	R—Q B 4
29. R (K 2)—B 2	K—Kt 3
30. Kt—K 4	R × R
31. R × R	

The exchange of one pair of Rooks simplifies the position, and the passed K R P thereby assumes a greater significance.

| 31. ... | R—Q 1 |
| 32. Kt—Q 2! | |

Transferring the Kt to an excellent position on Q B 4.

32. ...	K—B 2
33. Kt—B 4	R—Q R 1
34. P—B 4	P—B 3
35. K—R 2	

Having confined the black pieces to the defence of the weak pawns on the Q-side, White plans P—K Kt 4 and K—Kt 3 followed by the systematic advance of his passed pawns.

| 35. ... | P—K 4 |

White could answer 35. ... P—K B 4 by 36. R—K 2, B—B 1; 37. Kt—K 5, R—R 3; 38. P—R 5 etc.

| 36. P × P | P × P |
| 37. B—K 4 | B—B 1 |

The situation was not changed by 37. ... P—B 4; 38. B × B, K × B; 39. K—Kt 2, and White brings his King to K 4.

After the text move White manœuvres his Kt to effect an exchange of pieces on Q 4, which further simplifies his task.

38. Kt—R 3!	B—Q 2
39. Kt—Kt 5 ch	K—Kt 3
40. Kt × B	P × Kt
41. R—B 4	R—Q Kt 1

112

112

42. P—Q Kt 4!

The most accurate continuation; now White rids himself of the backward Q Kt P. If 42. ... K—B 2, then 43. P—Kt 5.

42. ...	R—K 1
43. P × P ch	K—B 2
44. R × P	P—B 4
45. R—B 4	B—B 3
46. B × B	K × B
47. P—R 5	

The sealed move. The advance of the K R P decides the game in quick time.

47. ...	K—Q 4
48. R—B 1	R—K 5
49. K—R 3	R × P
50. P—R 6	R × P
51. P—R 7	R—R 1
52. K—Kt 4	R—R 1
53. R—K R 1	P—B 5
54. K—Kt 5	P—B 6
55. K—Kt 6	P—B 7

Black resigned without waiting for White's reply 56. K—Kt 7.

No. 41. French Defence

V. SMYSLOV   R. LETELIER

(Venice, 1950)

1. P—K 4	P—K 3
2. P—Q 4	P—Q 4
3. Kt—Q B 3	B—Kt 5
4. P—K 5	P—Q B 4
5. P—Q R 3	B × Kt ch
6. P × B	Kt—K 2
7. P—Q R 4	Q—R 4
8. Q—Q 2	Q Kt—B 3
9. Kt—B 3	P × P

For this opening see game No. 6 Smyslov–Boleslavsky.

Black forces an ending. A more flexible reply is 9. ... B—Q 2, which preserves the possibility of opening the game by P × P as well as blocking the position on the Q-side by P—B 5.

| 10. P × P | Q × Q ch |
| 11. B × Q | |

One result of the exchange is that White no longer has doubled pawns; since he has prevented Kt—Q R 4, the two Bishops give White good chances in the ending.

| 11. ... | Kt—B 4 |
| 12. B—B 3 ! | |

Black played Kt—B 4, reckoning on 12. P—B 3, Kt—R 4. However, White retains control of Q R 5 and at the same time frees Q 2 for his King.

12. ...	B—Q 2
13. B—Q 3	R—Q B 1
14. K—Q 2	O—O
15. P—R 5	R—B 2
16. K R—K 1	

A prophylactic move aimed at Black's counterplay by P—B 3. Black ought to resort to waiting tactics in reply, trying to regroup his pieces by P—Q R 3, Kt—R 2 and B—Kt 4.

His next move falls in with his opponent's plans.

| 16. ... | P—B 3   *112a* |

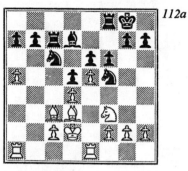

112a

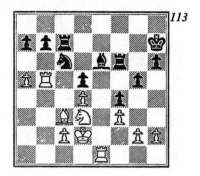

113

17. B × Kt!

The correct solution to the problem: by this capture White prevents the opening of the K B-file and steers the game along lines favourable to him.

17. ...   P × B
18. P × P   R × P
19. Q R—Kt 1

The beginning of a systematic attack on the opponent's pawn weaknesses. It is the squares K 4 and Q B 4 that are the real weak points in Black's position. As White has the better pawn formation, so he has the better chances in the ending.

19. ...   P—K R 3
20. R—Kt 5!   B—K 3
21. R (K 1)—   R (B 3)—B 2
      Q Kt 1
22. Kt—K 1   P—B 5
23. P—B 3   P—Kt 4
24. Kt—Q 3

The Kt is in a strong position at Q 3. All White's pieces are mobilized for a decisive attack, and it rapidly becomes difficult to ward off the combination of threats.

24. ...   K—R 2
25. R—K 1   R—B 3   *113*

26. R—B 5

Threatening to win a pawn by 27. Kt—Kt 4 and beginning a forced manœuvre, which ensures in the end a clear advantage. Black cannot answer 26. ... P—Kt 3 because after 27. P × P, P × P; 28. R—Kt 5 he has not the defence 28. ... R—Q Kt 2 on account of 29. Kt—B 5.

26. ...   R—Q B 1
27. Kt—Kt 4   Kt × Kt

The alternative 27. ... Kt—K 2 allowed the effective combination 28. Kt × P!, Kt × Kt; 29. R × B!, R (B 1) × R; 30. R × R, R × B; 31. R—Q 6, regaining the piece and remaining a pawn up; or 30. ... Kt × R; 31. P × R, Kt— Q 2; 32. K—Q 3!, Kt × P ch; 33. K—B 4 and the White King marches over to the Q-side pawns.

28. R × B!   R (B 3) × R
29. R × R   Kt—B 3   *114*

It appears that Black has safely disentangled himself from a difficult position, for if 30. R—B 7 ch, then there is 30. ... R—K 2. However the following pawn sacrifice shatters Black's position on the Q-side.

30. P—R 6!	P × P
31. R—B 7 ch	K—Kt 3
32. R—Q 7	Kt—K 2
33. B—Kt 4	Kt—B 4
34. R × Q P	

White was aiming for this position when he made his 26th move. He has two passed pawns in the centre which threaten to advance rapidly, while Black's counterplay on the K-side is obviously too slow.

34. ...	Kt—K 6
35. R—Q 8	Kt × Kt P
36. P—Q 5	R—Kt 3
37. B—B 5	R—Kt 2 *115*
38. R—Q B 8!	

Ensuring the stability of the position and at the same time supporting the advance of the white pawns.

38. ...	Kt—R 5
39. K—K2	Kt—B 4
40. R—B 6 ch	K—R 4

A little more resistance was offered by 40. ... K—B 2. White intended to continue 41. R × Q R P, R—B 2; 42. R × Q R P, remaining a pawn up. The text move leads to a quick debacle.

41. P—Q 6	R—Q 2
42. R—B 7	Black
	resigned.

42. ... R—Q 1 is answered by 43. P—Q 7, P—Kt 5; 44. P × P ch, K × P; 45. R × P, and 46. B—Kt 6 cannot be stopped.

No. 42.   Queen's Pawn, Nimzovitch Defence

I. BONDAREVSKY   V. SMYSLOV

(Eighteenth Soviet Championship, Moscow, 1950)

1. P—Q 4	Kt—K B 3
2. P—Q B 4	P—K 3
3. Kt—Q B 3	B—Kt 5
4. P—K 3	P—Q 4
5. P—Q R 3	B—K 2

The alternative here is 5. ... B × Kt ch; 6. P × B, P—B 4; 7. B P × P, K P × P; 8. B—Q 3, O—O; 9. Kt—K 2, P—Q Kt 3, proposing to exchange the white-squared Bishops by 10. ... B—R 3.

In playing the text move Black must take into account the reply 6. P—B 5. In the game Alatortsev–Smyslov (Eighteenth Soviet Championship) there occurred 6. P—B 5, P—B 3; 7. P—B 4, Kt—K 5; 8. Kt × Kt, P × Kt; 9. Q—B 2,

P—B 4; 10. B—B 4, Kt—R 3, and Black had sufficient counterplay.

6. Kt—B 3   O—O
7. B—Q 3   P—Q Kt 3
8. O—O   P—B 4
9. Q—K 2

White maintains the tension in the centre. Should he have played 9. B P × P, K P × P; 10. P × P, P × P; 11. P—K 4!, Black preserved the equilibrium by 11. ... P × P; 12. Kt × P, B—R 3!

9. ...   Kt—B 3
10. R—Q 1   B P × P
11. K P × P   B—R 3

11. ... B—Kt 2 seems more natural. In developing the Bishop on Q R 3 Black intends to promote a fight over the point Q B 5.

12. P—Q Kt 3   R—B 1
13. R—Kt 1   Q—B 2
14. Kt—Q Kt 5   Q—Kt 1

Taking the Kt is unsatisfactory, as after 14. ... B × Kt; 15. P × B there is no way of defending the weak square Q B 3.

15. B—Kt 5   P—R 3
16. B—R 4   Kt—K R 4!

Preventing 17. B—Kt 3. There is no danger for Black in 17. P × P, Kt—B 5; 18. Q—K 4, Kt × B; 19. P × Kt, B × B; 20. P—B 7, Q—R 1; 21. Q × Kt, B—K 2.

17. B × B   Kt × B
18. Kt—K 5   Kt—K B 3
19. P—Q R 4   Kt—B 3
20. P—B 4   116

White offers a pawn, reckoning to get an attack after 20. ... B × Kt; 21. R P × B, Kt × P; 22. Q—K B 2, Kt—B 4; 23. P—K Kt 4, Kt—Q 3; 24. P—Kt 5, K Kt—K 5; 25. Q—K Kt 2. Apparently he has underestimated Black's reply.

116

20. ...   Kt—Q Kt 5!
21. P—K B 5   Kt × B
22. Q × Kt   K P × P
23. Q × P   B—Kt 2
24. Q R—B 1   P—R 3
25. Kt—Q B 3   Q—Q 3

Threatening to occupy Q Kt 5 with the Queen. Bondarevsky finds a clever way of complicating the struggle anew.

26. P—R 5   Q P × P

Black first of all opens the diagonal for his Bishop. If now 27. Kt × Q B P, then 27. ... Q—B 3; 28. Q—R 3, P—Q Kt 4 with good play for Black. 26. ... Kt P × P was bad on account of 27. P—B 5.

27. Kt P × P   P—Q Kt 4!
28. P—B 5

28. P × P, P × P; 29. Kt × Kt P is impossible because of 29. ... Q—Q 4. Now White has two connected passed pawns, but he does not succeed in advancing them. At the same time Black's passed pawn threatens to rush forward. By moving the attacked Queen with gain of tempo Black seizes the initiative.

28. ...   Q—Q 1
29. R—R 1   P—Kt 5
30. Kt—K 2

After this retreat Black's initiative develops without a hindrance. A much more complex struggle resulted from 30. Kt—R 4!, B—K 5; 31. Q—B 2, Kt—Q 4; 32. Kt—Q Kt 6, R—B 2, and if 33. Q—Kt 2, then 33. ... Q—Kt 4 with chances for both sides.

30. ...	B—K 5
31. Q—R 3	B—B 7
32. R—K B 1	*117*

117

32. ...   P—Kt 6

It is interesting to see how quickly the situation on the board has changed. To blockade the enemy pawn now White must transfer his Queen to a passive position. This allows Black to start an attack on the K-side, using Q 4 as a base for his pieces.

33. Q—Q B 3	Kt—Q 4
34. Q—Kt 2	Kt—K 6
35. K R—K 1	

Not 35. R—B 3, Kt—Q 8!

35. ...   Q—Q 4

First the Kt and now the Queen occupies the key square Q 4. If 36. Kt—K B 4, one possibility is 36. ... Q—K 5; 37. P—Kt 3, K R—Q 1; 38. K—B 2 (or 38. Kt—Kt 4, Kt—B 5!), Q × P; 39. Q × Q, R × Q; 40. K × Kt, R—K 5 ch; 41. K—Q 2, P—Kt 7! winning material.

36. Kt—K B 3   K R—K 1

Black consolidates his position. He is not satisfied with 36. ... Kt—B 5; 37. Q—B 3, P—Kt 7; 38. Q × B, P × R=Q ; 39. R × Q, and, although Black wins the exchange for a pawn, White has freed his game.

37. Q R—B 1	R—B 3
38. Kt—B 3	Q—B 4
39. Kt—Q 1	

White takes advantage of the pin to exchange the dangerous Kt, but he still does not succeed in equalizing. Now Black's heavy pieces burst in on the open file.

39. ...	R (B 3)—K 3
40. Kt × Kt	R × Kt
41. R × R	R × R
42. K—B 2	

White cannot mobilize his passed pawns, for after 42. P—B 6, Q × P Black threatens 43. ... Q—B 6. The continuation 42. R—K 1, R × R ch; 43. Kt × R, Q—K 5 leads to a position analogous to that which occurs in the game.

42. ...	Q—K 5
43. R—K 1	R × R
44. Kt × R	*118*

118

44. ...   B—Q 8!

A "quiet" move, threatening 45. ... Q—K 7 ch! 46. Q × Q, B × Q; 47 P—B 6, P—Kt 7; 48. P—B 7, B—Kt 5 and wins. 45. P—R 3 does not help because of the manœuvre 45. ... Q—B 5 ch; 46. K—Kt 1 (46. Kt—B 3, B × Kt; 47. P × B, Q—R 7 ch), Q—K 6 ch; 47. K—B 1, Q—K 7 ch; 48. Q × Q, B × Q ch; 49. K × B, P—Kt 7 and the pawn queens.

| 45. P—B 6 | Q × P |
| 46. Kt—Q 3 | Q—B 5 |

| 47. K—K 3 | B—B 7 |
| 48. Kt—K 1 | |

If 48. Kt—B 5, then 48. ... Q—Kt 5 (threatening 49. ... Q—K 8 ch); 49. K—K 2, Q × R P; 50. Kt × Kt P, Q—Kt 4 ch and wins.

48. ...	B—B 4
49. K—Q 2	Q—Kt 4
50. K—Q 1	B—Kt 5 ch
51. K—B 1	Q—B 5 ch

White resigned.

No. 43. English Opening

L. ARONIN   V. SMYSLOV

(*Eighteenth Soviet Championship, Moscow, 1950*)

1. P—Q B 4	P—K 3
2. Kt—Q B 3	Kt—K B 3
3. P—K 4	P—B 4
4. P—K 5	Kt—Kt 1
5. P—Q 4	P × P
6. Q × P	Kt—Q B 3
7. Q—K 4	P—B 4!?

Usually 7. ... P—Q 3 is played here. The continuation in the text has not been investigated deeply; it leads to a complicated struggle. In the event of 8. P × Pe.p., Kt × P Black gets active play. But in leaving the pawn at K 5 White is forced to retreat the Queen to a bad position, since a strong reply to 8. Q—K 3 is 8. ... Kt—R 3.

| 8. Q—K 2 | K Kt—K 2 |
| 9. Kt—B 3 | |

9. P—B 4, strengthening the centre pawn, was worth considering. The text move conforms to the needs of development of the pieces, but helps Black to organize an attack on the K P.

9. ...	Kt—Kt 3
10. B—Q 2	P—Q R 3
11. O—O—O	Q—B 2
12. R—K 1	B—B 4
13. P—K R 4	Kt—Q 5
14. Kt × Kt	B × Kt
15. P—B 4	*119*

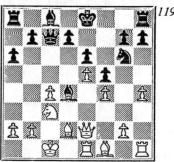

119

| 15. ... | P—Kt 4! |

The unusual pawn structure gives the development of the game a tense character. Black's counterattack is based on the opening of lines on the Q-side; at the same

time the Q B gets a square at Q Kt
2. If 16. P ×P, P × P; 17. Q × P,
then Black can win the pawn back
by either 17. ... R × P or 17. ...
B × Kt; 18 B × B, Kt × B P.

16. P—R 5	Kt—K 2
17. Q—Q 3	B—B 7
18. R—Q 1	B—Kt 2
19. Q—Q 6	Q—B 1

Black declines to exchange
Queens, reckoning on answering
20. P × P with 20. ... Kt—Q 4;
21. P × P, B × R P with the threat
of B—B 4, catching the enemy
Queen in a trap.

20. R—R 3 !

A strong defensive manœuvre.
If 20. ... P × P, then White
removes Black's dangerous Bishop
by 21. B—K 3, B × B; 22. R × B.

20. ...	B—B 4
21. Q—Q 3	P × P
22. Q × Q B P	Kt—Q 4
23. Kt × Kt	B × Kt
24. Q—B 2	Q—Kt 2 !
25. K—Kt 1	

Of course, not 25. Q × B,
R—Q B 1. If 25. R—Q B 3, then
25. ... B—Q 5; 26. R—B 7, B × P
ch; 27. K—Kt 1, Q—Kt 1, punishing
the premature activity of the White
Rook.

| 25. ... | R—Q B 1 |
| 26. R—Q B 3 | K—B 2 ! |

Safely completing his development. 26. ... O—O could after
27. R—B 1, B—K 5; 28. B—Q 3,
B × B; 29. Q × B, B—K 2 lead
to simplification. Now 27. R—B 1
is answered by 27. ... B—Q 5;
28. R × R, R × R with threats that
cannot be averted.

27. B—B 1

After this natural-looking move
White's position becomes difficult.

Obviously 27. R × B was impos-
sible because of 27. ... B—K 5.
He ought to have played 27. B—
B 4, to answer 27. ... B—K 5 with
28. B—Q 3, B—Q 5; 29. B × B,
P × B; 30. R—Q Kt 3! Therefore
Black would have continued 27. ...
B × B; 28. R × B, B—K 2 and
then played for control of the open
Q B-file.

27. ...	B—Kt 5
28. R × R	R × R
29. Q—R 4	P—R 4
30. B—Kt 5	*120*

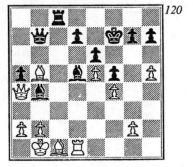

120

White wards off the threat of
30. ... B—B 3; 31. Q—Kt 3, P—R 5
and seeks safety in tactical complications.

| 30. ... | R—B 4 ! |
| 31. B × P | K—K 2 |

Both players were already experi-
encing a shortage of time. Much
stronger was 31. ... B—K 5 ch;
32. K—R 1, B—B 7; 33. B × P ch,
K—K 2!; 34. R—Q 7 ch, K × B!,
and Black remains a piece up. By
letting slip this opportunity Black
makes his task more difficult.

32. B—K 3 !

Against 32. B—K 8 Black had
prepared 32. ... B—K 5 ch; 33. K—
R 1, B—B 7; 34. R—Q 7 ch, K ×
B with a won position.

32. ...	Q × B
33. Q × Q ch	K × Q
34. P—R 3!	

A fine move. Nevertheless, although White recovers his piece, the active placing of Black's pieces ensures him some advantage.

34. ...	B × R P
35. P × B	R—B 6
36. B—B 1	R—Kt 6

In spite of the presence of Bishops of opposite colours Black has very real winning chances.

It is difficult for White to defend his K Kt and K R pawns. So he correctly decides to double his opponent's pawns on the K R-file.

37. P—R 6	P × P
38. R—R 1	R—Kt 3
39. R—R 2	B × P
40. B—Q 2	P—R 5
41. B—Kt 4	

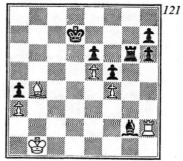

121
121

| 41. ... | B—B 6 |

The sealed move. Also strong was 41. ... K—B 3!; 42. B—B 8, K—Q 4; 43. R × P, R—Kt 5; 44. R × R P, R × P, and Black has an active King as well as an extra pawn.

42. K—B 2	P—R 4
43. R—R 3	R—Kt 7 ch
44. K—B 3	R—B 7
45. K—Q 4	B—Kt 5
46. R—Q 3	K—B 3!

Preventing the White King from reaching Q B 5. If 47. R—B 3 ch, then 47. ... K—Kt 2; 48. K—B 5, R—Q 7; 49. K—Kt 5, P—R 5!

47. K—B 3	K—Kt 4
48. R—Q 6	R—B 6 ch
49. K—Q 2	R × P
50. R × P	R—K 5!

Black ties down the White Rook to the defence of the K P; as a result Black's passed pawns quickly decide the game.

51. K—Q 3	P—R 5
52. R—K 7	P—R 6
53. B—Q 6	P—R 4
54. P—K 6	B—K 7 ch
55. K—Q 2	B—B 5
56. R—K R 7	R—Q 5 ch

White resigned.

No. 44.   Queen's Pawn Opening

V. SMYSLOV   A. TOLUSH

(Tchigorin Memorial Tournament, Leningrad, 1951)

1. P—Q B 4	Kt—K B 3
2. P—Q 4	P—K 3
3. P—K Kt 3	P—B 4

Black avoids the hackneyed variations starting with 3. ... P—

Q 4 and allows White's centre pawn to cross the half-way line and so establish a clear advantage in space.

4. P—Q 5

Embarking upon a complicated struggle. 4. Kt—K B 3 is a quieter reply.

4. ...	P × P
5. P × P	P—Q 3
6. Kt—Q B 3	

White aims for play with his pieces. The alternative plan is to build up a pawn centre by 6. P—B 3 and 7. P—K 4.

6. ...	P—K Kt 3
7. B—Kt 2	B—Kt 2
8. Kt—B 3	O—O
9. O—O	R—K 1
10. B—B 4	P—Q R 3
11. P—Q R 4	Q—B 2 *122*

122

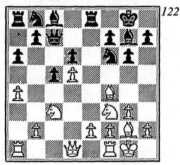

12. Q—Q 2

It was also worth considering 12. Kt—Q 2, manœuvring the Kt to Q B 4. For example: 12. ... Kt—R 4; 13. Kt—B 4, Kt × B; 14. P × Kt, P—B 4; 15. P—R 5, Kt—Q 2; 16. Kt—R 4, Kt—B 3; 17. Kt (R 4)—Kt 6, R—Kt 1; 18. R—B 1, intending 19. P—Kt 4.

12. ...	Q Kt—Q 2
13. K R—B 1	P—B 5

An interesting idea—to take advantage of the weakness of White's Q Kt 3 by threatening Kt—B 4. On the negative side there is the loss of control of the centre square Q 5.

14. B—R 6   B—R 1

He does not want to exchange his valuable Bishop. If 14. ... Kt—B 4, White could continue 15. B × B, Kt—Kt 6; 16. B × Kt with three minor pieces for the Queen.

15. Q—B 4

Here the Queen is in an active position attacking the Q B P, which thereby hinders Black's initiative on the Q-side.

15. ...   R—Kt 1

Planning the advance of the Q Kt P. White would have answered 15. ... Kt—K 4 with 16. Kt × Kt, R × Kt; 17. Q—Q 2 followed by transferring the Bishop to Q 4 via K 3.

16. P—R 3

This is directed against a possible Kt—Kt 5 at some time in the future. White does not prevent the push 16. ... P—Q Kt 4, but reckons that his pieces are well enough placed to beat off his opponent's pawn attack on the Q-side. 16. P—R 5, P—Q Kt 4; 17. P × Pe.p., R × Kt P was weaker, as Black gets pressure along the Q Kt-file.

16. ...	P—Q Kt 4
17. P × P	P × P
18. Kt—Q 4	Kt—R 4
19. Q—R 4	P—Kt 5

Black is consistent in his plans. 19. ... B—B 3; 20. B—Kt 5, B × Kt; 21. Q × B, Kt—B 4 was weaker, for example: 22. R—Q 1, Kt—Kt 6; 23. R—R 7, Kt ×Q; 24. R × Q, Kt × P ch; 25. Kt × Kt, R × Kt; 26. B—K 7 or 22. ... P—Kt 5; 23. Kt—K 4, B × P; 24. Kt × Kt, P × Kt; 25. P—Q 6, Q—Q 2; 26. Q × P (B 4), and in both cases White gets a powerful passed pawn on the Q-file.

20. Kt—Q 1   Kt—K 4 *123*

123

21. Kt—B 6!

This shows up the weaknesses in the enemy position, caused by the impetuous advance of the Q-side pawns.

21. ...   Kt × Kt
22. R × P

The only correct continuation. Against 22. Q × P Black had prepared a cunning rejoinder: 22. ... Kt × P!; 23. B P × Kt, Q—Kt 3 ch; 24. K—R 2, Kt—K 4. 22. P × Kt is met by 22. ... B—K 3, when Black has a strong position with the threat of 23. ... P—Q 4.

22. ...   B—B 3!

A counter-thrust. Black counts on answering 23. B—Kt 5 with 23. ... B × B; 24. Q × B, Q—Q 1, remaining a piece up. However, White had planned an exchange sacrifice, which brings about a sharp endgame.

23. R × Kt   Q × R
24. P × Q   B × Q
25. P—B 7!

An important intermediate move. The Black Rook is pushed to Q Kt 3, where it is badly placed.

25. ...   R—Kt 3
26. P × B   *124*

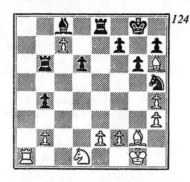

124

In the position reached White has a far advanced pawn, actively placed Bishops and can transfer his Kt to the centre square Q 5; all this puts Black in a difficult position in spite of his material advantage. If now 26. ..., R—K 2, then 27. Kt—K 3, R × P; 28. Kt—Q 5, and White recovers the exchange, retaining his positional advantage. If 26. ... R × P, then 27. Kt—K 3, R—R 3; 28. R—Q B 1, R—R 2; 29. Kt—Q 5 etc.

For an appraisal of the ending we point out the following variations: 26. ... B—Kt 2; 27. Kt—K 3, B × B; 28. K × B, R—B 3 (28. ... Kt—B 3; 29. R—Q B 1, R—Q B 1; 30. R—Kt 5, P—Q 4; 31. B × Kt, R × B; 32. Kt × P, R—K 3; 33. R—B 4); 29. Kt—Q 5, R—B 4; 30. P—K 4, P—B 4; 31. R—R 7, P × P; 32. R—Kt 7, R × Kt; 33. R—Kt 8, R—K 4; 34. R—Q 8! and White wins; 26. ... Kt—B 3; 27. Kt—K 3, P—Q 4; 28. Kt × P, Kt × Kt; 29. B × Kt, and Black's position is still difficult, for example: 29. ... R × P; 30. R—R 8, R—K 1; 31. R—Kt 8, R—R 3; 32. B—Kt 7, R—R 2; 33. R × B, R × R; 34. B × R, R × P; 35. B—R 6 or 29. ... R—K 2; 30. B—Kt 5, R × B P; 31. B—Q 8, R—Q 2; 32. B × R, R × B; 33. R—

R 8, R—Q 8 ch; 34. K—R 2, R—
Q B 8; 35. B—R 5, winning the
Q Kt P. If 29. ... R—R 3, then 30.
R—Q 1, threatening R—Q 8, is
strong. A Rook and a pawn on the
seventh rank creates dangerous
threats to the enemy King, so Black
decides to lighten the atmosphere
by exchanging a pair of Rooks.

26. ...   R—R 3
27. R × R   B × R
28. Kt—K 3   Kt—B 3

Black brings the Kt back to
defend the square Q 4, but in doing
so he loses a pawn. 28. ... P—Kt 6
would have made it more difficult
for White to keep the initiative.
In that case his attacking possibilities are nicely illustrated by the
following variations :
29. B—B 6, R—K 4 (29. ... R—
K 2; 30. B—Q Kt 5, B—Kt 2;
31. Kt—Q 5!); 30. Kt—Q 5, R ×
P; 31. B—Q Kt 5, R—K 8 ch;
32. K—R 2, B—Kt 2; 33. B—B 6,
B—R 3; 34. B—R 4. If now 34. ...
R—Q Kt 8, then 35. Kt—K7 ch,
K—R 1; 36. B—Q 2, and the
Q Kt P cannot be taken because of
37. B—B 3 ch.
After 34. ... B—Kt 2; 35. B—Q 2,
Black could try 35. ... R—Q Kt 8;
36. B—B 3, R—Q B 8; 37. B × P,
and the Q B P eventually costs him
a piece, or 35. ... R—K 7; 36. B—

B 6, B—B 1; 37. Kt—Kt 6, B—R 3;
38. B—Q Kt 5!
However, after his best reply 35.
... R—Q 8; 36. B—B 6, B—R 3;
37. B—B 3, R—Q B 8 Black had
chances of saving the game.

29. B—Kt 5   K—Kt 2

29. ... Kt—K 5 is no better because of 30. Kt—Q 5, K—Kt 2; 31.
Kt × P, B—B 1; 32. B—Q 8, con-
solidating the passed pawn.

30. B × Kt ch   K × B
31. Kt—Q 5 ch   K—K 3
32. Kt × P

With the win of this pawn White
gets two connected passed pawns,
which decide this tense struggle.
Black cannot continue 32. ... B ×
P because of 33. B—Kt 7, K—Q 2;
34. B—B 6 ch and wins.

32. ...   B—Kt 4
33. B—Kt 7   B—Q 2
34. Kt—Q 5   B—B 1

White threatened 35. Kt—Kt 6
and 36. P—B 8=Q.

35. B—B 6   R—Kt 1
36. P—Kt 4   P—Kt 4
37. P—R 5   P—Kt 5
38. P—R 4   B—R 3
39. P—Kt 5   B—B 1
40. P—Kt 6   P—Kt 6

Black resigned without waiting
for White's reply.

No. 45.   Catalan System

V. SMYSLOV   M. TAIMANOV

(Tchigorin Memorial Tournament, Leningrad, 1951)

1.	P—Q 4	Kt—K B 3
2.	P—Q B 4	P—K 3
3.	P—K Kt 3	P—Q 4
4.	B—Kt 2	P × P

5.	Q—R 4 ch	B—Q 2
6.	Q × B P	B—B 3
7.	Kt—K B 3	B—Q 4
8.	Q—R 4 ch	B—B 3

In this variation it is important for Black to carry through the advance P—Q B 4. Instead of the text move, which blocks the path of the Q B P, attention should have been given to 8. ... Q—Q 2 and if 9. Q—Q 1, then 9. ... P—B 4; 10. Kt—K 5, Q—B 2.

9. Q—Q 1	Q Kt—Q 2
10. O—O	P—K R 3
11. Q Kt—Q 2	

The Q Kt is usually developed on Q B 3. In this game White chooses a plan based on transferring the Kt to K 5.

11. ...	B—Kt 5
12. Kt—B 4	O—O
13. B—B 4	Kt—Kt 3

A characteristic deployment of pieces. In the event of 13. ... Kt—Q 4; 14. B—Q 2, B × B; 15. Q × B, Kt (Q 4)—Kt 3 White gets positional pressure on the Q-side by 16. Kt—R 5.

14. Kt (B 4)—K 5	B—K 5	
15. Kt—Q 3	B—Q 3	*125*

125

16. Kt—B 5!

The manœuvring continues under the shadow of White's growing initiative. If now 16. ... B × B, then 17. Kt × B, Kt × Kt; 18. P × B, and White has a strong position in the centre and excellent prospects on the diagonal K R 1—Q R 8.

16. ...	K B × Kt
17. P × B	Q × Q
18. K R × Q	Kt—R 5
19. B × B P	

The exchange of Queens has left White with the more active game. 19. ... Kt × Kt P allows the Kt to be cut off by 20. R—Q 4.

19. ...	K R—B 1
20. B—Q 6	Kt × B P
21. R—Q 4	B—Q 4
22. B—B 1	

This is a basic part of White's plan, which proposes to prepare a pawn advance P—B 3 and P—K 4 after the Kt has been moved.

22. ...	R—B 3
23. B—K 7	B × Kt

23. ... R—K 1 could be answered by 24. B × Kt (B 3), P × B; 25. P—K 4, B × K P; 26. Kt—Q 2, threatening to win the exchange by 27. B—Kt 5. Black's calculation is based on the variation 24. P × B, Kt—Q 4; 25. B × Kt, R × B, and Black has a strong position in the centre.

24. B × Kt

The tactical basis of this move, which prevents Black from playing Kt—Q 4, is the variation: 24. ... B × P; 25. B × B, P × B; 26. P—Q Kt 4, Kt—R 5; 27. P—Kt 5, Kt—B 6; 28. R—Kt 4 ch and 29. P × R.

24. ...	B—K 5

Incorrect: if you are going to move the Bishop, then you must consent to 24. ... B—Q 4; 25. R—K Kt 4, P—K Kt 3; 26. P—B 3, and White has the initiative. But you will agree that the best choice of all was 24. ... P × B; 25. P × B, P—K 4 followed by Kt— K 3.

25. B—K 7	B—Q 4 *126*

The Bishop must hold the long diagonal, for after 25. ... B—Kt 3 there occurs 26. B—Kt 2, R—B 2; 27. B—Q 6, R (B 2)—B 1; 28. P—Q Kt 4 and then 29. B × P. But now the awkward distribution of the black pieces in the centre gives White the chance to start a dangerous attack. The further events are in the nature of being forced.

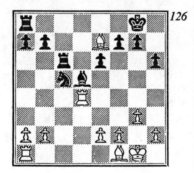

126

26. P—Q Kt 4!

Driving off the enemy Kt. Black's reply is forced.

26. ...   Kt—K 5

Necessary in view of the threat of P—K 4.

27. P—B 3   Kt—B 6
28. P—K 4   R—B 2

This is Black's best practical chance in this position; it points to a desire to create counterplay. If 28. ... B × R P, then 29. P—Kt 5, R—B 2; 30. B—Q 6, R (B 2)—B 1; 31. B—Kt 4, B—Kt 6; 32. R—R 3, and White wins a piece.

29. B—Q 6   R—Q 2
30. B—K 5   P—B 3

The point of Black's defence. It seems that he has managed to avoid the unpleasantnesses, but White's next move clarifies the situation.

31. R—Q 3!

Now both Black's minor pieces are attacked. 31. ... P × B is impossible on account of 32. R × Kt, B—B 3; 33. P—Kt 5, and the Bishop is caught.

31. ...   Kt—R 5
32. P × B   P × B
33. P × P

The second point of the Rook move becomes clear: it is defended on Q 3. Thanks to this White wins an important pawn.

33. ...   R × R
34. B × R   K—B 1

34. ... R—K 1 would not do because of 35. B—Kt 5, attacking both pieces. White quickly wins another pawn, after which his material advantage decides the issue.

35. R—K 1   R—Q 1
36. B—B 2   Kt—B 6
37. R × P   K—K 2
38. B—Kt 3   R—Q 7
39. R—B 5   Kt—K 7 ch
40. K—B 1   Kt—Q 5
41. R—B 7 ch   K—K 1
42. R × Q Kt P   Black
                resigned.

No. 46. Ruy Lopez
V. SMYSLOV   M. BOTVINNIK
(Nineteenth Soviet Championship, Moscow, 1951)

1. P—K 4	P—K 4		12. B—Kt 5	P—R 3
2. Kt—K B 3	Kt—Q B 3		13. B × Kt	
3. B—Kt 5	P—Q R 3			
4. B—R 4	Kt—B 3			
5. O—O	B—K 2			
6. R—K 1	P—Q Kt 4			
7. B—Kt 3	P—Q 3			
8. P—B 3	O—O			
9. P—K R 3	B—K 3			

The variation, characterized by 9. ... B—K 3, belongs to the creative legacy of M. I. Tchigorin. The exchange of the white-squared Bishops lessens White's attacking chances, while the doubled pawns, which result from 10. B × B, P × B are compensated for by the initiative on the open K B-file.

10. P—Q 4	B × B	
11. Q × B	Q—Q 2	127

The most solid reply. The attempt to create counterplay in the centre by 11. ... P × P; 12. P × P, P—Q 4; 13. P—K 5, Kt—K 5 is not good at the moment because of 14. Kt—B 3, Kt × Kt; 15. Q × Kt!, Q—Q 2; 16. B—Q 2, and White's position is clearly preferable. See also the game Boleslavsky-Flohr (Budapest, 1950).

After 13. B—R 4 Black could continue 13. ... Kt—K R 4 followed by Kt—B 5.

13. ...	B × B
14. P—Q 5	

This advance of the Q P is the point of the previous exchange. To rid himself of the backward Q B P Black must play P—Q B 3, but then after the exchange Q P × P the square Q 5 is free to be occupied by a White Kt.

14. ...	Kt—Q R 4
15. Q—B 2	P—B 3
16. P × P	Q × B P
17. Q Kt—Q 2	Q R—B 1
18. Q R—B 1	

Preventing the threat of P—Kt 5 by strengthening Q B 3 and also preparing for P—Q B 4 at the right moment.

18. ...	K R—Q 1
19. Kt—B 1	Kt—B 5
20. P—Q Kt 3	Kt—Kt 3
21. Kt—K 3	P—Q 4	128

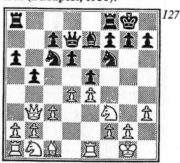

127

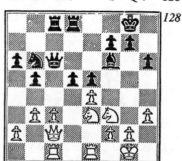

128

Black has succeeded in carrying through the freeing manœuvre in the centre. White threatened to fix the weak point Q 6 by Q—Q 3 and R—Q 1. The text move forestalls this threat.

22. Kt—Kt 4!

The best reply. White retains the initiative.

22. ... P—Q 5

The continuation 22. ... P × P; 23. Kt (B 3) × P, B × Kt; 24. Kt × B, Q—Kt 2 was insufficient because of 25. R × P!, R × P; 26. Q × R, Q × R; 27. Q—B 7. And if in the above variation Black plays 25. ... Kt—Q 4, then White maintains his material advantage by 26. R—Q 4!

23. Kt × B ch Q × Kt

If 23. ... P × Kt, then 24. Q—Q 2!, P × P; 25. Q × R P with an attack on Black's weakened King position.

24. Q—Kt 2

White has managed to keep the initiative. Now a serious problem confronts Black—how to maintain equality in the centre. The chief failing in his position is the poor position of the Kt on Kt 3, where it does not take part in the struggle for the centre squares.

24. ... P × P

24. ... P—Q 6; 25. R—K 3, R—Q 3; 26. R—Q 1, Q R—Q 1; 27. R—Q 2 was risky, as White begins to lay siege to the Q P, which after Q—Kt 1 and if necessary Kt—K 1 must fall.

25. R × P Kt—Q 2
26. K R—Q B 1

Seizing the open Q B-file. 26. R—Q 1 did not give White any advantage after 26. ... Kt—B 1!

26. ... R × R
27. Q × R Q—Q 3
28. Q—B 6 Kt—B 3!

Black conducts the defence skilfully, bringing the Kt to an active position. However, Black still has a number of difficulties to overcome in the ending.

29. Q × Q R × Q
30. Kt × P Kt × P
31. P—B 3 Kt—Kt 4

In spite of the limited material remaining on the board Black must play very accurately. The fact that the back rank is undefended allows White to organize a dangerous attack on the enemy King in some variations. Thus, for example, 31. ... P—B 3, which looks natural could be answered by 32. Kt—Kt 6, Kt—Kt 6; 33. K—B 2, Kt—B 4; 34. P—K Kt 4 with a threatening position on the K-side. The best reply to 31. ... Kt—Kt 6 is 32. K—B 2.

32. P—B 4 Kt—K 3
33. P—B 5 Kt—Q 1
34. R—B 8

White's position is the little more active. Now both sides centralize their Kings.

34. ... K—B 1
35. K—B 2 K—K 2 *129*

129

36. K—K 3

Here it was possible to simplify into a pawn ending by 36. R × Kt, R × R; 37. Kt—B 6 ch, K—Q 2; 38. Kt × R, K × Kt; 39. K—K 3, K—K 2; 40. K—Q 4, K—Q 3; 41. P—Q Kt 4, but after 41. ... P—B 3 Black can defend himself successfully.

36. ...   R—Q 8

Up to this moment Black had played a difficult defence very well, but now he commits an inaccuracy. He should play 36. ... R—Q 4! and, if 37. K—K 4, then 37. ... R—Q 7, attacking White's pawns. In the event of 36. ... R—Q 4; 37. Kt—Q 3, R × P; 38. R—R 8, Kt—B 3; 39. R × P, K—Q 2 Black could also continue to defend with success.

37. R—R 8!   K—B 3

After this move Black's game cannot be saved. 37. ... R—Q 3 would be bad because of 38. R × Kt! with a won ending for White. However, after 37. ... R—K 8 ch; 38. K—Q 4, R—K 7; 39. R × P, R × Kt P Black still had practical chances of a draw.

38. Kt—Q 3!

Splitting Black's forces.

38. ...   Kt—B 3

A blunder in time-trouble. But even after 38. ... Kt—Kt 2; 39. R × P ch, K × P; 40. R—Kt 6, Kt—Q 1; 41. R × P ch White must win.

39. R × P   Black
                                   resigned.

No. 47. Queen's Pawn, Nimzovitch Defence

I. LIPNITSKY   V. SMYSLOV

(Nineteenth Soviet Championship, Moscow, 1951)

1. P—Q 4   Kt—K B 3
2. P—Q B 4   P—K 3
3. Kt—Q B 3   B—Kt 5
4. Q—B 2   Kt—B 3

The Nimzovitch Defence is often met in contemporary tournament practice. Abounding in a great variety of ideas it belongs to the number of those openings where the possible transposition from one system of development to another is easy.

5. Kt—B 3   P—Q 4
6. P—Q R 3   B × Kt ch
7. P × B

White avoids the well-known variations based on 7. Q × B and instead proposes to solve in practical play an opening problem, which has been but a little investigated.

7. ...   Kt—Q R 4!

From the very opening moves the game follows unusual lines. The Kt is maintained on Q R 4, where it controls the important square Q B 5; 8. Q—R 4 ch is answered by 8. ... P—B 3.

8. Kt—K 5   Kt—Q 2

Continuing to fight for control of the white squares on the Q-side.

9. Kt × Kt   B × Kt
10. P × P   P × P
11. B—B 4   *130*

To all appearances an active method of development, but in fact it allows Black to seize the initiative by an unexpected manœuvre. He should play 11. P—K 3, to which the reply would be 11. ... O—O.

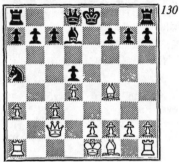

130

11. ...   B—Kt 4!

This makes it very difficult for White to develop his K-side normally. Now P—K 3 allows the exchange of the white-squared Bishops, as a result of which the Kt would occupy an impregnable position at Q B 5. Best seems 12. P—Kt 3, intending to prepare to castle by 12. ... O—O; 13. B—Kt 2, R—K 1; 14. B—B 3. White takes the risky decision to leave the King in the centre.

12. P—K R 4   O—O
13. R—Q Kt 1   Q—Q 2
14. R—R 3

Planning to develop the Rook on K Kt 3. Of course, 14. B × P was impossible because a piece is lost after 14. ... B—R 5.

14. ...   K R—K 1
15. R—K Kt 3   Kt—B 5
16. B—R 6

White creates play on the K-side; but it soon becomes clear that Black has sufficient resources at his disposal to repulse his opponent's assault.

16. ...   P—K Kt 3
17. Q—B 1   Kt—Q 3 !

This move, intending Kt—B 4, emphasizes the artificial nature of White's attacking set-up.

18. Q—B 4   B—R 3

But not 18. ... Kt—B 4 on account of 19. R × B!, Kt × R; 20. P × Kt, Q × R; 21. Q—B 6. After the text move White is in an impasse. The threats Kt—B 4, R—K 4, etc. are gathering round him.

19. P—K 3   *131*

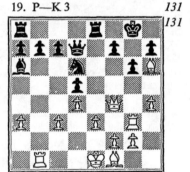

131

19. ...   Kt—B 4

The Kt has trod an interesting path from Q Kt 1—Q B 3—Q R 4 Q B 5—Q 3—K B 4. Black goes over to the counter-attack.

20. B × B   P × B
21. R—Kt 7

White seeks chances to complicate the struggle, but Black's reply shows that White's King is in a dangerous position.

21. ...   Q R—Kt 1 !
22. R × B P   R—Kt 8 ch
23. K—K 2   Q—R 5 !

White resigned.

This game bears witness yet again to the fact that it is risky to attack on the flank without first safeguarding your position in the centre.

No. 48.   Sicilian Defence
V. SMYSLOV   D. BRONSTEIN
(Nineteenth Soviet Championship, Moscow, 1951)

1. P—K 4	P—Q B 4
2. Kt—Q B 3	Kt—Q B 3
3. P—K Kt 3	P—K Kt 3
4. B—Kt 2	B—Kt 2
5. P—Q 3	P—Q 3
6. B—K 3	Kt—R 3

An unusual position for the Kt. Black's opening idea is disclosed in the variation 7. P—K R 3, P—B 4; 8. Q—Q 2, Kt—B 2 but White prefers to direct the game in another direction.

7. Q—B 1	Kt—K Kt 5
8. B—Q 2	Kt—Q 5
9. P—K R 3	Kt—K 4
10. Q Kt—K 2	

White prepares to advance his pawn chain and drive back the enemy pieces by P—K B 4 and P—Q B 3 with gain of tempo. The manœuvre Q Kt—K 2 when the K Kt is still undeveloped is characteristic of the treatment of the Closed Variation (compare game No. 24).

10. ...   Q—Kt 3

Here the Queen makes an indirect attack on the Q Kt P.

Black opposes the systematic development of the game with the threat of combinational complications.

11. P—K B 4

White does not lay aside his intended plan, but estimates that the prospects in the sharp struggle ahead will be favourable for him.

11. ...   Kt × B P ch!?

A tempting, but not absolutely correct, continuation. Black intends by his sacrifice to set up a pawn majority on the Q-side. All the same it was better to consent to 11. ... Kt (K 4)—B 3; 12. P—B 3, Kt × Kt; 13. Kt × Kt, when White has the freer game.

12. Q × Kt	Q × P
13. Q × Q	Kt × P ch
14. K—B 1!	

The correct way. Black's position was better after 14. K—Q 1, Kt × Q ch; 15. K—B 2, Kt—B 5, and the Kt is actively placed on Q B 5.

14. ...   B × Q

If 14. ... Kt × Q, then White could exchange the black-squared Bishops by 15. B—Q B 3.

15. R—Kt 1   B—K 3 *132*

Leading to a still sharper struggle. Now White could have made new material gains by 16. R × B, Kt × R; 17. B—Q B 3, but after 17. ... Kt—Q 8; 18. B × R, P—B 3; 19. B—Kt 7, B × Q R P the black passed pawns could become very dangerous.

132

16. B—Q B 3!

This reply resolves the tension. In the event of 16. ... B × B; 17. Kt × B, B—B 5; 18. K Kt—K 2, O—O—O; 19. B—B 3 and 20. K—Kt 2 White has completed his development and remains with the better chances.

16. ...   B × Q R P

Black strives to create an absolutely unopposed majority of pawns on the Q-side at any price. However in the further course of the game he does not succeed in showing the correctness of this decision. Possibly he ought to stop at 16. ... B × B; 17. Kt × B, B—B 5, when with three pawns for the piece he has good practical chances of organizing a defence.

17. R × B   Kt × R
18. B × Kt

An original situation, in which White has two Kts and a Bishop against a Rook and four pawns. Of course, White could have taken either of the attacked pieces, but after 18. B × R, P—B 3 the Bishop is out of play. For this reason he prefers the lesser material advantage, but his Bishop in an active position.

18. ...   R—K Kt 1

Black refrains from castling, keeping his King in the centre instead. 18. ... P—B 3 could be answered by 19. P—K 5, B P × P; 20. B × Kt P, R—Q Kt 1; 21. B—B 6 ch, K—Q 1; 22. B—Q B 3, and the long diagonals have been opened for the Bishops.

19. K—B 2   B—B 5
20. Kt—K B 3   B × Kt

Probably Black hoped by this exchange to cut down the activity of the White pieces so that he could carry on with his plan of sheltering his King on the Q-side.

If 20. ... P—Q Kt 4, then 21. Kt —Q 2, B × Kt; 22. K × B, threatening 23. P—K 5. As a result White now has the additional advantage of two Bishops.

21. K × B   K—Q 2
22. R—Q 1 !

White has the initiative. By bringing the Rook to the Q-file he defines the object of attack—the point Q 6. It rapidly becomes clear that the position of the Black King on Q 2 is also not very promising.

22. ...   P—Q R 4 *133*

Obviously, Black's chances are based on the advance of the pawns on the flank; on the other hand White has already succeeded in mobilizing his pieces for counter operations in the centre.

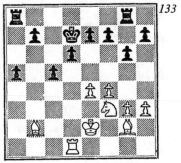

133

23. Kt—K 5 ch   K—B 2

Black gives up a pawn, for if 23. ... K—K 3, then 24. P—B 5 ch, P × P; 25. P × P ch, K × P; 26. P—Kt 4 ch with dangerous threats. If 23. ... K—K 1, then 24. Kt—B 4, P—Q Kt 4; 25. P—K 5, opening up the game.

24. Kt × B P   P—R 5
25. P—K 5   P—R 6
26. B—Q R 1   K R—K 1

In this way Black defends the point Q 6. 26. ... R—R 3 was not sufficient on account of 27. P × P ch, P × P; 28. Kt × P, R × Kt; 29. B—K 5, R—Q 1; 30. B × P, K × B; 31. R × R, etc. Now 27. P × P ch is met by 27. ... P × P ch—discovering check to the White King.

27. Kt—Kt 5

The centralization of the pieces carried out by this move is one of the basic principles of the strategic conduct of the struggle. The immediate threat is 28. Kt—K 6 ch, K—Q 2; 29. Kt × P ch. On the other hand the attack on Q 6 could not be maintained by 27. K—B 2, R—R 3; 28. P × P ch, P × P; 29. Kt × P, R × Kt; 30. B—K 5 because of 30. ... R × B.

27. ...   R—R 4
28. Kt—K 6 ch   K—Q 2
29. B—Q 5   P—R 7   134

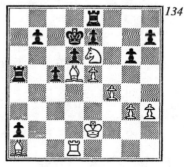

134

He cannot play 29. ... P—Q Kt 4 on account of 30. Kt × P ch, P × Kt; 31. B—B 7 ch, winning the Rook.

30. P—Kt 4!

White's pieces are successfully containing the enemy pawns; now his own rush forward to create a passed pawn on the K B file.

30. ...   R—Q B 1
31. Kt—Kt 5   R—B 1
32. P—B 5

White consistently completes his plan, exploiting his K-side pawn majority.

32. ...   P × B P
33. P × B P   P—R 3

And not 33. ... R × P on account of 34. B—K 6 ch.

34. B—K 6 ch   K—B 2
35. P × P ch   P × P
36. Kt—K 4

Already close at hand is the final moment in the struggle, when the Rooks will no longer be able to hold the attack of the minor pieces.

36. ...   R—R 6
37. Kt × Q P   R × R P
38. B—K 5   R—Q R 1
39. Kt—B 4 ch   Black
                resigned.

Mate next move cannot be avoided.

No. 49. English Opening

V. SMYSLOV   V. SIMAGIN

(*Nineteenth Soviet Championship, Moscow, 1951*)

1. P—Q B 4   P—Q B 4
2. Kt—Q B 3   Kt—Q B 3
3. Kt—B 3   P—K Kt 3
4. P—K 3

White prepares to advance his Q P and be able to answer P × P with P × P, so setting up a pawn centre. If you play 4. P—Q 4 at once, then after 4. ... P × P; 5. Kt × P, B—Kt 2 the Black Bishop exerts strong pressure on the long diagonal.

4. ...	P—Q 3
5. P—Q 4	B—Kt 5
6. B—K 2	B—Kt 2
7. P—Q 5	

Advancing with gain of tempo and guaranteeing an advantage in space. Now 7. ... Kt—K 4 is not possible on account of 8. Kt × Kt, B × B; 9. Q—R 4 ch, so the attacked Kt must retreat to a less satisfactory square.

7. ...	Kt—Kt 1
8. P—K R 3	B × Kt
9. B × B	Kt—K B 3
10. O—O	O—O
11. Q—Q 2	

Thus White prepares to fianchettoe his Q B. 11. P—Q Kt 3 could be answered by 11. ... Kt × P; 12. B × Kt, B × Kt; 13. B × P, B × R; 14. B × R, Kt—Q 2, and Black's opening troubles are behind him.

| 11. ... | P—Q R 3 |

Planning a pawn storm on the Q-side, and preparing to answer 12. P—Q Kt 3 with 12. ... P—Q Kt 4; 13. P × P, P × P, when 14. Kt × P is impossible on account of 14. ... Kt—K 5.

| 12. R—Kt 1 |

It is advisable to remove the Rook from the threatened diagonal. If now 12. ... P—Q Kt 4; 13. P × P, P × P, a possible continuation is 14. P—Q Kt 4, Kt—R 3; 15. P—R 3 with good play for White.

12. ...	Q Kt—Q 2
13. B—K 2	Kt—K 1
14. P—Q Kt 3	

White has managed to carry out his plan of development. From the opening he has obtained the freer position and favourable prospects.

| 14. ... | P—K 4 |
| 15. P × Pe.p. | |

This exchange is in keeping with the strategic demands of the position, for it is well known that the strength of the long-range Bishops increases in an open game. Besides, there is an object of attack on the Q-file—the backward Q P.

15. ...	P × P
16. B—Kt 2	Q—K 2
17. Q R—Q 1	Q R—Q 1
18. P—B 4	

Intending to transfer the Bishop to K B 3 and so set up the most appropriate arrangement of the White pieces. Such a set-up allows White to establish control over the centre squares and also create the necessary requisites for active operations on the K-side.

| 18. ... | Kt (Q 2)—B 3 |
| 19. B—B 3 | Kt—B 2 _135_ |

Black gives up a pawn in order to alter the rather unsatisfactory course of the game by tactical complications. After 20. B × P, P—Q 4 Black gets counterchances thanks to the isolated position of White's Bishop.

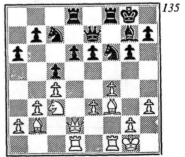

_135_

20. P—K Kt 4!

White avoids problematic variations with the win of a pawn and instead prefers to carry out an attack against the enemy King.

20. ...	P—Q Kt 4
21. P—Kt 5	Kt (B 3)— K 1
22. P—K R 4	

More logical seemed 22. Kt—K 4, which makes it difficult for Black to create any counterplay in the centre. The text move could be answered by 22. ... P—Q 4 and if 23. P × Q P, then 23. ... P—Kt 5; 24. Kt—Q R 4, P × P with an attack on the K P. Probably White would have had to play 23. P—R 3, and after 23. ... P—Kt 5; 24. R P × P, B P × P; 25. Kt—R 4 he still had the better chances.

22. ...	P—Kt 5
23. Kt—K 4	B × B
24. Q × B	P—Q 4
25. Kt—B 2	Q—Kt 2

A dangerous attack based on Kt—Kt 4 was building up, so it is natural that Black should strive to exchange Queens.

26. Q × Q ch	Kt × Q
27. Kt—Kt 4	Kt—B 4
28. K—B 2	

In the ending White's advantage has assumed real proportions in the shape of the more active distribution of his pieces and pawns. Already 29. Kt—B 6 ch is threatened, which forces Black to disclose his plans in the centre. The K R P cannot be taken, as White has threats along the K R-file after 28. ... Kt × R P; 29. Kt—B 6 ch, K—Kt 2; 30. R—K R 1.

28. ...	P × P

In opening the file Black counts on getting a pawn majority on the Q-side. The alternative plan, with 28 ... P—Q 5, led after 29. P—K 4, Kt—Q 3; 30. K—Kt 3 to a position, in which White could prepare an attack by doubling Rooks on the K R-file followed by P—K R 5.

29. P × P	P—Q R 4 *136*

136

30. Kt—B 6 ch

The beginning of a forced manœuvre, which leads to the win of the Q B P.

30. ...	K—Kt 2
31. Kt—Q 7	R—B 2

Black is forced to give up the fight for the open file, otherwise it is difficult to maintain material equality. If, for example, 31. ... K R—K 1, then 32. P—R 5 is possible, e.g. 32. ... P R 3; 33. R —K Kt 1, and White gets a direct attack on the enemy King.

32. Kt × P	R × R
33. R × R	Kt × R P
34. Kt—Q 7!	

This prevents Black from ridding himself of the backward pawn by P—K 4.

34. ...	Kt × B
35. K × Kt	Kt—Q 4

An unsuccessful attempt to transpose into a Rook and pawn ending; after 36. P × Kt, R × Kt; 37. P—Q 6, K—B 2; 38. K—K 4, R—Q 1; 39. K—K 5, R—Q Kt 1, threatening

R—Kt 4 ch, Black had counter-chances.

36. Kt—B 5   Kt—B 2
37. K—K 4

White follows the well-known principles governing endgame play: the King has taken up a strong position in the centre and the Rook controls the open file. In spite of the material equality Black has no chance of preventing White's pieces from becoming even more active. 37. ... R—B 4 cannot be played because of 38. R—Q 7 ch, R—B 2; 39. R × Kt, R × R; 40. Kt × P ch and 41. Kt × R.

Black takes his best chance, trying to relieve a little his cramped position by advancing his K R P.

37. ...   P—R 3
38. R—Q 6   P × P
39. P × P   K—B 1
40. R—B 6   K—K 1
41. K—K 5!

Keeping strictly to his plan to invade his opponent's position with his pieces. Now the King is aiming for Q 6; this is stronger than the prosaic solution of the problem by 41. Kt × P, R—K 2; 42. R × Kt, R × Kt ch, and Black has rid himself at the cost of a pawn of his "bad" Kt at Q B 2.

41. ...   K—Q 1   *137*

137

42. R—Kt 6!

Making the necessary room for the successful penetration of the King to the sixth rank. 42. K—Q 6 at once was premature on account of 42. ... Kt—K 1 ch; 43. K × P, R —K 2 ch and 44. ... R × P.

The text move considerably increases the effectiveness of the final attack. Now if 42. ... R—B 4 ch, there follows 43. K—Q 6, Kt—K 1 ch; 44. K—B 6, K—K 2; 45. R—Kt 7 ch, K—B 1; 46. Kt × P ch, K—Kt 1; 47. R—K 7 etc. If 42. ... K—K 2, then 43. P—K 4, R—B 7; 44. R—Kt 7, K—Q 1; 45. K—Q 6, R—Q 7 ch; 46. K—B 6, and Black is again lost.

42. ...   K—B 1
43. K—Q 6   R—B 7

In search of counterchances. If he plays 43. ... Kt—K 1 ch, then 44. K—B 6, R—B 2 ch; 45. K—Kt 5, and the black pawns are attacked.

44. K—B 6!

Of course, not 44. R—Kt 7 on account of 44. ... Kt—R 3. The King has now taken the opposition; the end is not far off.

44. ...   R—B 7
45. R—Kt 7   Kt—K 1

The "sacrifice" 45. ... Kt—Q 4 does not help because of 46. P × Kt, R × Kt ch; 47. K × R, K × R; 48. P × P, and the pawn ending is easily won for White.

46. R—Q R 7   K—Kt 1
47. R—K 7   Black
                   resigned.

No. 50. Ruy Lopez

V. SMYSLOV   G. BARCZA

(International Team Tournament, Helsinki, 1952)

1. P—K 4	P—K 4
2. Kt—K B 3	Kt—Q B 3
3. B—Kt 5	B—B 4

An old system, which has been successfully rehabilitated by O'Kelly. With best play White is able to get a slight but enduring advantage.

4. P—B 3!

This is stronger than 4. O—O, which allows Black to ease his position by exchanges, e.g. 4. O—O, Kt—Q 5; 5. Kt × Kt, B × Kt; 6. P—Q B 3, B—Kt 3; 7. P—Q 4, P—Q B 3; 8. B—Q B 4, P—Q 3 with approximate equality (Szily–O'Kelly, Budapest, 1952).

4. ...	Kt—B 3
5. P—Q 4	P × P

It is unwise to give up the centre in this way. Better is 5. ... B—Kt 3, though White has slightly the better chances after either 6. B—Kt 5, P—K R 3; 7. B—K R 4, P—Kt 4; 8. B—Kt 3, Kt × K P; 9. B × P or 6. O—O, O—O; 7. P × P, K Kt × P; 8. Q—Q 5, Kt—B 4; 9. B—Kt 5, Kt—K 2; 10. Q—Q 1, Kt—K 5; 11. B—K R 4, P—Q 4; 12. Q Kt—Q 2, P—Q B 3; 13. B—Q 3, P—K B 4; 14. P × Pe. p., Kt × P (B 3); 15. Q—B 2, P—Kt 3; 16. Q R—K 1 (Bronstein–O'Kelly, Hastings, 1953-1954).

6. P—K 5   Kt—Q 4?

Surrendering the centre without a fight. Correct is 6. ... Kt—K 5; even then White gets some pressure in the centre by 7. O—O, P—Q 4; 8. Kt × P (or 8. P × Pe.p., O—O;

9. P × B P, Q × P, and according to Keres Black has compensation for the pawn; this is an interesting idea, which needs to be thoroughly tested), B—Q 2; 9. B × Kt, P × B; 10. P—B 3.

7. O—O	O—O
8. P × P	B—Kt 3 *138*

138

9. B—Q B 4!

A fine move, which shows up the awkward positions of Black's pieces and prevents him from completing his development.

9. ...   Kt (B 3)—K 2

Even worse is 9. ... Kt (Q 4)—K 2 because of 10. P—Q 5!, Kt—Kt 1 (or 10. ... Kt—R 4; 11. B—K 2, threatening to win a piece by 12. P—Q Kt 4); 11. P—Q 6, cutting Black's position in two.

10. B—K Kt 5!   Q—K 1

If 10. ... P—Q B 3, then 11. K B × Kt, P × B; 12. Kt—B 3 wins a pawn, while 10. ... P—K B 3 also leads to loss of material after 11. P × P, P × P; 12. B—K R 6, R—B 2; 13. Kt—B 3, P—B 3; 14. Q—Kt 3.

11. Q—Kt 3

Forcing Black to create an irreparable weakness in his position —a hole at Q 3.

11. ...   P—Q B 3 *139*

139

12. Q Kt—Q 2

The Kt is aiming for Q 6, where it would have a stranglehold on Black's position. Black can only free his game by sacrificing his Q P, but this can only be to White's good as he is ahead in development as well. The game is really already over.

12. ...   P—K R 3

Neither 12. ... B—B 2; 13. Kt—K 4, Kt—Q Kt 3; 14. Kt—Q 6, B × Kt; 15. P × B, Kt × B; 16. P × Kt nor 12. ... Kt—B 2; 13. Kt—K 4, Kt—B 4; 14. Kt—Q 6, Kt × Kt; 15. P × Kt, Kt—K 3; 16. B—K 7 offered any chance of salvation.

13. Q B × Kt   Kt × B

13. ... Q × B simply lost a pawn for nothing after 14. B × Kt.

14. Kt—K 4   P—Q 4

The only chance. After 14. ... Kt—B 4; 15. Kt—Q 6, Kt × Kt; 16. P × Kt Black's Q-side is completely blockaded. White would easily build up a winning K-side attack.

15. P × P e.p.   Kt—B 4

He might as well have given up a second pawn by 15. ... Kt—Q 4 to free himself of the threats to his K B 2; however, after 16. B × Kt, P × B; 17. Q × P, B—K 3; 18. Q × K 5 White should have no difficulty in realizing his material advantage.

16. K R—K 1   Q—Q 1   *140*

140

17. Kt—K 5!

Black can no longer defend his K B P. If 17. ... Kt × P (Q 5), then 18. B × P ch, K—R 1 (or 18. ... K—R 2; 19. B—Kt 6 ch, K—R 1; 20. Kt—B 7 ch); 19. Kt—Kt 6 ch, K—R 2; 20. Kt × R ch, Q × Kt; 21. Q—B 4.

17. ...   Kt × P (Q 3)
18. Kt × Kt   Q × Kt
19. B × P ch   R × B

The exchange is also lost after 19. ... K—R 1; 20. Kt—Kt 6 ch of 19. ... K—R 2; 20. B—Kt 6 ch, K —R 1; 21. Kt—B 7 ch.

20. Q × R ch   K—R 2
21. Kt—B 4   Black
                              resigned.

He is the exchange down with the inferior position.

No. 51.   French Defence

V. SMYSLOV   G. STAHLBERG

(*Candidates' Tournament, Zurich, 1953*)

1. P—K 4	P—K 3
2. P—Q 4	P—Q 4
3. Kt—Q B 3	Kt—K B 3
4. B—Kt 5	P × P

A solid, but slightly passive, continuation. White has a small space advantage, which, however, can be neutralized by accurate play.

5. Kt × P	B—K 2
6. B × Kt	B × B
7. Kt—K B 3	Kt—Q 2
8. B—B 4	

As in the game Smyslov–Stahlberg, from the previous Candidates' Tournament, Budapest, 1950. On that occasion White was able to preserve a slight advantage, so he was not averse to following the same lines again.

8. ...	O—O
9. Q K 2	Kt—Kt 3

This move does not fully answer the needs of the position: the Kt is passively placed on Q Kt 3 as it can always be driven from the one square it might aspire to—Q 4—by P—Q B 4; but, what is more important, the Kt is required on Q 2 to help carry through the thematic freeing move—P—Q B 4. In fact the immediate 9. ... P—B 4 should equalize, and it is surprising that Stahlberg did not play it considering his lack of success with the text move in the above-mentioned game.

10. B—Kt 3

If 10. B—Q 3, Black can safely take the Q P, e.g. 10. ... B × P; 11. O—O—O, B—B 3 or 11. Kt (K 4)—Kt 5, P—K B 4; 12. Kt ×

B, Q × Kt (Kt 4); 13. Kt × K P, B × Kt; 14. Q × B ch, K—R 1 or finally 11. R—Q 1, B—B 3; 12. Kt (K 4)—Kt 5, B × Kt; 13. B × P ch, K × B; 14. R × Q, B × R.

10. ...	B—Q 2
11. O—O	*141*

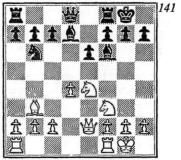

141

11. ...   Q—K 2

It was already difficult to find a satisfactory plan for Black simply because he had neglected to free his game by P—Q B 4. The text is an improvement on the unfortunate 11. ... B—Q R 5, which Stahlberg played in the other game. After 11. ... B—Q R 5 White continued 12. Kt × B ch, P × Kt (Black was forced to weaken his K-side because 12. ... Q × Kt loses a pawn after 13. B × B, Kt × B; 14. Q—B 4); 13. P—B 4, B × B; 14. P × B, P—B 3; 15. Q—K 3, K—R 1; 16. Kt—Q 2!, R—K Kt 1; 17. Kt—K 4, and White's advantage was clear. The alternatives 11. ... B—B 3 and 11. ... P—Kt 3 are both answered by 12. Kt × B ch Q × Kt; 13. Kt—K 5, and Black is still far from freeing himself.

12. K R—K 1   Q R—Q 1

An alternative plan was 12. ...
K R—Q 1; 13. Q R—Q 1, B—B 3;
14. Kt × B ch, Q × Kt; 15. Kt—
K 5, B—K 1, followed by Q R—B
1 and, if necessary, Kt—Q 2 in
preparation for P—Q B 4. Nevertheless, White's space advantage
would give him the better
prospects.

13. Q R—Q 1   B—Q R 5
14. B × B   Kt × B
15. Q—Kt 5

Taking the initiative on the Q-
side and at the same time increasing
his advantage in space. He could
have doubled Black's K B Ps by
15. Kt × B ch as 15. ... Q × Kt
would again lose a pawn, but the
doubled pawns are not so easily
exploited at the moment, and
exchanges are generally to the
defender's advantage.

15. ...   Kt—Kt 3
16. P—B 4   P—B 3
17. Q—Kt 3   Q—B 2

Allowing his K-side pawns to be
seriously weakened, after which
White is able to go over to a direct
attack on the King. He should have
played 17. ... R—Q 2, but there is
still a long and difficult defence in
prospect.

18. Kt × B ch   P × Kt   *142*

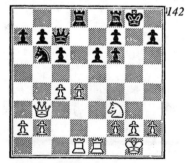

19. Q—K 3!

Threatening 20. Q—R 6, which,
however, is not decisive against the
most accurate defence—19. ...
K—R 1; 20. Q—R 6, Kt—Q 2
(but not 20. ... Q—K 2; 21. Kt—
R 4, followed by 22. Kt—B 5 etc.).

On the other hand he cannot take
the pawn by 19. ... Kt × P,
because after 20. Q—R 6, Kt—
Q 3 (or 20. ... Q—K 2; 21. R—
K 4); 21. Q × P White has an
overwhelming position, as the
following variations show:

(1) 21. ... Kt—K 1; 22. Q—R 6,
and to prevent Kt—Kt 5 Black
must play 22. ... P—B 3, which
loses the K P.

(2) 21. ... Kt—B 4; 22. R—K 4,
and now

(a) 22. ... K R—K 1; 23. R—Kt
4 ch, K—B 1; 24. Kt—Kt 5.

(b) 22. ... P—K R 3; 23. R—Kt
4 ch, K—R 2; 24. Kt—Kt 5 ch,
P × Kt; 25. R × P and 26. R—
R 5 ch.

(3) 21. ... K R—K 1; 22. R—K 5,
Kt—B 4; 23. R—K 4, P—K R 3;
24. R—Kt 4 ch, K—B 1 (or 24. ...
K—R 2; 25. Kt—Kt 5 ch); 25. Kt—
K 5.

19. ...   K—Kt 2   *143*

20. Kt—K 5!
A surprising finesse, which
threatens to win the Queen by
21. Q—Kt 3 ch, K—R 1; 22. Kt—

Kt 6 ch. If 20. ... P × Kt, then
21. Q—Kt 5 ch, K—R 1; 22. Q—
B 6 ch, K—Kt 1; 23. R—Q 3, K R
K 1; 24. Q—R 6, P × P; 25. P—
B 4! and wins.

20. ...   Q—K 2

Black could have resisted a little
longer by 20. ... P—K R 3;
21. Q—Kt 3 ch, K—R 2; 22. Kt—
Kt 6!, Q × Q; 23. Kt × R ch,
R × Kt; 24. R P × Q, Kt × P.

21. Kt—Kt 4!   R—K Kt 1

Loses the exchange. Only 21. ...
K—R 1; 22. Q—R 6, R—K Kt 1
(if 22. ... Kt—Q 2, then 23. P—
Q 5, B P × P; 24. P × P, P—K 4;
25. R—K 3, R—K Kt 1; 26. R—
K R 3, R—Kt 2; 27. Kt—K 3 etc.);
23. Kt × P, R—Kt 2 gave Black any
hope of survival, though it could

not be for long, as White is a pawn
up with the superior position.

22. Kt—R 6   Q—B 2

22. ... Kt × P was of no avail
on account of 23. Kt—B 5 ch, K—
R 1; 24. Q—R 6, Q—B 1; 25.
Q × B P ch, R—Kt 2; 26. Kt ×
R, Q × Kt; 27. Q × R ch. The
rest needs no explanation.

23. Kt × R	R × Kt
24. P—Q Kt 3	K—R 1
25. Q—R 6	R—Kt 3
26. Q—R 4	Kt—Q 2
27. R—K 3	Q—R 4
28. R—R 3	Kt—B 1
29. R—Kt 3	Q × P
30. R × R	Kt × R
31. Q × B P ch	K—Kt 1
32. Q—B 3	Q—B 7
33. Q—Q 3	Black
	resigned

No. 52.   Queen's Pawn Opening

P. KERES   V. SMYSLOV

(Candidates' Tournament, Zurich, 1953)

1. P—Q B 4	Kt—K B 3
2. Kt—Q B 3	P—K 3
3. Kt—B 3	P—B 4
4. P—K 3	B—K 2
5. P—Q Kt 3	O—O
6. B—Kt 2	P—Q Kt 3
7. P—Q 4	

At last White decides to advance
his centre pawn. He could go on
temporizing by 7. B—K 2, B—Kt 2;
8. O—O, Kt—B 3; 9. R—B 1, but
it would certainly not bring him
any advantage.

7. ...   P × P
8. P × P   P—Q 4

Now White always has to reckon
with P × P, which leaves him with
hanging pawns; should he try to

avoid this by playing P × P himself, then he has an isolated Q P.

9. B—Q 3	Kt—B 3
10. O—O	B—Kt 2
11. R—B 1	R—B 1
12. R—K 1	*144*

More natural seems 12. Q—K 2
and 13. K R—Q 1. White need have
no fears about the safety of his
Q P, for it would always be too
dangerous for Black to take it. For
example: 12. Q—K 2, P × P;
13. P × P, Kt × P; 14. Kt × Kt,
Q × Kt; 15. Kt—Q 5, Q—B 4; 16.
B × Kt!, P × B (not 16. ... B × B;
17. Q—K 4); 17. B × P ch, K × B;
18. Q—R 5 ch, K—Kt 1; 19. R—
B 3 with a winning attack; or 12.

Q—K 2, Kt—Q Kt 5; 13. B—Kt 1,
P × P; 14. P × P, B × Kt; 15.
P × B, Q × P; 16. Kt—K 4, Q—
Q 2; 17. Kt × Kt ch, P × Kt;
18. K—R 1, and once again White's
attack is decisive.

144

12. ...   **Kt—Q Kt 5**

Forcing White's attacking Bishop
to retreat to K B 1, where, although
t supports the centre—the Q B P,
it is less active than on Q Kt 1.

13. B—B 1   **Kt—K 5**
14. P—Q R 3

If 14. Kt × Kt, P × Kt, the
advanced K P would prove a
strength rather than a weakness,
e.g. 15. Kt—Q 2, P—B 4; 16. P—
B 3, B—K B 3!

14. ...   **Kt × Kt**
15. R × Kt   **Kt—B 3**
16. Kt—K 5

He cannot play for a pawn storm
on the Q-side by 16. P—B 5 on
account of 16. ... P × P; 17. P × P,
B—B 3; 18. R—B 2, B × B; 19.
R × B, Q—R 4, winning a pawn.

16. ...   **Kt × Kt**
17. R × Kt

He should now have contented
himself with 17. P × Kt, P × P;
18. B × P, Q × Q; 19. R × Q,
K R—Q 1; the ending is slightly in
Black's favour, but not enough

to win against exact play. Nevertheless, Keres had to win this game to
have a chance of first place in the
tournament, and this explains his
attempt to attack at all costs.

17. ...   **B—K B 3**
18. R—R 5

After 18. R—K 1, P × P; 19.
P × P Black's position is clearly
the better.

18. ...   **P—Kt 3**
19. R (B 3)—R 3   145

145

19. ...   **P × P!**

The only sure way of meeting a
violent assault on the wing is to
counter-attack in the centre. Accep-
ting the Rook would allow White
a most dangerous attack. For
example: 19. ... P × R; 20. Q × P,
R—K 1, and he has a choice
between 21. Q—R 6, B—Kt 4 (or
21. ... P × P; 22. P—Q 5!, B × B;
23. R—Kt 3 ch, K—R 1; 24. R—
R 3 and draws); 22. R—Kt 3, P—
B 3; 23. P—K R 4! and 21. P—
Q R 4! with the following variations:

(1) 21. ... P × P; 22. Q × R P
ch, K—B 1; 23. B—R 3 ch, R—K 2;
24. R—Kt 3 etc.

(2) 21. ... Q—Q 3; 22. P—B 5
and now

(a) 22. ... P × P; 23. Q—R 6!,
B—Kt 2 (or 23. ... Q—K 2; 24. R—

Kt 3 ch, K—R 1; 25. B—Q 3);
24. Q × P ch, K—B 1; 25. P × P.
(b) 22. ... Q—Q 1; 23. P—B 6,
R × P; 24. B—R 3, R—Q 3;
25. Q—R 6, B × P (25. ... B—Kt
2; 26. R—Kt 3); 26. B—Q 3 etc.
(c) 22. ... Q—B 5; 23. P—B 6!
R × P (if 23. ... B × B P, then
24. B—Q 3 is very strong and if
23. ... B × Q P, then 24. Q × R P
ch, K—B 1; 25. B—R 3 ch, B—B 4;
26. R—K B 3, Q × R—not 26. ...
Q—B 2; 27. B × B ch, P × B;
28. P × B, Q × P; 29. Q—R 8 ch,
K—K 2; 30. R × P ch!—27.
B × B ch, P × B; 28. P × Q,
B × P; 29. P—B 4 with chances
for both sides); 24. Q × P ch,
K—B 1; 25. B—R 3 ch, R—K 2;
26. R—Kt 3, K—K 1; 27. Q—Kt 8
ch, K—Q 2; 28. R—K B 3, Q × P;
29. Q—Kt 8, B—B 1; 30. B × R,
B × B; 31. R × P, and Black's
position is still not safe.

20. R × P

White could not leave his Rook
en prise any longer, e.g. 20. P × P,
P × R; 21. B—Q 3 (21. Q × P,
B—K 5), R—B 4; 22. P × R,
B × B; 23. B × P ch, K—Kt 2;
24. Q × P, B—B 8!; 25. R—Kt 3
ch, K—B 3; 26. Q—R 4 ch, K—
K 4, and Black survives.

However, 20. R—R 6 would
have put up more resistance: the
point is the Rook is not en prise on
K R 6, and so 20. ... P—B 6 can be
met by 21. B × P; if 20. ... B—
Kt 2, then 21. R × P, and White
can answer 21. ... P—B 6 by 22.
B × P, R × B; 23. R × B ch! By
continuing 20. ... P × P; 21. Q ×
P, Q—Q 4, Black would preserve
a big advantage, as the White
Rooks are misplaced on the K R-
file.

20. ...   P—B 6!

Decisive: Black will now be able
to capture the Q P and thus protect
K R 1 yet again. 21. B × P is, of
course, answered by 21. ... R × B
and 22. ... K × R.

21. Q—B 1   146

A last ingenious attempt to snare
his opponent. The Bishop cannot
be taken on account of 22. Q—R 6,
Q × P; 23. R—R 8 ch, B × R;
24. Q—R 7 mate. Nor is 21. ... B ×
Kt P sufficient to win, e.g. 22. B ×
B, P × B; 23. Q—R 6, R—B 8 ch;
24. B—B 1, R × B ch; 25. K × R,
P—Kt 8 = Q ch; 26. K—K 2!, and
Black has no more than a draw by
perpetual check.

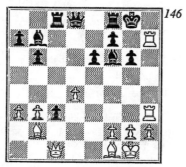

146

21. ...   Q × P!

Now the attack is completely
burnt out; all White's pieces are
scattered about the edges of the
board, while Black's dominate the
centre. The rest is easy.

22. Q—R 6	K R—Q 1
23. B—B 1	B—Kt 2
24. Q—Kt 5	Q—B 3
25. Q—Kt 4	P—B 7

Threatening 26. ... R—Q 8.

26. B—K 2	R—Q 5
27. P—B 4	R—Q 8 ch
28. B × R	Q—Q 5 ch

White resigned.

No. 53.   French Defence
V. SMYSLOV   M. BOTVINNIK
(*World Championship Match, Moscow, 1954*)

1. P—K 4	P—K 3
2. P—Q 4	P—Q 4
3. Kt—Q B 3	B—Kt 5
4. P—K 5	P—Q B 4
5. P—Q R 3	B—R 4
6. P—Q Kt 4	P × Q P
7. Q—Kt 4	

The most aggressive continuation; in the first and third games of the match 7. Kt—Kt 5 was played, but it did not lead to any advantage for White.

7. ...	Kt—K 2

If 7. ... K—B 1, White gets a dangerous attack by either 8. Kt—Kt 5, B—Kt 3; 9. B—Q 3 or 8. P × B, P × Kt; 9. Kt—B 3.

8. P × B

This is much stronger than 8. Q × Kt P at once. In that case Black can get a dangerous counter-attack by 8. ... R—Kt 1; 9. Q × P, B—B 2; 10. Kt—Kt 5, P—R 3; 11. Kt × P, B × P; 12. K Kt—B 3, Q—B 2 (Estrin-Khasin, Moscow Championship, 1953).

8. ...	P × Kt
9. Q × Kt P	R—Kt 1
10. Q × P	Kt—Q 2

Black brings another piece over to the defence of his K-side. This is very necessary, as White is already threatening to build up a formidable assault on the K-side by Kt—B 3 and Kt—Kt 5.

11. Kt—B 3	Kt—B 1

More accurate was 11. ... Q—B 2, so as to tie the White pieces down to the defence of the K P. As a result of this White is able to

develop his pieces on their most active squares.

12. Q—Q 3	Q × P
13. P—K R 4	

In this way White makes K Kt 5 a strong square for one of his minor pieces and at the same time threatens to advance the passed K R P even further.

13. ...	B—Q 2
14. B—Kt 5	

So the Bishop has taken up its most aggressive position.

14. ...	R—B 1 *147*
	147

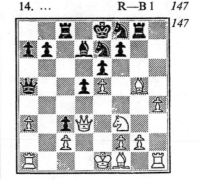

15. Kt—Q 4!

Now the Kt is centralized; the threatened R—B 5 is met by 16. Q—K 3, R—R 5 (or 16. ... Kt—B 4; 17. Kt × Kt, and if 17. ... R—K 5, then 18. Kt—Q 6 mate); 17. R—Q Kt 1, R × P; 18. Kt—Kt 5.

15. ...	Kt—B 4
16. R—Q Kt 1!	

White does not want to exchange on K B 5 unnecessarily, as then Black's pieces would become more active (Kt—K 3). The text move prevents the exchange of the white-squared Bishops, which would be to Black's advantage, and forces him to look to the defence of the Q Kt P.

16. ...   R—B 5

Black embarks upon a variation involving an exchange sacrifice, which though attractive is not completely sound. He ought to content himself with 16. ... P—Kt 3; 17. P—Kt 4, Kt × Kt; 18. Q × Kt, Q × P; 19. B—Q 3, when White has the better prospects though Black is not without his.

17. Kt × Kt   P × Kt

And not 17. ... R—K 5 ch; 18. Q × R, R × B (18. ... P × Q; 19. Kt—Q 6 mate); 19. Kt—Q 6 ch, winning easily.

18. R × P   R—K 5 ch?

148

An inadvertent transposition of moves · which loses immediately. Botvinnik had intended to play first 18. ... R × B; 19. P × R and then 19. ... R—K 5 ch, but even then White should be able to ward off the attack. For example: 20. B—K 2 (not 20. K—Q 1, Q × P; 21. R— Q Kt 1, Kt—K 3; 22. Q—R 6, R—Q 5 ch with a

draw by perpetual check), Kt—Kt 3 (20. ... Kt—K 3 is bad on account of 21. P—Kt 6!); 21. K—B 1 , and now either 21. ... Kt—B 5; 22. R—R 8 ch, K—K 2; 23. Q—Kt 5 or 21. ... B—B 3; 22. R—Kt 8 ch, K—K 2; 23. Q—R 6, and Black's chances of saving the ending would be very slight indeed.

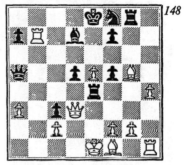

148

19. Q × R!   Q P × Q
20. R—Kt 8 ch   B—B 1
21. B—Kt 5 ch   Q × B
22. R × Q   Kt—K 3
23. B—B 6

Now the advance of the K R P quickly decides the game.

23. ...   R × P
24. P—R 5   B—R 3
25. P—R 6   Black
                 resigned.

No. 54. Queen's Pawn, King's Indian Defence

M. BOTVINNIK   V. SMYSLOV

(World Championship Match, Moscow, 1954)

1. P—Q 4	Kt—K B 3	7. O—O	P—K 4
2. P—Q B 4	P—K Kt 3	8. P—K 4	P—B 3
3. P—K Kt 3	B—Kt 2	9. B—K 3	
4. B—Kt 2	O—O		
5. Kt—Q B 3	P—Q 3		
6. Kt—B 3	Q Kt—Q 2		

More usual is 9. P—K R 3. The text move allows 9. ... Kt—Kt 5, but White expects to regain

the tempo by attacking the Black
Queen. However, by a fine temporary piece sacrifice on the 11th move
Black is able to assume the initiative.

9. ...　　　　　　　　Kt—Kt 5
10. B—Kt 5　　　　　Q—Kt 3
11. P—K R 3　　　　　　　*149*

11. B—K 7 would not lead to
any advantage after 11. ... R—
K 1; 12. B × P, P × P; 13. Kt—
Q R 4, Q—R 3.

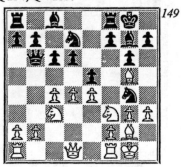

149

11. ...　　　　　　　　P × P!

The most vigorous continuation.
White is well placed after 11. ...
K Kt—B 3; 12. Q—Q 2, P × P;
13. Kt × P, Kt—B 4; 14. Q R—
Q 1, R—K 1; 15. K R—K 1, K Kt
—Q 2; 16. B—K 3 (Lilienthal–
Konstantinopolsky, Sochy, 1952).

12. Kt—Q R 4　　　　Q—R 3
13. P × Kt　　　　　　P—Kt 4
14. Kt × P

Playing for the win of the
exchange, which is his best chance.
Both 14. P—B 5, P × P; 15. Kt
× B P, Kt × Kt; 16. B—K 7,
Kt—K 3 and 14. B—K 7, R—K 1;
15. B × P, P × Kt; 16. Kt × P,
Kt—K 4! give Black excellent
prospects. First 14. P × P, P × P
does not help, as Black can always
play his Q B on to the long
diagonal.

14. ...　　　　　　　　P × Kt
15. Kt × P

White has no time to consolidate
his position, e.g. 15. P—Kt 3,
Kt—K 4; 16. P—B 3 (or 16. B—
K 7, B × P; 17. P—B 3, K R—
K 1; 18. B × P, Q R—Q 1), P—
Q 4! As well as winning the
exchange the text move has the
merit of delaying Kt—K 4 for the
moment.

15. ...　　　　　　　　Q × Kt
16. P—K 5　　　　　　Q × P
17. B × R　　　　　　Kt × P

At last the Kt reaches K 4, where
it dominates the centre and
threatens White's weakened K-
side. In spite of being the exchange
up White is in a very difficult
position, and only the most accurate play will suffice to hold the
game. For example: 18. Q × Q P,
B—K 3; 19. B—Kt 2, Q × Kt P,
and Black has a strong attack or
18. B—K 7, B × P; 19. Q—Q 5,
Q—B 1; 20. B × R, B—B 6 or
finally 18. B—Q 5, Q—Kt 4,
threatening Kt—Q 6.

18. R—B 1

The alternative continuation 18.
B—Kt 2, B—K 3; 19. Q × Q P,
Q × Kt P; 20. B—B 4, Kt—B 6 ch;
21. B × Kt, Q × K B; 22. Q—Q 1,
Q—Kt 2; 23. P—B 3 also offered
good chances of defending the
position, although Black's active
Bishops would be difficult to fight
against.

18. ...　　　　　　　　Q—Kt 5

Better than 18. ... Q—Kt 4,
which can be answered by 19. B—
K 7, B × P; 20. Q—Q 5.

19. P—R 3

In this way White succeeds in
removing the advanced Q R P,
which could have become very

dangerous supported by the two Bishops.

19. ...   Q × Q Kt P
20. Q × R P   *150*

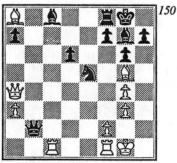

150

20. ...   B—Kt 2!

Eliminating the White K B, the chief defender of the K-side. 20. ... B × P was not dangerous, as after 21. Q × P Black has no more pawns left on the Q-side.

21. R—Kt 1

A serious error allowing Black to make a decisive combination. Correct is 21. B × B, Q × B; 22. R— B 3, Kt—B 6 ch; 23. R × Kt, Q × R; 24. B—K 7, R—B 1; 25. B × P, and although White still has some difficulties to face in the defence of his K-side, they should not prove overwhelming.

21. ...   Kt—B 6 ch
22. K—R 1   *150a*

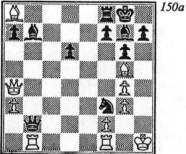

150a

22. ...   B × B!

Black gets three minor pieces for his Queen; this would normally be an advantage, but here it is absolutely decisive on account of the open position of the White King.

23. R × Q   Kt × B ch
24. K—R 2   Kt—B 6 ch
25. K—R 3   B × R

White's position is hopeless; he cannot prevent Black from building up a mating attack.

26. Q × P   B—K 5

This forestalls R—Q Kt 1 followed by R—Kt 8, exchanging the Rooks. If White could succeed in achieving this, he would have a better chance: the Black King would be more exposed to checks, and there would be less force with which to carry out the final attack.

27. P—R 4   K—Kt 2
28. R—Q 1   B—K 4
29. Q—K 7   R—B 1!

White would have liked to sacrifice the exchange by 30. R × P, but now he would find himself mated after 30. ... R—B 8.

30. P—R 5   R—B 7
31. K—Kt 2

31. R—K B 1 fails to 31. ... B—Q 6.

31. ...   Kt—Q 5 ch
32. K—B 1   B—B 6
33. R—Kt 1   Kt—B 3

White resigned.

There is no way of stopping Black from massing his pieces against K B 7 by B—Q 5 and Kt—K 4 followed by Kt × P or Kt—Q 6.

No. 55. Queen's Pawn, Old Indian Defence

V. SMYSLOV   A. FUDERER

(Hastings, 1954-55)

1. P—Q B 4	P—K 4
2. Kt—Q B 3	P—Q 3
3. Kt—B 3	P—Q B 3

Black commits himself to a formation, which, although solid, does not offer so many prospects of counterplay as those normal to the King's Indian Defence itself. More flexible is 3. ... Kt—K B 3; 4. P—Q 4, Q Kt—Q 2.

4. P—Q 4	Q—B 2
5. P—K Kt 3	Kt—B 3
6. B—Kt 2	B—K 2

It is no longer advisable to attempt to transpose into the King's Indian by 6. ... P—K Kt 3 as the Queen would be rather passively placed on Q B 2 in that case.

7. O—O	O—O
8. P—K 4	P—Q R 4

This move does not fit in with Black's set-up, which is principally aimed at maintaining the strong-point K 4 rather than surrendering it for a counter-attack on White's centre. He should play 8. ... B—Kt 5 to be followed by Q Kt—Q 2, K R—K 1 and B—B1, after which the struggle in the centre would become intense.

9. P—K R 3

A move typical of such positions: B—Kt 5 is prevented and 10. B—K 3 can no longer be answered by Kt—Kt 5.

9. ...	Kt—R 3

The Kt is not well placed on Q R 3; 9. ... Q Kt—Q 2 preserved more possibilities of organizing a satisfactory defence.

10. B—K 3	R—K 1
11. R—B 1	Kt—Q 2

And now Black starts to decentralize his other Kt with the result that White gets a strong initiative both in the centre and on the King-side. A better plan would seem to be 11. ... B—B 1 followed by P—K Kt 3 and B—Kt 2.

12. Q—K 2	B—B 1
13. K R—Q 1	*151*

White has now completed his development; he has a strong centre and all his pieces are in active positions—a marked contrast to the sorry picture made by Black's pieces.

151

13. ...	P × P

By this move Black gives up the centre and bases his hopes on a counter-attack on White's centre; however, as his pieces are badly placed compared with his opponent's this strategy has little hope of success. He should still try 13. ... P—K Kt 3 followed by B—Kt 2, though White would even so have much the better of it.

14. Kt × P   Kt (Q 2)— B 4

More natural seems 14. ... Kt (R 3)—B 4, which at least has the merit of bringing the Q Kt into play. After the text move the Q Kt remains out of play for the rest of the game with the result that White is able to carry through his K-side attack virtually a piece to the good.

15. K—R 2   B—Q 2
16. Q—B 3

White wishes to play Kt—B 5 and answer B × Kt with Q × Kt; the text move also removes the Queen from the line of the enemy Rook.

16. ...   P—R 5
17. Kt—B 5   R—K 3

An artificial manœuvre which only leaves the Rook awkwardly placed. A better defence was 17. ... B—K 3; 18. B—B 1, Q R—Q 1, after which Black's pieces are more co-ordinated for the defence of his position.

18. Q—B 4   R—B 3

The Rook is rather worse off here than on K 3. He should play 18. ... R—Q 1 followed by B—B 1 to have the Q P adequately defended before trying for counterplay by Q—R 4. The immediate 18. ... Q—R 4 loses the Q P without compensation, e.g. 18. ... Q—R 4; 19. Kt × Q P, B × Kt (or 19. ... R—B 3; 20. Kt—B 5, Q—Kt 5; 21. B—Q 4); 20. R × B, R × R; 21. Q × R, Q—Kt 5; 22. Kt—Q 1.

19. P—K Kt 4

Not only supporting the Kt and thus threatening to bring more pieces to bear on the Q P by Q—Kt 3 and B—B 4 but also exploiting the position of the Rook to prepare a K-side attack.

19. ...   R—K 1
20. Q—Kt 3   P—R 3

He is practically forced to weaken his K-side, otherwise the Rook on K B 3 is jeopardized. 20. ... Q—R 4 is once again insufficient after 21. Kt × Q P, B × Kt; 22. R × B, R × R; 23. Q × R, Q—Kt 5; 24. Kt × P!

21. R—Q 2

Before starting a direct attack on the K-side White strengthens his control over the Q-file.

21. ...   B—B 1

Slightly better than this retreat is 21. ... Q—R 4; 22. B—B 4, B × Kt; 23. Kt P × B, Q—Kt 5, but after 24. B—K 3! with the threat of 25. B—Q 4 White's advantage would be obvious. The text move leads to a similar variation a move later.

22. R (B 1)—Q 1   Q—R 4

Black is now forced to go in for this counterplay, although there is scarcely a chance of it succeeding. If 22. ... B × Kt; 23. Kt P × B, there is no answer to the threat of 24. B—Q 4.

23. B—B 4   B × Kt

The alternative 23. ... Q—Kt 5 is no better after 24. B × Q P, Q × B P (or 24. ... B × Kt; 25. Kt P × B, B × B; 26. R × B, R × R; 27. R × R); 25. P—K 5, R—Kt 3 (not 25. ... R (B 3)—K 3; 26. R—Q 4, trapping the Queen) 26. Kt—R 4.

24. Kt P × B

By capturing this way White exposes the enemy King to attack along the K Kt-file.

24. ...   Q—Kt 5
25. B × Q P

Though this maintains his advantage, there is an even stronger way of continuing—25. B—K 3, and there is no way of preventing White from winning material by B—Q 4, e.g. 25. ... Q × B P?; 26. R—Q 4 or 25. ... Kt—Q 2; 26. B—Q 4, Kt—K 4; 27. P—B 4. Black would have to give up the exchange by either 25. ... Kt—Q 2; 26. B—Q 4, Kt (R 3)—B 4; 27. P—B 4!, Q × B P; 28. B × R, Kt × B; 29. R—Q 4, Q—R 3; 30. P—K 5 or 25. ... B—K 2; 26. B—Q 4, Q × B P; 27. B × R, B × B; 28. P—B 4, and in both cases he has little to show for it.

25. ...	R × B
26. R × R	B × R
27. R × B	K—R 2

Both 27. ... Q × B P and 27. ... Q × Kt P are answered by 28. R × R P, threatening 29. P—B 6.

| 28. P—K 5 | Q × B P 152 |

Better than 28. ... Q × Kt P, which would leave the Queen out of play on the Q-side and allow 29. P—K 6 at once. But now White strengthens his attack by a neat finesse.

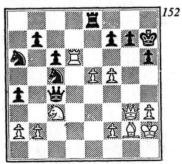

152

29. R—Kt 6	R—K Kt 1
30. R—Kt 4	Q—Q 6
31. B—K 4	Q—Q 7

After this White is able to force home his attack; a longer resistance could have been put up by 31. ... Q × Q ch; 32. K × Q, R—Q 1 (32. ... R—K 1; 33. K—B 4), but after 33. B—Kt 1 White's K-side pawn majority would be decisive.

32. P—K 6

The decisive break-through: the passed K P will prevent Black from successfully defending his K-side.

| 32. ... | P × P |
| 33. P × P ch | Kt × B |

Or 33. ... K—R 1; 34. P—K 7.

34. Kt × Kt	Q × P
35. Q—B 4	Kt—Kt 5
36. P—K 7	Kt—Q 6 *153*

Allowing a pretty finish, but there is no defence anyway: if 36. ... Kt—Q 4, then 37. Q—B 5 ch, K—R 1 (37. ... P—Kt 3; 38. P—K 8=Q); 38. Kt—Kt 5!, P—K Kt 3 (or 38. ... P × Kt; 39. R—R 4 ch, P × R; 40. Q—R 5 mate); 39. Kt—B 7 ch, K—R 2; 40. P—K 8=Q etc.

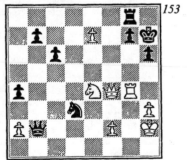

153

37. Kt—B 6 ch!   Black resigned.

If 37. ... Q × Kt, then 38. Q × Q, P × Q; 39. R × R and the pawn queens; if 37. ... P × Kt, then 38. Q—B 5 ch, K—R 1; 39. R × R ch etc., and finally if 37. ... K—R 1, then 38. Q × P ch!, P × Q; 39. R × R mate.

No. 56.   Queen's Pawn, King's Indian Defence
V. SMYSLOV   V. SCHERBAKOV
(*Twenty-second Soviet Championship, Moscow, 1955*)

1. P—Q B 4	Kt—K B 3
2. Kt—Q B 3	P—K Kt 3
3. P—Q 4	B—Kt 2
4. P—K 4	P—Q 3
5. K Kt—K 2	

The usual moves here are 5. Kt—B 3, 5. P—K Kt 3 and 5. P—B 3. The text move in conjunction with the following move is an attempt to start an attack against the enemy King. It leads to sharp play, which, however, does not seem unfavourable to Black.

5. ...	O—O
6. B—Kt 5	P—B 3

Black plans to make use of his slight lead in development to carry out a vigorous counter-attack.

7. Q—Q 2	P—Kt 4!

Offering a pawn, which it would be very dangerous for White to accept. For example: 8. P × P, P × P; 9. B × Kt, B × B; 10. Kt × P, B—R 3; 11. K Kt—B 3, Kt—B 3; 12. P—Q 5 (12. B—K 2, B × Kt; 13. Kt × B, P—Q R 3), Kt—R 4; 13. B—K 2, Q—Kt 3, and Black's play on the Q-side is more than adequate compensation for the pawn.

8. P × P	

If 8. Kt—Kt 3, then 8. ... P × P; 9. B × P, P—Q 4, and Black has an excellent position.

8. ...	P × P
9. P—Q R 3	Kt—B 3
10. P—K Kt 3	Kt—Q R 4
11. Q—B 2	P—K R 3 154

A mistake which loses a tempo and so surrenders the initiative, which his previous vigorous play had earnt him. Correct was 11. ... B—Kt 2; 12. B—Kt 2, R—B 1, and Black has a slight advantage.

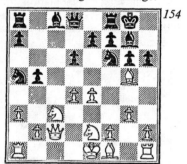
154

12. B × Kt	B × B
13. P—Q Kt 4	

Now Black cannot continue 13. ... Kt—B 5 because of 14. Kt × P, attacking the Kt once again.

13. ...	Kt—B 3
14. Kt—Q 5!	

14. Kt × P would simply hand back the initiative to Black after 14. ... P—R 3; 15. Q × Kt, B—Q 2.

14. ...	B—Q 2

Unfortunately he cannot avoid the weakening of his pawn formation because if 14. ... B × P; 15. Q × Kt, B × R; 16. Q × R, White is left a piece up.

15. Kt × B ch	P × Kt
16. B—Kt 2	P—Q R 4

This is the best chance: Black is still ahead in development, so he should try to open lines of play.

17. O—O	P × P
18. P × P	Q—Kt 3

If 18. ... Kt × Kt P, then White recovers the pawn by 19. Q—Q 2 and 20. Q × P.

| 19. Q—Q 2 | K—Kt 2 |

After this White is able to take advantage of the awkward positions of Black's pieces to smash open the enemy position. To avoid the following combination he should first exchange Rooks himself, but White would then have a fine game.

| 20. R × R | R × R | *155* |

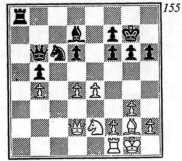

155

| 21. P—K 5! | Q P × P |

If 21. ... P—B 4, White can continue 22. P × P, e.g. 22. ... R—Q B 1; 23. R—B 1, Kt × Q P; 24. R × R, Kt × Kt ch; 25. Q × Kt, B × R; 26. Q—K 5 ch, K—R 2; 27. Q—K 7 and wins; or 22. ... R—K 1; 23. B × Kt, Q × B (23. ... B × B; 24. P—Q 5, B—Q 2; 25. Kt —B 3, Q × P; 26. Q—Q 4 ch with a clear advantage to White); 24. P—Q 5, Q × P (6); 25. Q—Q 4 ch with the same advantage.

| 22. P × P | R—Q 1 |

Other moves are worse: 22. ... B—K 3; 23. P × P ch, K—R 2 (23. ... K × P; 24. Q—B 3 ch); 24. Q—Q 6, and the pins cost Black a piece.

| 23. P × P ch | K—R 2 |
| 24. Q—K 3! | |

A subtle move which either forces Black to concede more ground by 24. ... Q—R 3; 24. Q— B 5 or brings about a favourable ending.

| 24. ... | Q × Q |
| 25. P × Q | Kt × P |

This leads to the loss of the exchange in the long run, but other moves such as 25. ... B—K 1 and 25. ... R—Q B 1 result in a hopeless ending after 26. B × Kt.

| 26. R—Q 1 |

The point of White's 24th move: to escape the pin Black must lose material. If now 26. ... Kt—R 3, then 27. B—B 6, Kt—Kt 1; 28. B × P, and all the Black pieces are completely tied up.

26. ...	Kt—B 7
27. B—B 6	B × B
28. R × R	

The rest is easy and needs no explanation.

28. ...	Kt × P
29. Kt—Q 4	B—Q 4
30. Kt × P	P—Kt 4
31. Kt—B 7	B—B 5
32. R—Q 4	B—R 7
33. R—Q R 4	B—Kt 8
34. K—B 2	Kt—B 4
35. Kt—Q 5	K—Kt 3
36. R—R 6	P—Kt 5
37. Kt—K 7 ch	K—Kt 4
38. Kt × Kt	B × Kt
39. K—K 3	K—Kt 3
40. K—B 4	B—K 3
41. K—K 5	B—B 4

The game was adjourned here, and Black resigned without resuming. He can do nothing against 42. R—R 8, B—K 3; 43. R—Kt 8 ch, K—R 4; 44. K—Q 6, B—B 5; 45. R—Kt 7, B—K 3; 46. K—K 7 and 47. R × B P.

No. 57. King's Indian Attack

V. SMYSLOV   M. BOTVINNIK

(Twenty-second Soviet Championship, Moscow, 1955)

1. Kt—K B 3	Kt—K B 3
2. P—K Kt 3	P—K Kt 3
3. B—Kt 2	B—Kt 2
4. O—O	O—O
5. P—Q 3	P—B 4
6. P—K 4	Kt—B 3
7. Q Kt—Q 2	P—Q 3
8. P—Q R 4	

White adopted a similar system in his match with Botvinnik, but here he tries a different strategic plan: he avoids the advance of the K B P and strives to transfer the centre of gravity of the struggle to the Q-side. The text move safeguards the position of the Kt on Q B 4.

8. ...	Kt—K 1
9. Kt—B 4	P—K 4

Botvinnik also used this manoeuvre in one of the match games.

10. P—B 3   P—B 4   *156*

One might take this move simply as the start of active operations on the K-side, and since Black has strengthened his hold on the central point Q 5 operations on the flank are justified from a strategic

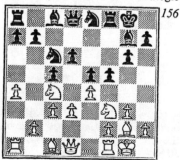

156

point of view. However, as the further course of the game shows, the World Champion is really aiming to stifle the initiative, which White is planning on the Q-side.

11. P—Q Kt 4!

White goes on with his plan. The tactical basis of the move is found in the variation 11. ... P × P; 12. P × P, Kt × P?; 13. Q— Kt 3.

11. ...   P × Kt P

The beginning of a manœuvre leading to the win of a pawn. 11. ... P—B 5 was very tempting.

Against 11. ... P—B 5 it is dangerous to play 12. P × Q B P, P—K Kt 4; 13. P × Q P, P—Kt 5; 14. K Kt—Q 2, P—B 6; 15. B—R 1. And scarcely any better is 12. P × K B P, P × B P; 13. P × P, B × P; 14. R—Kt 1, P × P; 15. Q—Kt 3, Kt—Q 5!; 16. Kt × Kt, B × Kt; 17. Kt—Kt 6 ch, K—R 1; 18. Kt × R, P—B 6. White does best to continue 12. P × Q B P, P—K Kt 4; 13. P—R 3, P—K R 4; 14. Kt—R 2, threatening both 15. Q × P and 15. P × Q P.

12. P × Kt P   P × P

This exchange weakens the position of the Kt on Q B 4, and so Black wins a tempo by attacking it. Now 12. ... P—B 5; 13. P—Kt 5, Kt—Kt 1; 14. P × P, P × P; 15. B—Kt 2 is not very attractive for Black.

13. P × P	B—K 3
14. Kt—K 3!	

A move which White had to fore-
see when he played 11. P—Q Kt 4.

| 14. ... | Kt × P |
| 15. R—Kt 1 | P—Q R 4 |

Also worth consideration was
15. ... Kt—R 3, after which 16.
R × P, Kt—B 4; 17. R—Kt 4,
P—Q R 4; 18. R—Kt 1, Kt × K P;
19. Kt × P, Kt—B 6 led to Black's
advantage (20. Kt—B 6, Q—Q 2,
and White loses the exchange).
In reply to 15. ... Kt—R 3 White
intended to start an attack by
16. P—R 4. For example: 16. ...
Kt—B 4; 17. Kt—Kt 5, Q—K 2;
18. B—Q R 3, and the pressure is
worth a pawn.

16. B—Q R 3

Winning back the pawn by force
and preserving a slight positional
advantage.

16. ...   Kt—B 2

After this weak move it is difficult for Black to defend the Q P.
He wanted to prevent White from
occupying Q 5 with a Kt, and the
continuation 16. ... B—R 3; 17.
B × Kt, B × Kt; 18. P × B, P ×
B; 19. R × P, Q—R 4; 20. R × P,
Q × P; 21. Kt—Kt 5 led to loss of
material.

Probably either 16. ... Q—K 2 or
16. ... R—B 2 would enable Black
to equalize the position.

| 17. B × Kt | P × B |
| 18. R × P | B—R 3 |

Better was 18. ... Kt—R 3; 19.
R × P, Kt—B 4; 20. R—Kt 4, R ×
P; 21. R × R, B—Kt 6.

19. R—Kt 6!

Now Black must lose a pawn.
Any attempt to avoid loss of
material leads to a speedy catas-
trophe.

19. ...	B × Kt
20. P × B	B—B 5
21. R × Q P	Q—K 1
22. R--K 1	R—B 2

22. ... R × P does not work on
account of 23. R—Q 7, attacking
two pieces. Also bad for Black is
22. ... Q × P; 23. Q × Q, R × Q;
24. Kt × P.

23. Kt—Kt 5   R—K 2   *157*

157

24. B—B 1!

The decisive move: White indirectly defends the Q R P (24. ...
Q × P; 25. R—Q 8 ch, K—Kt 2;
26. R × R, Q × R; 27. B × B or
25. ... R—K 1; 26. R × R, R × R;
27. B × B ch, Q × B; 28. Q—Q 7)
and gains control of both the
K B-file and the diagonal Q R 2—
K Kt 8.

| 24. ... | B × B |
| 25. R × B | Q × P |

Otherwise 26. Q—Kt 3 ch
follows.

| 26. R—Q 8 ch | R—K 1 |

Or 26. ... K—Kt 2; 27. Q—Q 6.

27. Q—B 3!	Q—B 5
28. R—Q 7	Black
	resigned.

If 28. ... R—K B 1, White intended to continue 29. Kt—B 7 with
the threats of 30. Kt—R 6 ch and
30. Q—B 6.

No. 58. Queen's Pawn, Nimzovitch Defence
V. SMYSLOV   A. BISGUIER
(Match, U.S.S.R.–U.S.A., Moscow, 1955)

1. P—Q 4	Kt—K B 3
2. P—Q B 4	P—K 3
3. Kt—Q B 3	B—Kt 5
4. P—K 3	O—O
5. B—Q 3	P—Q 4
6. Kt—B 3	P—Q Kt 3

An excellent system of development. Recently the variation 6. ... P—B 4; 7. O—O, Kt—B 3 has enjoyed great popularity and been subjected to most careful study. The text move is also not new, but it has the advantage that it is met less often in tournament practice.

7. O—O	B—Kt 2
8. P × P	P × P

If 8. ... Kt × P, then 9. Q—B 2, P—K R 3; 10. P—K 4 is good.

9. B—Q 2	Q Kt—Q 2
10. R—B 1	P—Q R 3
11. Kt—K 5	B—Q 3
12. P—B 4	

Under the cover of a strong outpost in the centre White plans an attack on the K-side; Black seeks counterplay on the Q-side.

12. ...	P—B 4
13. Q—B 3	P—Q Kt 4

Of course, not 13. ... P—B 5 on account of 14. B × P.

14. Q—R 3	P—Kt 3 *158*

158

15. Kt × Kt	

A concrete solution to the problem. White is willing to exchange his strong Kt for the sake of a direct attack on his opponent's weakened King position. If 15. ... Q × Kt, one possibility is 16. P × P, Q × Q; 17. P × Q, B × Q B P; 18. Kt × Kt P, P × Kt; 19. R × B, R × P; 20. B—B 3, Kt—K 5; 21. B × Kt, P × B; 22. R—B 2 with the better ending. The alternative is (15. ... Q × Kt) 16. P—B 5, P—B 5; 17. B—Kt 1, maintaining the tension.

15. ...	Kt × Kt
16. P—B 5	B—K 2

16. ... P—B 5 is impossible on account of 17. P × P, R P × P; 18. B × Kt P!, P × B; 19. Q—K 6 ch, K—Kt 2; 20. Q × B etc.

17. B P × P	R P × P
18. P × P	Kt × P
19. B—Kt 1	Kt—Q 2?

In a sharp position every tempo is valuable. Correct was 19. ... P—Kt 5!; 20. Kt—K 2, Kt—K 5; 21. B—K 1, R—B 1; 22. R—Q 1, Q—Kt 3; 23. Kt—Q 4 with chances for both sides.

20. Kt—K 2	P—Kt 5
21. Kt—Q 4	Kt—B 3 *159*

If 21. ... Kt—K 4, then 22. Kt—K 6!, P × Kt; 23. Q × P ch etc.

Black comes back to the right idea—transfer of the Kt to K 5—but now he is two tempi behind. This fact means that White has a decisive advantage.

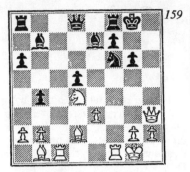

159

22. Kt—B 5!

The beginning of a forced manœuvre, based on the threat of 23. Kt × B ch, Q × Kt; 24. Q— R 4. The Kt cannot be taken on account of 23. R × P, Kt—K 5; 24. B × Kt, P × B; 25. Q—Kt 4 ch.

22. ...	Kt—K 5
23. B × Kt	P × B
24. Q—Kt 3!	

White now threatens 25. Kt × B ch, Q × Kt; 26. R—B 7. Since 24. ... Q × B; 25. Kt × B ch, K—Kt 2; 26. R—B 7 leads to a quick debacle, Black's next move is virtually forced.

| 24. ... | R—B 1 |
| 25. Q R—Q 1! | Q—K 1 |

25. ... Q—B 2 is unplayable because of 26. Q × Q, R × Q; 27. Kt × B ch, R × Kt; 28. B × P.

| 26. Kt—Q 6 | B × Kt |
| 27. Q × B | |

Now White's idea becomes clear: Black loses a pawn, since 27. ... P —R 4 is answered by 28. Q—Kt 6. However, the real trouble is not so much the loss of the pawn as the fact that White's Bishop gets on to the weakened long diagonal.

27. ...	P—Kt 6
28. P × P	Q—K 3
29. Q—Kt 4	B—B 3
30. B—B 3	*160*

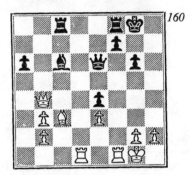

160

The Bishop has taken up an excellent attacking position, while Black's Bishop is blocked in by its own K P. The presence on the board of Bishops of opposite colours is not a saving factor here but rather the reason for White's superiority.

30. ...	Q R—Q 1
31. R × R	R × R
32. Q—Kt 6	Q—B 1
33. P—R 3	R—Q 4
34. Q—Kt 4	

Intending to answer 34. ... Q— Kt 2 with 35. Q—R 3.

34. ...	Q—K 1
35. B—Q 4	B—Kt 4
36. R—B 1	R—Q 1
37. Q—B 5	B—Q 2
38. Q—K Kt 5	Black resigned.

If 38. ... R—B 1, then 39. R— B 1, followed by either 40. Q—R 6 or 40. Q—B 6 is decisive.

No. 59. Reti Opening
V. SMYSLOV   P. TRIFUNOVIC
(*Zagreb, 1955*)

1. P—Q B 4	Kt—K B 3
2. Kt—Q B 3	P—K 3
3. Kt—B 3	P—Q 4
4. P—K 3	B—K 2
5. P—Q Kt 3	O—O
6. B—Kt 2	P—B 4
7. P × P	Kt × P

This variation has often been met in tournament practice. It is well known that, if 7. ... P × P; 8. P—Q 4, Black has trouble with the defence of his Q P.

8. Kt × Kt	Q × Kt
9. B—B 4	Q—Q 1
10. Kt K 5	Kt—Q 2
11. O—O	

More consistent was 11. P—B 4, Kt × Kt; 12. P × Kt, opening the K B-file for an attack. The text move allows Black to simplify the game.

11. ...	Kt × Kt
12. B × Kt	B—B 3
13. P—Q 4	

White has a minimal positional advantage. If 13. ... B × B; 14. P × B, White gets an outpost for his heavy pieces at Q 6. For example: 14. ... Q—B 2; 15. Q—Q 6, Q × Q; 16. P × Q, R—Q 1; 17. K R—Q 1, B—Q 2; 18. P—K 4, and the ending is better for White.

13. ...	P × P
14. P × P	B—Q 2
15. Q—R 5	B—B 3
16. Q R—Q 1	B—K 5

The transfer of the Bishop to the K-side loses time. Equal chances were offered by 16. ... B × B; 17. P × B, Q—R 4, followed by exchanging Rooks on the Q-file.

17. K R—K 1	B—B 7
18. R—Q 2	B—Kt 3
19. Q—K 2	B—K 2

No better is 19. ... B × B; 20. Q × B, Q—Kt 3; 21. P—K R 4, and White has a fine game.

20. R (Q 2)—Q 1	Q—Kt 3

Preference should have been given to 20. ... B—Kt 5; 21. R—K B 1, Q—K 2, parrying the threat of the break 22. P—Q 5 by 22. ... P × P; 23. R × P, K—R 1 and then P—B 3.

21. P—Q 5!	P × P
22. R × P	B—B 3
23. R—Q 6	Q—B 4 *161*

161

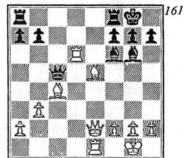

24. R × B!

A combinational blow. Now the game enters a sharper phase.

24. ...	P × R
25. B × P	Q—K R 4

It is not easy to demonstrate the best way of defending against the threats on the long diagonal. If, for example, 25. ... Q—B 3, then 26. Q—Kt 2, K R—K 1; 27. R—Q B 1, P—Kt 4; 28. B—R 8, K—B 1; 29. B—Kt 7 ch, K—Kt 1; 30. B—R 6.

26. Q—K 3   P—K R 3
27. P—K R 3   Q—K B 4
28. B—B 3   K—R 2
29. P—K Kt 4!

Beginning a pawn storm against the enemy King. The reply is forced, for 29. ... Q—B 7 is met by 30. B—Q 2.

29. ...   Q—K Kt 4
30. P—B 4   Q—R 5 *162*

162

31. K—Kt 2!

In this way White gives extra force to the threat of 32. P—B 5, B × P; 33. Q—K 5! The immediate 31. P—B 5 would be rash on account of 31. ... Q R—K 1; 32. P × B ch, P × P; 33. B—K 5, R × B; 34. Q × R, Q—B 7 ch; 35. K—R 1, Q—B 6 ch with perpetual check.

31. ...   R—K Kt 1

Bad was 31. ... Q R—K 1; 32. Q × R, R × Q; 33. R × R, P—B 3; 34. R—K 7 ch, K—R 1; 35. P—Kt 5 or 35. B—K 1.

32. Q—K 7   Q × Q
33. R × Q   Q R—K 1
34. R × R   R × R
35. P—B 5

The logical completion of the attack: the Black Bishop is caught. Now the chess prose begins—the realization (true, in this case it is not difficult) of an advantage gained. The further course of the game needs no explanation.

35. ...   P—R 3
36. K—B 3   R—Q B 1
37. B—Q 4   P—Kt 4
38. B—Q 3   R—B 8
39. P × B ch   P × P
40. P—K R 4   R—Q 8
41. K—K 2   R—K R 8
42. P—R 5   R—R 7 ch
43. B—B 2   K—Kt 2
44. P × P   P—K R 4
45. P × P   R × P
46. B—Q 4 ch   K—Kt 1
47. B—K 4   P—R 4
48. K—B 3   Black
                    resigned.

No. 60.   Ruy Lopez

V. SMYSLOV   A. DUCKSTEIN

(Zagreb, 1955)

1. P—K 4   P—K 4
2. Kt—K B 3   Kt—Q B 3
3. B—Kt 5   Kt—B 3
4. O—O   B—B 4
5. P—Q 3

White refrains from the theoretical continuation 5. Kt × P, preferring to develop quietly.

This game was played in the penultimate round, and I did not wish to risk my position in the tournament.

5. ...	P—Q 3
6. Kt—B 3	O—O
7. B—Kt 5	

The game has transposed into a line of the Four Knight's with the small difference that Black has his Bishop on Q B 4.

7. ...	P—K R 3
8. B—K R 4	B—K Kt 5
9. B × Q Kt	P × B
10. P—K R 3	B × Kt

A sensible decision, as after 10. ... B—K 3 White could continue 11. P—Q 4, B—Q Kt 5; 12. Q—Q 3 with the better position. In the event of 10. ... B—R 4; 11. P—K Kt 4, B—K Kt 3; 12. Q—K 2 the Bishop would be out of play for a long time.

11. Q × B	P—Kt 4
12. B—Kt 3	Kt—R 2
13. Kt—R 4	B—Kt 3
14. Kt × B	R P × Kt *163*

163

15. P—Q 4!

At the cost of a pawn White makes a sharp attempt to widen the sphere of action of his Bishop. If Black wished to be cautious he would now play 15. ... P—B 3, however he takes up the challenge.

| 15. ... | P × P |
| 16. Q—Q 3 | P—K B 4 |

Having accepted the sacrifice it was worth thinking about 16. ... P—Q B 4. After 16. ... P—Q B 4; 17. P—K B 4, R—K 1; 18. Q R—K 1, there would be a complicated position giving chances to both sides (18. ... R × R P would be dangerous on account of 19. P × P Kt × P; 20. P—R 4, Kt—K 3; 21. P—K 5 with a strong attack).

17. P × P	R—R 4
18. Q × P	Q—Q 2
19. Q—B 4 ch	K—Kt 2
20. P—Kt 4	Q R × B P
	164

164

21. P—Q R 4!   •

The play has resulted in a clear advantage for White. He creates a passed pawn on the Q R-file to deflect Black's pieces to the Q-side and then takes advantage of the open position of the Black King. Play on both flanks—that is the typical strategy in positions of this nature.

21. ...	Kt—B 3
22. P—R 5	P × P
23. P × P	R—B 4
24. Q—Q R 4	R—Q R 1
25. P—R 6	Q—B 4
26. K R—K 1	K—B 1

If 26. ... Kt—Q 4, then 27. Q— Q 4 ch, Q—B 3; 28. B—K 5! or 27. ... K—Kt 1; 28. P—Q B 4 etc.

27. P—Q B 4!

Depriving the Rook of Q Kt 5. White now threatens to transfer his

Queen to Q Kt 7, against which Black has no satisfactory defence.

27. ...	Kt—Q 2
28. Q—Kt 4	Kt—Kt 3
29. B × P ch	P × B
30. Q × Kt	Black resigned.

No. 61.　Queen's Pawn, Nimzovitch Defence

E. GELLER　　V. SMYSLOV

(Candidates' Tournament, Amsterdam, 1956)

1. P—Q 4	Kt—K B 3
2. P—Q B 4	P—K 3
3. Kt—Q B 3	B—Kt 5
4. P—Q R 3	

Grandmaster Geller's favourite continuation. After the exchange on Q B 3 White gets the two Bishops and a strong pawn centre. However, the doubled pawns on the Q B-file provide Black with sufficient counterplay on the Q-side.

4. ...	B × Kt ch
5. P × B	P—B 4
6. P—K 3	P—Q Kt 3
7.' Kt—K 2	

The usual line here is 7. B—Q 3, B—Kt 2; 8. P—B 3. By a small transposition of moves White wishes to avoid the advance of the K B P, which blocks the Queen's path to an attacking position.

7. ...	Kt—B 3
8. Kt—Kt 3	O—O
9. B—Q 3	B—R 3
10. P—K 4	Kt—K 1

To take the pawn by 10. ... P × P and 11. ... Kt × Q P was dangerous on account of 12. P—K 5! with excellent attacking prospects for White.

11. B—K 3	Kt—R 4
12. Q—K 2	R—B 1
13. P—Q 5	

A critical decision. White's centre becomes less mobile and more readily exposed to attack. 13. R—Q B 1 was preferable.

| 13. ... | Q—R 5! |

A powerful reply: the Queen hinders the activity of the White pieces on the K-side and indirectly attacks the Q B P. Bad was 13. ... Kt—Q 3 because of 14. P—K 5, Kt (Q 3) × P; 15. Q—R 5, P—Kt 3; 16. Q—R 6 with the threat of 17. Kt —R 5.

14. O—O　　　　　　　*165*

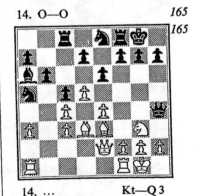

165

| 14. ... | Kt—Q 3 |

The final link in the plan to surround the Q B P. Black has avoided P—Q 3, leaving the square free for his Kt.

15. Q R—Q 1   P—B 4

Of course, the attacked pawn could be taken. But Black prefers to limit the activity of the White Bishops. The weak pawns on the Q-side will always be a source of trouble for White.

16. Q P × P   Q P × P

16. ... P—B 5 was risky on account of 17. P × P, R (Q B 1)— Q 1; 18. P—K 5.

17. P × P   P × P
18. Q—B 3

Threatening 19. Q—Q 5 ch. White does everything possible to give himself chances.

18. ...   B—Kt 2
19. Q—B 4   Q—B 3

In the event of 19. ... Q × Q; 20. B × Q, Kt—K 5; 21. P—B 3, Kt × Kt; 22. P × Kt, B—R 3; 23. K R—K 1 the White Rooks threaten to invade the seventh rank. Therefore Black declines to exchange Queens.

20. B—Kt 1   Kt—K 5
21. R—Q 7

After 21. Kt × Kt, P × Kt; 22. Q × Q, R × Q; 23. R—Q 7, R— K B 2; 24. K R—Q 1, B—B 3 the ending is favourable for Black. The text move attests to a desire to complicate the issue.

21. ...   Q—B 3
22. R × B

If 22. R—K 7, then 22. ... Kt × P (B 6); 23. P—B 3, Kt × B; 24. Kt— R 5, R—K B 2 or 24. Kt × P, Q— Kt 3 with advantage to Black.

22. ...   Q × R
23. Kt × P

Against 23. Kt × Kt Black could continue 23. ... P × Kt; 24. B × K P, R × Q; 25. B × Q, Kt × B; 26. B × R, R—Q 1; 27. R— K 1, Kt—R 4, and he has the better ending.

23. ...   Q R—K 1

Not 23. ... Kt × P (B 6) on account of 24. Q—R 4!, threatening Kt—K 7 ch.

24. Q—Kt 4   K—R 1
25. Kt—Kt 3   Kt × Kt
26. R P × Kt   *166*

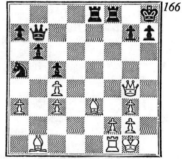
166

26. ...   Q—K B 2

Combining defence of the King and attack on the pawn weaknesses. For the exchange White has a pawn as well as the two Bishops. This makes it difficult for Black to realize the advantage he has obtained.

27. Q—R 4   P—K R 3
28. B—Q 3   Q—B 3
29. Q—R 5   R—Q 1

Now the Bishop must abandon the dangerous diagonal Q Kt 1— K R 7, otherwise the Q B P is lost.

30. B—K 2   Q—B 4
31. Q—R 4   Q—B 3
32. Q—R 5   Kt—B 3

The Kt comes over to the other wing to take a more active part in the struggle.

33. P—Kt 4

White's only chance is to open up the enemy King position.

33. ...	Q—B 2
34. Q—R 4	Kt—K 2
35. Q—R 3	Kt—Kt 3
36. Q—R 2	

A little better was 36. P—Kt 3, although even then after 36. ... K —Kt 1; 37. P—Kt 5, P × P; 38. B × Kt P, Q R—K 1; 39. B—Q 3, R—K 8!; 40. P—B 4, K R—K 1 and then Kt—B 1 Black preserved his advantage.

36. ...	Kt—B 5
37. B—B 3	Q × P
38. P—Kt 5	R—Q 3
39. R—B 1	R—Kt 3
40. P × P	R × P
41. Q—Kt 3	

The game was adjourned in this position. Black sealed his move. *167*

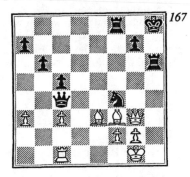

167

41. ...   Q—K 5!

An effective manœuvre based upon the threat of Q—R 2. If 42. B × Q, then there follows 42. ... Kt—K 7 ch; 43. K—B 1, Kt × Q ch; 44. K—K 1, R—R 8 ch; 45— K—Q 2, Kt × B ch. Therefore White is forced to simplify, getting a lost ending.

42. Q × Kt	Q × Q
43. B × Q	R × B
44. R—K 1	R—Q R 5

Quieter is 44. ... R (R 3)—K B 3, which does not allow any counter-chances. But Black presumed that White's initiative was not danger-ous.

45. R—K 8 ch	K—R 2
46. B—K 4 ch	P—Kt 3
47. P—Kt 4	R × P
48. R—K 6	R × P
49. K—Kt 2	

If 49. P—Kt 5, then 49. ... R— R 5; 50. B × P ch, K—Kt 2; 51. B—B 5, R—K B 5. White tries to strengthen the force of P—Kt 5.

49. ...	P—Kt 4
50. P—B 3	P—Kt 5
51. P—Kt 5	R—R 5
52. B × P ch	K—Kt 2
53. K—Kt 3	R—Q 5
54. B—K 8	

Or 54. B—R 5, R—Q 2, prevent-ing the perpetual check.

| 54. ... | P—Kt 6 |
| 55. P—Kt 6 | R—Q 1 |

White lost on time.

If 56. R—K 7 ch, then 56. ... K— B 3; 57. P—Kt 7, R × B!

No. 62. Sicilian Defence

V. SMYSLOV   O. PANNO

(Candidates' Tournament, Amsterdam, 1956)

1. P—K 4	P—Q B 4
2. Kt—K B 3	P—Q 3
3. P—Q 4	P × P
4. Kt × P	Kt—K B 3
5. Kt—Q B 3	P—Q R 3

Argentinian players use this popular system with especial regularity.

6. B—K 2

White chooses the positional treatment. Sharp play results from 6. B—K Kt 5, P—K 3; 7. P—B 4, which was tested out in the Interzonal Tournament at Gothenburg, 1955.

6. ...	P—K 4
7. Kt—Kt 3	B—K 2
8. O—O	O—O
9. B—K 3	B—K 3

9. ... Q—B 2 has been more often played recently; the position of the Q B is not decided for the moment, and so the possibility of developing it on Q Kt 2 is preserved.

10. P—B 4   P × P

This exchange is practically forced. After 10. ... Q—B 2; 11. P—B 5, B—B 5; 12. P—Q R 4 Black's position is clearly inferior because of the weakness of his Q 4 square.

11. B × B P	Kt—B 3
12. K—R 1	Q—Kt 3
13. Q—Q 2	Q R—B 1
14. B—K 3	Q—B 2
15. Kt—Q 4	Kt × Kt

Black exchanges the Kts as he does not wish to allow 16. Kt—B 5.

16. B × Kt	Kt—Q 2
17. Q R—Q 1	Kt—K 4
18. Q—K 3	P—Q Kt 4
	168

Panno advances his Q-side pawns without sufficient justification. He should continue 18. ... K R—K 1 followed by 19. ... B—B 1. Black would then have a solid position.

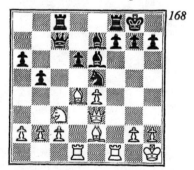

168

19. Q—Kt 3   P—Kt 5

Continuing with an incorrect plan. But now even after 19. ... P—Kt 3; 20. P—Q R 4!, P—Kt 5; 21. Kt—Q 5, B × Kt; 22. P × B White would stand better.

20. Kt—Q 5	B × Kt
21. P × B	P—Kt 3

21. ... Q × P would be answered by 22. B × P, R—R 1; 23. B—Q 3, Q—B 2; 24. B—Kt 1 and 21. ... P —Q R 4 by 22. P—B 3, P × P; 23. B × P with advantage to White in both cases.

22. B × P

Also worth consideration was 22. P—B 3. The text move leads to more lively play.

22. ...	R—R 1
23. B—Kt 5	R—R 4

Best. 23. R × P was not good on account of 24. Q—Kt 3, R—R 4; 25. Q × P, R—Kt 1; 26. P—B 4, and White has an extra pawn.

24. B—B 6	Kt × B
25. P × Kt	Q × P *169*

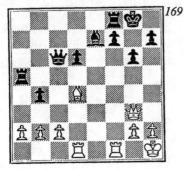

169

26. P—B 3

A series of forced moves has led to a position, in which White has good attacking prospects on the K-side.

26. ...	R—K Kt 4

After this move Black quickly gets into a position where he cannot fight against White's two connected passed pawns on the Q-side. He ought to go in for 26. ... P × P; 27. B × P, R × P; then White could either transpose into the better ending by 28. Q—K 3, B—Q 1; 29. Q—Q 4, P—B 3; 30. Q × Q P or play for an attack by 28. K R—K 1, R—R 2; 29. Q—B 2, Q—Q 2; 30. Q—Q 4, P—B 3; 31. Q—Q 5 ch.

27. Q—B 2	Q—R 3
28. Q—K 3	Q—Kt 2
29. R—B 2	R—Kt 5
30. P × P	Q × P
31. B—B 3	Q—R 5

No better is 31. ... Q—K 5; 32. Q—R 6, P—B 3; 33. R—K 1, Q—Kt 2; 34. Q—K 3, R—B 2; 35. Q—K 6.

32. P—Q Kt 3	Q—B 3 *170*

The passive 32. ... Q—Q 2 is cold comfort.

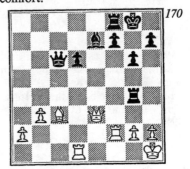

170

33. Q × B

The simplest solution to the problem. White wins a pawn, and in the heavy piece ending the Q R and Q Kt pawns guarantee victory.

33. ...	Q × B
34. Q × P	P—R 4
35. P—K R 3	R—Kt 6
36. K—R 2	P—R 5

This eases White's task since the R P becomes weak. 36. ... R—K 6 offered more resistance.

37. Q—B 4	P—Kt 4
38. Q—B 5	Q—B 2
39. K—R 1	

Avoiding the trap 39. R—Q 7?, R × R P ch.

39. ...	Q—B 1
40. R—Q 7	Q—B 8 ch
41. K—R 2	Black resigned.

No. 63. Ruy Lopez

V. SMYSLOV   M. FILIP

(Candidates' Tournament, Amsterdam, 1956)

1. P—K 4	P—K 4
2. Kt—K B 3	Kt—Q B 3
3. B—Kt 5	P—Q R 3
4. B—R 4	Kt—B 3
5. O—O	B—K 2
6. R—K 1	P—Q Kt 4
7. B—Kt 3	P—Q 3
8. P—B 3	O—O
9. P—K R 3	Kt—Q R 4
10. B—B 2	P—B 4
11. P—Q 4	Q—B 2
12. Q Kt—Q 2	

This position has been met innumerable times in tournament practice and has undergone detailed investigation, but Black's system of defence still preserves its essence and vitality.

12. ...	K—R 1	*171*

The search for new methods continues. But this move is not new: Tchigorin used it in a game against Duras (Nuremberg, 1906), which went on 13. Kt—B 1, Kt—Kt 1; 14. Kt—K 3, B—K 3; 15. Kt—B 5, B—B 3.

171

13. P—Q Kt 4

A sharp attempt to liven up the game. It is entirely appropriate to open the Q B-file here, as after 13. ... P × Kt P; 14. B P × P Black cannot place a Rook on the Q B-file but must retreat the Kt.

13. ...	P × Kt P
14. B P × P	Kt—B 3
15. P—R 3	P × P

Otherwise White gets an advantage by P—Q 5. After the exchange Black is left with a weak Q P, but he gets good play for his pieces on the Q-side.

16. B—Kt 2	Kt—Q 2
17. Kt × P	B—B 3
18. Kt (Q 2)—Kt 3	Kt—Kt 3
19. Q—Q 3	

By threatening P—K 5 White transfers the Queen to an attacking position.

19. ...	Kt—K 4
20. Q—Kt 3	Kt (Kt 3)—B 5

The point of playing the Queen to K Kt 3 is found in the variation 20. ... Kt—R 5; 21. B—B 3, Kt—B 3; 22. B—K 3, and if 22. ... Kt × Kt; 23. Kt × Kt, B × Kt; 24. B × B, the Bishop on Q B 2 cannot be taken because of the threat of mate.

21. B—B 3	B—Q 2
22. Kt—K 2	

Intending to play P—B 4 and also planning to transfer the Kt to Q 5 via K B 4.

22. ...	Q—Q 1
23. Kt—B 4	B—R 5
24. Q—R 2	

The only square for the Queen. The Black pieces are now actively placed, but there is a weakness in his pawn formation at Q 3. This gives the struggle a double-edged character.

| 24. ... | R—B 1 |
| 25. Kt—Q 4 | |

White wards off the threat of 25. ... Kt × P by defending the Bishop on Q B 2. 25. Kt—Q 5 was not good on account of 25. ... Kt—Q Kt 3.

25. ...	Kt—Q Kt 3
26. Kt (B 4)—K 2	B—K B 3
27. K R—Q 1	Kt—R 5
28. B × Kt	P × B
29. Q—Kt 3	B—R 5 172

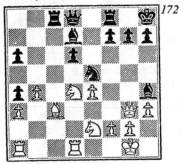

172

Up to this moment Black has played consistently, but here 29. R—K 1 seems stronger.

30. Q—K 3	B—K Kt 4
31. P—B 4	Kt—B 5
32. Q—B 3	B—K B 3
33. Kt—K Kt 3	P—Kt 3

Black must weaken his King position as he cannot allow Kt—R 5. As a result of his unsuccessful Bishop manœuvre his position has grown difficult. His

initiative has been exhausted while the pawn weaknesses remain. Now White can increase the pressure on the Q P without hindrance.

34. Kt (Q 4)—K 2	B—B 3
35. Q R—B 1	B—Q Kt 2
36. B—Q 4	K—Kt 1
37. K—R 2	R—K 1
38. B × B	Q × B
39. R—Q 4	Kt—Kt 3
40. R × R	Kt × R
41. Q—Q 3	

By doubling his heavy pieces on the Q-file White cuts down the mobility of the Black Kt, which is playing a modest defensive role on Q B 1. Black seeks counterchances in an attack on White's centre pawns.

| 41. ... | P—K R 4   *173* |

173

The game was adjourned in this position, and White sealed his 42nd move. Evidently 42. P—Kt 5 was the strongest move since it leads to the win of the Q R P. The sealed move preserves the positional advantage, but does not force events.

42. Kt—B 1	Q—K 2
43. Kt—B 3	Q—B 3
44. Q—Q 2	P—R 5

This lessens Black's chances of defence since now he has lost control of K Kt 5; a White Kt quickly aims for this square. In addition, the K R P becomes weak.

45. K—Kt 1	R—K 3
46. Kt—R 2	Q—K 2
47. P—B 5	P × P
48. P × P	R—K 6

49. Kt—B 1	Black resigned.

There is no defence: if 49. ... R —K 4 (49. ... R—K 8; 50. K—B 2), then 50. Q—R 6 is decisive.

No. 64. Ruy Lopez

B. IVKOV   V. SMYSLOV

(Match, Yugoslavia—U.S.S.R., Belgrade, 1956)

1. P—K 4	P—K 4
2. Kt—K B 3	Kt—Q B 3
3. B—Kt 5	P—Q R 3
4. B—R 4	P—Q 3
5. B × Kt ch	

This exchange, which guarantees White a rapid development, is recommended by many opening experts. However, I prefer 5. P— B 3 and 6. P—Q 4, retaining the white-squared Bishop.

5. ...	P × B
6. P—Q 4	P—B 3

The logical reply. Black's pawn configuration in the centre is very solid, and it is hardly possible to take advantage of his slight lack of piece development without the white-squared Bishop. The alternative 6. ... P × P; 7. Kt × P, P—Q B 4 gives White the better chances.

7. B—K 3	Kt—K 2
8. Kt—B 3	Kt—Kt 3
9. Q—Q 2	B—K 2
10. O—O—O	B—K 3
11. P—K R 4	P—K R 4
12. P × P	

In this way White establishes control over K Kt 5, aiming for the initiative on the K-side.

As this game shows, this plan does not bring White any success.

Black's threats on the Q Kt-file are the more real.

12. P—Q 5 also was not dangerous for Black on account of 12. ... P × P; 13. Kt × P, Q—Kt 1; 14. P—B 4, Q—Kt 2 with sufficient counterplay.

12. ...	B P × P
13. Kt—K Kt 5	

Tempting was 13. B—Kt 5 with the idea of exchanging the black-squared Bishops and so guaranteeing K Kt 5 for the Kt. However, 13. B—Kt 5 could be answered by 13. ... B—B 3! and if 14. B × B, then 14. ... P × B.

13. ...	B × Kt
14. B × B	174

Or 14. P × B, Q—Kt 1; 15. P— B 3, P—R 5, preventing the advance of the white pawns (P— K Kt 3 and P—K B 4).

174

14. ...   Q—Kt 1!

Black's counter-attack is based on the transfer of the Queen to the Q Kt-file. The position of the White King on the Q-side is more vulnerable than that of the Black King in the centre; Black threatens to start active play, while it is not easy for White to think of a reasonable plan of campaign. 15. P—K Kt 3 is bad because of 15. ... B—Kt 5 and 16. ... B—B 6, blockading the White pawns; but he should have considered 15. P—B 4, P × P; 16. B × P, O—O; 17. B—Kt 3.

In the game Ivkov did not succeed in finding an appropriate piece grouping. As a result White got a lost position without making any obvious mistakes.

15. P—Q Kt 3	Q—Kt 5
16. P—B 3	P—R 4
17. Kt—R 4	P—B 4
18. K—Kt 2	O—O
19. Q × Q	

White exchanges Queens to lessen Black's attacking chances. However, the ending does not bring the desired relief.

19. ...	R P × Q
20. P—B 3	K R—Kt 1
21. P × P	R × P
22. Kt—B 3	P—B 5
23. Kt—Q 5	*175*

175

23. ...   R—Kt 2!

Now there is no satisfactory defence against the threat of P—B 3. If 24. R—Q B 1, then 24. ... P—B 3; 25. Kt—K 3, P—Q 4; 26. P × P, P × Q P; 27. K R—Q 1, R—Kt 4 followed by doubling Rooks on the Q Kt or Q R files.

White decides to give up a pawn and seek salvation in an ending with Bishops of opposite colours.

24. Kt—K 7 ch	Kt × Kt
25. B × Kt	P—B 6 ch!

Stronger than 25. ... P × P; 26. P—R 3, and White can still organize a defence.

Now if 26. K—Kt 1, then 26. ... P—B 7 ch, so White has to take the pawn and allow the Black Rook to invade the seventh rank.

26. K × P	R × P
27. R—Q Kt 1	R × P
28. K R—K B 1	R—Q R 7
29. P—B 4	

White had to undertake something because of the threat of R—R 6. But now unpleasantness comes from the other side.

29. ...	B—R 6!
30. R—Q R 1	R—K 7
31. R (B 1)—K 1	R × R
32. R × R	P × P
33. B—Kt 5	P—B 6
34. B—K 3	K—B 2
35. R—Q R 1	P—B 4

The big material advantage ensures Black an easy victory. The remaining moves were:

36. R—R 6	B—K 3
37. R—R 3	R—Kt 5
38. P—K 5	R—K 5
39. K—Q 2	R × K P
40. R—R 7 ch	K—Kt 3
41. R—K 7	K—B 3

White resigned.

No. 65. Queen's Pawn, Queen's Indian Defence
V. UHLMAN   V. SMYSLOV
(Alekhine Memorial Tournament, Moscow, 1956)

1. P—Q 4	Kt—K B 3
2. P—Q B 4	P—K 3
3. Kt—K B 3	P—Q Kt 3
4. P—K Kt 3	B—R 3

One of Nimzovitch's original ideas which leads to interesting and little investigated play. The usual development of the Bishop at Q Kt 2 is undoubtedly more solid, but also more studied.

5. P—Kt 3

A quiet positional reply. The alternative here is 5. Q—R 4 with a possible continuation 5. ... B—K 2; 6. B—Kt 2, O—O; 7. O—O, P—B 3; 8. Kt—B 3, P—Q 4; 9. Kt—K 5, Q—K 1!, and Black threatens P—Q Kt 4.

5. ...   P—Q 4
6. B—K Kt 2   B—Kt 5 ch

The Q B P is indirectly defended, for on 6. ... P × P there would follow 7. Kt—K 5, B—Kt 5 ch; 8. B—Q 2 etc.

7. K Kt—Q 2   *176*

A pretentious manœuvre. More natural seemed 7. B—Q 2, to which Black proposed to reply 7. ... B—K 2.

176

7. ...   P—B 4!

Only by energetic measures is it possible to cast doubt on White's last move, which deflects the Kt from the fight for the centre squares. Otherwise White would succeed in driving off the Bishop and then playing P—K 4.

8. Q P × P	K B × P
9. B—Kt 2	O—O
10. O—O	Kt—B 3
11. Kt—Q B 3	R—B 1
12. P × P?	

A careless exchange. The isolation of the centre pawn does not play an important role here, while the opening of the position increases the activity of Black's pieces. Preference should have been given to 12. Kt—R 4 and only after 12. ... B—Kt 5; 13. P × P.

12. ...   P × P
13. Kt—R 4   Kt—Q 5!

A strong attacking move. Now 14. R—K 1 is impossible on account of 14. ... Kt—B 7; 15. Q × Kt, B × P ch.

14. Kt—Q B 3   Q—K 2

14. ... B—Kt 5 did not achieve its aims because of 15. Kt (Q 2)—Kt 1! By the text move Black prepared an interesting combination against White's next move.

15. R—K 1   *177*

Natural, but not good. It is true that White's position is already very difficult.

177

15. ...   Kt—B 7!

An effective manœuvre. If 16. Q
× Kt, there is the sacrifice 16. ...
B × P ch!; 17. K × B (or 17. K—
R 1, B × R; 18. R × B, P—Q 5
etc.), Kt—Kt 5 ch with a decisive

attack. For example: 18. K—Kt 1,
Q—K 6 ch; 19. K—R 1, Kt—B 7
ch; 20. K—Kt 1, Kt—R 6 ch;
21. K—R 1, Q—Kt 8 ch; 22. R ×
Q, Kt—B 7 mate or 18. K—B 3,
Q—K 6 ch; 19. K × Kt, R—B 5
ch; 20. P × R, B—B 1 ch, and
mate is unavoidable.

16. R—K B 1

White is unwilling to allow
combinational beauty, preferring
to give up the exchange at once.
The rest is just prosaic.

16. ...   Kt × R
17. Q × Kt   K R—Q 1
18. B—B 3   B—R 6

White resigned.

No. 66.   Queen's Pawn, Grunfeld Defence

V. SMYSLOV   M. BOTVINNIK

(World Championship Match, Moscow, 1957)

1. P—Q 4   Kt—K B 3
2. P—Q B 4   P—K Kt 3
3. Kt—Q B 3   P—Q 4
4. Kt—B 3   B—Kt 2
5. Q—Kt 3   P × P
6. Q × B P   O—O
7. P—K 4   B—Kt 5
8. B—K 3   K Kt—Q 2

The World Champion follows
a system which was first worked
out and put into practice by his
opponent. The struggle of the
pieces against the pawn centre
remains one of the most controver-
sial and difficult problems of
modern opening theory.

9. O—O—O

A most aggressive continuation.
Usually 9. Q—Kt 3 is played here,

as in Euwe-Smyslov, World Championship Tournament, 1948 (Game
No. 34).

9. ...   Kt—Q B 3

More natural and better is at
once 9. ... Kt—Kt 3. After 10. Q—
Kt 3 Black can build up adequate
counterplay by 10. ... P—Q R 4;
11. P—Q R 4, Kt—B 3; 12. P—
Q 5, Kt—Kt 5.

10. P—K R 3   B × Kt
11. P × B   Kt—Kt 3
12. Q—B 5

Here the Queen is more actively
placed than on Q 3. Now 12. ...
Kt—Q 2 can be answered by
13. Q—R 3, and the white centre
remains firm.

12. ...   P—B 4

Black boldly strikes at White's centre even at the expense of weakening his position. A more careful but also more passive continuation was 12. ... P—K 3.

13. Kt—K 2

This does indeed meet the threat of 13. ... P—B 5, but simpler was, 13. P—Q 5, Kt—K 4; 14. B—K 2, and the white pawn centre is threatening to become dangerous.

13. ...   Q—Q 3

Preparing not only to bring pressure to bear on the centre by doubling on the Q-file but also to lessen the power of White's pawns by an exchange of Queens. 13. ... P — K 3 with the idea of restraining the centre and bringing the K R to Q 2 via K B 2 is well met by 14. Kt—B 4, and if 14. ... Q—K 1, then 15. B—B 4, Kt × B; Q × Kt, Kt—Q 1; 17. P—Q 5!

14. P—K 5   178

Otherwise Black plays a Rook to Q 1 after which he has little to fear.

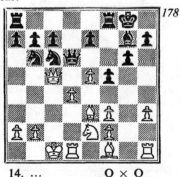

178

14. ...   Q × Q

An incorrect exchange which leaves White with a winning advantage. Correct was 14. ...Q—Q 4; 15. Kt—B 3, Q × Q (not 15. ... Q × B P; 16. B—K 2,

Q—Kt 7; 17. Q R—Kt 1, winning the Queen); 16. P × Q, P—B 5; 17. P × Kt, P × B; 18. P × B P, B × P with equal chances.

15. P × Q   Kt—B 5

Of course, 15. ... P—B 5 is no longer possible on account of 16. Kt × P, Kt—B 1; 17. Kt—K 6 with a winning advantage.

16. P—B 4

The game is really already decided: the black Bishop has no future, while White's K B has such a free hand on the white squares that Black is soon unable to prevent loss of material.

16. ...   K R—Q 1

The Q-file must be contested, but more accurate was 16. ... Q R —Q 1, since the Q R is forced to move shortly in any case.

17. B—Kt 2   Kt × B
18. P × Kt   Kt—Kt 5

It would be even worse to allow 19. B × Kt, P × B; 20. Kt—Q 4.

19. B × P   Q R—Kt 1

Now it is clear that had this Rook been at Q 1 Black would have had the resource 19. ... Kt— Q 6 ch; 20. K— B 2, Kt × Q B P.

20. P—B 6   K—B 2

The alternatives are no better. For example, (*i*) 20. ... Kt × P ch; 21. K—Kt 1, Kt—Kt 5; 22. Kt— Q 4, and Black cannot prevent both 23. Kt—K6 and 23. Kt—Kt 5 or (*ii*) 20. ... Kt—Q 6 ch; 21. K— B 2, Kt—B 4 (or 21. ... Kt—B 7; 22. R × R ch, R × R; 23. R— K B 1 followed by 24. Kt—Q 4); 22. R × R ch, R × R; 23. R—Q 1 and if 23. ... R—Kt 1, then 24. R —Q 7! while if 23. ... R × R; 24. K × R, then 25. Kt—Q 4 will again be decisive.

21. Kt—Q 4   P—K 3
22. Kt—Kt 5   Kt—Q 4 *179*

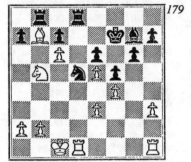

179

23. R × Kt!

The decisive blow. Black will in any case be forced to return the

exchange, and in the meantime his Q B P is lost leaving White's passed pawn a winning factor.

23. ...   P × R

After 23. ... R × R ; 24. Kt × B P, R—B 4 ch; 25. K—Kt 1 there is no answer to the threat of 26. Kt—R 6. The rest is easy.

24. Kt × B P   K R—Q B 1

If he does not give back the exchange, the Q B P will cost even more.

25. B × R   R × B
26. Kt × P   R × P ch
27. K—Q 2   K—K 3
28. Kt—B 3   Black
                          resigned.

No. 67. French Defence

V. SMYSLOV   M. BOTVINNIK

(*World Championship Match, Moscow, 1957*)

1. P—K 4   P—K 3
2. P—Q 4   P—Q 4
3. Kt—Q B 3   B—Kt 5
4. P—K 5   P—Q B 4
5. P—Q R 3   B × Kt ch
6. P × B   Q—B 2
7. Q--Kt 4   P—B 3

Desperately in need of a win at this stage of the match the World Champion varies from the usual 7. ... P—B 4, which he had played earlier. However the text move can certainly not be considered an improvement.

8. Kt—B 3   Kt—B 3

White has a fine game after 8. ... P × Q P; 9. B—Kt 5 ch, K—B 1; 10. O—O, P × K P (or 10. ... P × B P; 11. P × P, Kt × P; 12. Q—K R 4 with a terrific

attack); 11. P × P, Kt—K B 3; 12. Q—Kt 3.

9. Q—Kt 3   Q—B 2

The inadequacy of 7. ... P—B 3 is making itself felt: after 9. ... K Kt—K 2; 10. Q × P the K B P is en prise as well as the Rook. Better than the text move were both 9. ... P—B 4, which would have been an admission of failure, and 9 ... P × Q P; 10. P × Q P, Q—B 2; 11. B—Q 3, K Kt—K 2.

10. Q P × P

Although White has to saddle himself with tripled pawns to win a pawn he is justified by getting open lines for his Bishops.

10. ...   K Kt—K 2
11. B—Q 3   P × P

A poor solution to the problem of the centre. He should increase the pressure by 11. ... Kt—Kt 3. However, White still has the better prospects after 12. P × P, e.g. (*i*) 12. ... Q × P; 13. O—O, O—O; 14. B × Kt, P × B (or 14. Q × B; 15. Q × Q, P × Q; 16. R—K 1); 15. Kt—R 4, K—R 2; 16. B—Kt 5. or (*ii*) 12. ... P × P; 13. P—B 4, P—Q 5; 14. Q—Q 6, P—K 4; 15. B—K 4, B—Q 2; 16. B—Q 5, Q—K 2; 17. B—R 6.

12. Kt × P	Kt × Kt
13. Q × Kt	O—O
14. O—O	Kt—B 3
15. Q—Kt 3	P—K 4
16. B—K 3	

For the moment all is well with Black's position: his pawns occupy the centre and he has free play for his pieces; however, this is only of a temporary nature and it will not be long before White is ready to break up the centre, after which his extra pawn will gain in importance.

| 16. ... | B—B 4 |

Natural, but not the best. Correct is 16. ... B—K 3, though White still has the better of it after 17. P—K B 4.

| 17. Q R—Kt 1 | |

White takes advantage of Black's last inaccuracy very neatly: Black must now either admit his error by playing 17. ... B—K 3 or improve White's pawn position.

| 17. ... | B × B |
| 18. P × B | Q R—K I *180* |

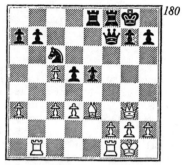

180

19. P—K B 4!

At last White achieves his object: Black can no longer hold his ideal formation in the centre.

| 19. ... | Q—B 2 |

The B 2 squares prove unfortunate for the black Queen. The obvious 19. ... P—K 5 was correct. After 20. P—Q 4, Kt—R 4; 21. P—B 5, Kt—B 5; 22. B—B 4 White preserves his advantage, but Black is not without counterplay. The text move allows White to bring about a won ending.

| 20. P × P | R × R ch |
| 21. R × R | Q × P |

21. ... Kt × P is strongly met by 22. B—Q 4 followed by R—B 5.

| 22. Q × Q | Kt × Q |

Still worse is 22. ... R × P; 23. B—B 4, R—K 7; 24. B—Q 6, and the white pieces dominate the position.

23. R—Q 1	K—B 2
24. P—R 3	Kt—B 3
25. B—B 4	

Now White threatens to win the Q Kt P by 26. B—Q 6 and 27. R—Kt 1. To defend his weak points Black is forced to doom his pieces to passive positions while White's sweep the board.

25. ...	R—K 2
26. B—Q 6	R—Q 2
27. R—B 1 ch	K—K 3
28. R—K 1 ch	K—B 2
29. K—B 2	P—Q Kt 3

Black is so constricted that any attempt to free himself only reacts to his own detriment. Yet defeat is just as sure if he does nothing, e.g. 29. ... R—Q 1; 30. R—Q Kt 1, R—Q 2; 31. K—K 3, and White forces a passed Q P by P—Q 4, K—Q 3 and P—B 4.

30. R—Q Kt 1	K—K3
31. R—Kt 5	P—Q 5

Every new bid for play leads to a worsening of his position in the face of White's unrelenting accuracy. White even gets his pawns on ideal squares now, and the black Q P must eventually fall.

32. P—B 4	P × P	181

181

33. B—R 2

A fine move which emphasizes Black's helplessness. The B P must fall anyway, and this way the Kt cannot go to K 4.

33. ...	R—B 2 ch
34. K—K 2	R—K 2

After 34. ... R—B 4; 35. P—Kt 4, R—Kt 4; 36. B—B 4 the Rook would be forced to give up the defence of the pawn.

35. R × P	K—Q 2 ch
36. K—Q 2	R—K 3
37. R—K Kt 5	

Again the most accurate. The immediate 37. B—Kt 1 would allow Black some counterplay with 37. ... R—Kt 3.

37. ...	P—Kt 3
38. R—Q 5 ch	K—B 1
39. B—Kt 1	

Winning the Q P after which the win is easy.

39. ...	R—B 3
40. B × P	Kt × B
41. R × Kt	R—B 7 ch
42. K—B 3	

The game was adjourned, but Black resigned without resuming since White's passed pawns win easily.

LaVergne, TN USA
06 January 2011
211398LV00004B/98/A